International acclaim for
CHINA SHAKES THE WORLD

"This sharply penned warning shows how China's silken threads pervade every aspect of global commerce and geopolitics." — *Wired*

"A particularly well-written book . . . [Kynge] combines a fresh perspective with an eye for arresting detail." — *Economist*

"Kynge has the eyes and ears of a skilled journalist, as well as an insatiable curiosity about what is going on around him."
— *Foreign Affairs*

"James Kynge captures both the dynamism of China's growth and the powerful worldwide trends, some of them dismal, that growth has accelerated. Clear-eyed and straightforward."
— **Bill McKibben, author of** *The End of Nature*

"Reveal[s] the complexity and scale of what's happening [in China] in a way that is gripping."
— **Jeffrey Garten, author of** *The Mind of the CEO*

"China is a changing world and James Kynge's book captures the essence of that change."
— **Lloyd Blankfein, chairman and chief executive of Goldman Sachs**

"A sweeping and fluent account of how China is changing every aspect of the modern world." — *Sunday Times* (London)

"Captures the ambivalence that many intelligent people feel about the rise of China . . . excellent reporting."
— *Far Eastern Economic Review*

"This is journalism at its best: relevant, provocative, balanced, and highly readable." — *Irish Times*

"Kynge breathes life into the story of an emerging China . . . fascinating, informative, and more than a little scary." — *The Australian*

"Both authoritative and eye-opening." — *Publishers Weekly*

CHINA
SHAKES THE
WORLD

A TITAN'S RISE AND TROUBLED
FUTURE — AND THE
CHALLENGE FOR AMERICA

JAMES KYNGE

A MARINER BOOK
HOUGHTON MIFFLIN COMPANY
BOSTON • NEW YORK

First Mariner Books edition 2007

Copyright © 2006 by James Kynge

www.houghtonmifflinbooks.com

Library of Congress Cataloging-in-Publication Data
Kynge, James.
China shakes the world : a titan's rise and troubled
future — and the challenge for America / James Kynge.
p.   cm.
Includes bibliographical references and index.
ISBN-13: 978-0-618-70564-1
ISBN-10: 0-618-70564-3
1. China — Economic conditions — 2000– 2. China — Foreign
economic relations. I. Title.
HC427.95.K96 2006
330.951 — dc22   2006012084

ISBN-13: 978-0-618-91906-2 (pbk.)
ISBN-10: 0-618-91906-6 (pbk.)

Book design by Melissa Lotfy
Typefaces: Palatino, Michaelangelo

PRINTED IN THE UNITED STATES OF AMERICA

MV 10 9 8 7 6 5 4

To Lucy, Tom, Ella, and Ollie

Contents

★

ACKNOWLEDGMENTS

This book was researched and written over a year and a half, beginning in mid-2004, but it is the product of many influences and impressions formed during an association with China that goes back to 1982, when I arrived in Jinan, in Shandong province, as a wide-eyed student. I am indebted, therefore, not only to the many people who helped in several ways with the book project itself but also to those who have shown me kindness, hospitality, wisdom, and many corrective prods in the years since China became my fascination. I wish to thank the teachers and administrators of Shandong University's foreign students department in the early 1980s for their generosity and humor during difficult times. I am also indebted to the Edinburgh University Chinese department's inspiring lecturers, in particular William Dolby and John Scott.

My career as a journalist would never have gotten off the ground had it not been for Graham Earnshaw and Mark O'Neill, who took me under their wings in Beijing in 1985. Since then, countless others have helped shape my evolving understanding of China, at times by teaching me things I did not know and at others by challenging my point of view. Among these, I feel particularly grateful to Robert Thomson, Jasper Becker, Li Jiehua, William Kazer, Gui Minhai, Andrew Higgins, Jane Macartney, Jean-Pierre Cabestan, Andrew Browne, Wang Xiaohong, Fang Xinghai, Graham Hutchings, Song Fengming, Yu Yongding, Martin Wolf, Li Yang, Hu Angang, James Harding, John Pomfret, James Miles, Karin Finkelston, Kenneth Lieberthal, Yukon Huang, Cao Siyuan, Xu Zhongbo, Andy Rothman, Xu Xiaonian, Zhang Weiying, Giles

Chance, Fang Ying, Wang Rujun, Hong Huang, Zhang Xin, Hu Shuli, Anthony Galsworthy, Richard McGregor, Mure Dickie, Andrew Yeh, Adam Williams, Clinton Dines, Peter Batey, David Mahon, Joerg Wuttke, Nicholas Lardy, Denis Simon, David Shambaugh, Dan Rosen, Jim Walker, Murray Scott Tanner, James Mulvenon, Jim Harkness, Liu Chaowei, Wang Wei, Wang Min, Ge Xiaomei, Xing Houyuan, Patrick Horgan, Shi Junbao, as well as Joe Studwell and Arthur Kroeber at the excellent *China Economic Quarterly*. Needless to say, the opinions in the book are my own, and I take responsibility for them.

My greatest debt in researching the book is to Yang Li, who, first as a colleague at the *Financial Times* and later as a full-time researcher on this project, showed enormous resourcefulness, intelligence, and good humor in tracking down elusive facts, arranging meetings with many hard-to-get-to people, and helping me understand what we experienced. She alone knows the many places in which it would have been more accurate for me to have written "we" instead of "I." Alia Malik also did sterling and much-appreciated work researching the context and economic history of several issues.

Many friends supplied generous advice, support, and insights during the ups and downs of the writing process. Among these, I am particularly thankful to Tim Clissold, David Murphy, Jim McGregor, Rob Gifford, Nancy Fraser, Zhang Lijia, Calum Macleod, Catherine Sampson, Charles Hutzler, Gerry Bourke, and Rupert Wingfield-Hayes. An old friend, Keith Abel, did a fastidious job reading drafts and in telling the truth with sensitivity. At Houghton Mifflin, I wish to thank most warmly my editor Webster Younce, for his encouragement, unfailing professionalism, and friendship, and also Larry Cooper, who did marvelous work on the manuscript. My agents, Felicity Bryan and George Lucas, guided me from the start of a long process to the end with judgment, patience, and good humor.

My many excellent former colleagues at the *Financial Times* have been an unfailing source of inspiration and intellectual stimulation. I thank Richard Lambert for posting me to China in the first place, Peter Montagnon, John Thornhill, and Dan Bogler for the care they took to keep the phone lines open and the story ideas flowing, and Graham Watts, Victor Mallet, and Guy de Jonquieres for their help at crucial times. I am also very grateful to John Ridding, who, having engineered the time for me to write, spared plenty of his own to debate many of the issues and arguments.

My parents, to add to their countless indulgences over the years, put up a "cuckoo" who was writing about one appetite while developing another during several glorious weeks in Potto. My love and gratitude go to them, as well as to Marian and Howard Rogers and Lucy and Iain Nicholson, for their hospitality and endless good cheer.

This book is dedicated to Lucy, who, throughout this book, as in all things, has made the difficult parts seem easier and the distant closer by. It is also dedicated to our wonderful children, Tom, Ella, and Ollie, for whom China is quite simply home.

Introduction

★

THE RISE OF great powers and their subsequent decline from
eminence are processes that can rarely be traced in a simple, linear
fashion. They are full of twists and turns, false dawns and deceptive signals. Who could have predicted, for example, that Britain's
retreat from empire in America would come to be symbolized by
the actions of settlers masquerading as Mohawk Indians, dumping tea chests into Boston harbor? Similarly, when a Japanese
company bought Rockefeller Center, a New York icon, in the late
1980s, few could have known that the purchase would come to be
remembered less as a sign of economic strength than as a portent
of Japan's incipient stagnation.

Sometimes the biggest events are telegraphed by the merest of
harbingers. The first inkling the British had, for instance, of the
Mongol invasion of Europe—a cataclysm for the civilization of
the continent—was when the price of fish at Harwich, a harbor
on the North Sea, suddenly rose. The reason for this, people later
learned, was that fishing fleets along the Baltic coast, abruptly
deprived of sailors required to face the horse-borne enemy ap-
proaching from the east, had remained at their moorings. That
had reduced the supply of cod and herring to Harwich, and prices
had gone up accordingly.

So when historians come to chronicle the rise of China in the
late twentieth and early twenty-first centuries, it may be that the
motifs they use to illustrate the renaissance of an ancient nation
will be quite different from those we commonly employ today. A
few decades from now, it may not be Beijing's accession to the

★

World Trade Organization in 2001 that sticks in the mind. The handover of Hong Kong from British to Chinese sovereignty in 1997 may by then warrant no more than a few snapshots in the story of China's ascent. Even the many elements of domestic transformation that today elicit expressions of awe — that the economy has been growing at an average of more than 9.5 percent annually for the past twenty-eight years and that over the same period more than four hundred million people have been lifted above the poverty line of one U.S. dollar a day — may in the future appear somehow less remarkable. But what is less likely to fade from the global consciousness is the appetite that the world's most populous nation unleashed on the planet in the first few years of the twenty-first century.

It is difficult to say exactly when the influence of a rising China first became a palpable global force. In the 1990s there had been early soundings of Beijing's growing international clout. An economic boom in the middle of the decade helped create a glow of prosperity in some of China's neighbors. Then, in 1997 and 1998, when the Asian financial crisis tore through the region, the world looked to Beijing for stability in the storm. Nevertheless, even in the increasingly cosmopolitan 1990s my assignment with the *Financial Times* was occupied much more with how the world was affecting China than how China was affecting the world. Then, quite suddenly, or so it seemed, there was a reversal. Reports surfaced in all corners of the planet describing how one or another aspect of a far-off economy or society had been altered by China's voracious need for resources, jobs, markets, energy, and myriad other things. For me, this new trend reached its crescendo in the several weeks beginning in mid-February 2004, when, slowly at first but with mounting velocity, manhole covers started to disappear from roads and pavements around the world.

As Chinese demand drove up the price of scrap metal to record levels, thieves almost everywhere had the same idea. As darkness fell, they levered up the iron covers and sold them to local merchants, who cut them up and loaded them onto ships to China. The first displacements were felt in Taiwan, the island just off China's southeast coast. The next were in other neighbors such as Mongolia and Kyrgyzstan. Soon the gravitational pull of a resurgent "Middle Kingdom" (or Zhongguo, the Mandarin name for China) was reaching the farthest places. Wherever the sun set, pilferers worked to satisfy China's hunger. More than 150 covers disappeared during one month in Chicago. Scotland's "great drain robbery" saw more than a hundred vanish in a few days. From Montreal to Gloucester to Kuala Lumpur, unsuspecting pedestrians stumbled into holes.

From then on, some of the disconnectedness that used to characterize life in Beijing seemed to fall away. The Communist Party still restricted the inflow of foreign newspapers, books, and movies. Dissidents and others who spoke of human rights and democracy were still in danger of being hunted down and sent to prison. And China remained in many ways a strategic and military rival of the United States and of its ally in Asia, Japan. But the sense of muffled isolation from events abroad that I remembered from the 1980s and 1990s had gone. China had shifted from being a bystander to being an actor. Its appetite, though unpremeditated and inarticulate, had become a source of major change in the world.

Things seemed to evolve so quickly that, sitting in my office overlooking the Avenue of Eternal Peace, Beijing's main drag, I fancied I could actually *see* some of the economic forces that China was conjuring before it sent them hurtling overseas. People bought cars at such a rate that, week by week, the traffic on the avenue became noticeably more clogged. The buildings on the far side of the road that were Soviet-era apartment blocks when I started my assignment were pulled down to make way for high-rise towers with marble foyers and glass-and-chrome exteriors. Bicycles, once ubiquitous, began to disappear. The sibilant chorus of peddlers of pirated DVDs had proliferated. Even the Friendship Store, a relic of the first blush of China's opening, had changed. Its staff, who in the early 1980s were magnificently indifferent at the point of sale, had mellowed into an attitude of rumpled nonchalance. The sleepy patisserie that occupied one corner of the store and used to sell some of the only croissants in the capital when I was a student in 1982 had, by the early twenty-first century, ceded territory to a Starbucks, which offered blueberry muffins and tiramisu.

Napoleon, it is said, once remarked, "Let China sleep, for when she wakes, she will shake the world." The shaking, it seemed to me in 2004, had started. I resolved to explore how the influence of a rising China was being felt in the wider world. I wanted to link cause and effect and to trace external convulsions back to their internal combustions. I traveled to several countries in Europe and to parts of the United States, as well as to destinations in Asia, to gauge the manner and range of the impact. I was not only looking for the economic arguments and the facts to back them up, but also for personal stories, for the soft reverberations of human feeling and the delicate cartilage of cultural and social capital. As the manhole cover episode showed, it is possible in this era of globalization to follow a trend from the place where it originates out to the places where its influence is reflected. It is at that point — in the eddies of swash and backwash, at the interchange of cause and effect, and in the places where sound and echo merge — that reactions are formed.

These reactions, though derivative, are no less influential than the impulses that cause them. Thus the ways in which China is reshaping the world may be the direct results of Chinese actions or, just as often, manifestations of reactions to China's influence. The price of fish at Harwich did not rise as a direct consequence of the Mongol invasion of Europe but as a consequence of Europe's reaction to that invasion. Similarly now, one direct result of China's earthshaking competitiveness in manufacturing is that many businesses are finding it tougher to make money. And the reactions to this reality cover a wide canvas. Workers are being laid off. European factories are moving in a swelling tide to eastern Europe to cut costs, and commentators are questioning whether the whole expensive edifice of the European welfare state may one day topple and fall. Politicians, seeking votes from those to whom they must administer bitter medicine, are spinning themselves into ever more intricate rhetorical contortions.

In the United States, arguably even more profound shifts are happening, most of which spring from a peculiarity of millennial proportions: China, an authoritarian state ruled by a single, Communist party, has succeeded in fostering a capitalist economy so vibrant that in many ways it outcompetes America. Such a thing was not supposed to happen in a world painstakingly created under Pax Americana over the more than sixty years since the Second World War. When first Japan and then the Asian "tigers" rose to economic power and prominence, there was disquiet in certain quarters of the American establishment. But there was a measure of comfort too; these countries were in the main strategic allies of Washington, and their economic success had come with the espousal of the democracy and open markets that condition the American world order. China in many respects is different. Not only is it implacably opposed to the idea of multiparty democracy, it also strives to keep the commanding heights of the economy firmly under state control while eschewing free capital markets and a floating currency.

These essential differences, coupled with an emerging strategic rivalry in the Asia-Pacific region and intensifying competition to secure sources of energy and resources, have made the United States deeply wary of a rising China. Visceral aversions color the debate over the outsourcing of American jobs, perceptions of China's unfair trading practices, Chinese piracy of Western intellectual property, and several other irritants in the commercial relationship. But set against these, there are, of course, positive outcomes from engagement. The cost of consumer products has fallen significantly for U.S. buyers, and the downward pressure on retail prices has helped to keep American interest rates low — which in turn has powered a real estate boom.

In addition, it should be understood that not all the graphs charting Chinese economic performance go up. For all its prowess in manufacturing, the country is beset by profound frailties in other areas. The environment is in deep distress. Deserts in the north are marching toward the fertile agricultural plains to the south. Waterways that just a decade ago coursed with torrents and rapids have slowed to a trickle or dried up altogether. Air pollution is so bad that by 2010 about 380,000 people may die each year of respiratory ailments. Strange diseases such as SARS and bird flu appear with regularity, and in some areas whole towns are sinking into gaping subterranean holes, excavated by miners or emptied of the groundwater they used to hold. Never before has so large a country emerged so rapidly from so eviscerated an environmental base.

Nature's degradations are mirrored in society. A general crisis of trust exists in both personal and commercial relationships, and bedevils the functions of the government bodies charged with ensuring a measure of social equity. Corruption is virtually institutionalized in the legal system, the media, local and central government offices, and the police force. The intricate system of checks and balances that regulate Western-style democracies is largely absent in China, throwing up huge inefficiencies and incurring losses that must ultimately be paid for by the people. The financial system is particularly susceptible to such systemic failure: state banks regularly receive huge government bailouts, the stock market is little better than a casino, and many of the contributions to fund the pensions of hundreds of millions of elderly have simply gone missing. All of these deficits, though hidden from public view, will have to be paid for one day. When that day comes, the rapid emergence of Asia's giant may slow or even stumble.

But in the meantime, the world must learn to contend with a new, convulsive force. The question for the West — and the issue that concerns this book — is one of compatibility. Will the Western world be able to accommodate the manifestations of extreme strengths and profound weaknesses that are emanating from the vastly different presence in its midst? The answer to that question will define much of the course of the twenty-first century.

CHINA SHAKES
THE WORLD

1

Rags to Riches

BY THE TIME I got there, there was only a scar. A scar of ocher earth twenty-five times the size of a soccer field. A dozen excavators pawed ponderously at the soil as if absently searching for something lost. The place where one of Germany's largest steel mills had stood since before World War Two was now reduced to a few mounds of twisted metal scrap.

I approached a man in overalls by the side of the road. He was hoisting a huge length of pipeline onto the back of a truck. After he had settled it in place, I called over to him. He said he had dislodged, lifted, and loaded fourteen pieces of pipe like this already and there were only three left, enough for another week's work. Then it would all be over. I asked him where the pipeline was going. He straightened his back and made as if to throw something in a gentle arc far into the distance. "China," he said.

The rest of the equipment had gone earlier: the oxygen converters that were housed in a shed two hundred feet high, the hot-rolling mill for heavy steel plates that stretched out over two-thirds of a mile, a sinter plant, a blast furnace, and a host of other parts. They had all been packed into wooden crates, inserted into containers, and loaded onto ships, and then they were unpacked at their destination, near the mouth of the Yangtze. There, on the flat alluvial bed of that mighty river, they had been reconstructed exactly — to the last screw — as they had been in Germany. Altogether, 275,000 tons of equipment had been shipped, along with 44 tons of documents that explained the intricacies of the reassembly process.[1] The man in overalls shook his head at the convoluted nature of it all. "I just hope it works when they get it there," he said.

The Thyssen Krupp steel mill in Dortmund once employed around ten thousand people. The communities of Horde and Westfalenhutte, where workshops clustered around smokestacks that could be seen from all over the city, had depended on them for generations. People had made iron here for nearly two hundred years, and when the drums of German conquest rolled in 1870, 1914, and 1939, it was this corner of the Ruhr Valley that supplied first Prussia and then the German empire with field guns, tanks, shells, and battleship armor. A pride in practical things was evident everywhere. A stumpy-looking iron blast furnace from the nineteenth century with a sign saying that it had been brought over from England stood as a monument by one of the gates of the former plant. Nearby, a plaque memorialized a local engineer.

But on a warm, bright afternoon in June 2004, Horde was clearly no longer the pounding heart of the Ruhr. The place looked laid-back, becalmed. A few people sat in the sun outside an ice cream shop on Alfred Trappen Street, digging to the bottom of their sundaes with long spoons. Up the road, women fished into a wire basket outside Zeeman Textiel, a discount store, inspecting T-shirts for ninety-nine (euro) cents. There were three tanning salons in the vicinity and a tattoo parlor advertising its ability to emblazon *ai, fu,* and *kang,* the Chinese characters for "love," "wealth," and "health," on the bodies of its customers. But the tanning and tattoo places were shut.

I had come to Horde to try to understand how life was changing now that the steel plant was gone. But my inability to speak German was a handicap. I tried calling on local officials, but they were unwilling to talk. People on the street, when approached, seemed to find my questions unwarranted. So I went to the Lutheran church and phoned each of the five fathers listed in a leaflet, inviting them for a coffee. Pfarrer Martin Pense was busy, Pfarrer Klaus Wortmann was out of town, Pfarrer Bern Weissbach-Lamay did not answer, and Pfarrerin Angela Dicke would

have been happy to help but it was a holiday, so . . . sorry. Pfarrer Sven Frohlich, a soft-spoken man, was ready to give me a few
minutes on the phone.

The death of the steel mill, he said, had been the slow but inevitable result of a loss in competitiveness. In the early 1990s, when
efficient South Korean steel plants were undercutting the world,
Horde steelworkers were agitating for a thirty-five-hour work
week. And the reunification of West and East Germany had taken
its toll by forcing the government to raise taxes and by acting as
a drag on overall economic activity. By the mid-nineties, the ultimate fate of the Horde plant had become an issue of debate. To
start with, the management reacted as managements generally
do, by agreeing to merge with a competitor to derive operational
synergies, cost reductions, and improved competitiveness. But by
the time world steel prices had slumped into a trough around the
year 2000, such talk had died away. There seemed to be little that
could be done.

Pfarrer Frohlich said that nearly half the Lutheran church's
congregation had moved away as thousands of steelworkers lost
their jobs and the community, though not poor, had sunk into a
kind of numbness. Young people did not seem to feel the pull of
religion in spite of the strenuous efforts, evident in the church
newsletter, to lure them into all sorts of community activities.
"Our identity is lost," said Frohlich. "And that is the most important thing that can be taken away from somebody. It could take
more than a decade to recover it."

According to Thyssen Krupp, the Horde plant would have
been closed regardless of whether a buyer for it had been found.
But others had their doubts. The Chinese pounced so quickly on
the purchase, signing to buy it just one month after the plant was
idled, that some in Horde suspected a sweetheart deal. Whatever
the truth, the events that were to follow the Chinese acquisition
stunned the local population. As if out of nowhere, nearly one
thousand Chinese workers arrived. They bedded down in a makeshift dormitory in a disused building in the plant and worked
twelve hours a day, seven days a week throughout the summer.

Only later, after some of the German workers and managers complained, were the Chinese workers obliged to take a day off, out of respect for local laws.

Their industriousness alone was enough to give the hardened workers of the Ruhr pause for thought. But there was something else. Locals started to notice the Chinese deconstruction teams high up — as high as two hundred feet above ground — on exposed walkways, swinging on ladders and clinging from scaffolding poles, all without the use of safety harnesses. The spectacle became a media sensation. Some referred to it as the "ultimate Chinese takeaway," and on the day that a reporter from Deutsche Welle, the German broadcaster, showed up, a Chinese worker was spotted dangling by a thin wire from the top of the 300-foot-high Horde Fackel smokestack. "Have the Chinese acrobats come to town?" he asked in his dispatch.

By the end of 2002, in less than one year, the Chinese had finished the dismantling job — a year ahead of the schedule that the Chinese had agreed on with Thyssen Krupp and a full two years faster than the German company had initially estimated the job would take. Shortly before it was time to leave, a diplomat from the Chinese embassy in Berlin arrived to address the laborers. "The Chinese are known in Germany for washing dishes and running restaurants," he said. "When our companies want to do business here we sometimes have to beg just for an appointment. But through your work you have earned the Chinese people some face."

A few weeks after that, the workers pulled out, having invited local German officials and site managers to a banquet cooked in four different styles, reflecting the four hometowns of the deconstruction team chefs. The dormitories and kitchens they had been using for a year were left scrupulously clean and tidy, save for a single pair of black safety boots. These boots, it turned out, bore the brand name of Phoenix and were made in China.[2] That was curious, said Germans who had worked at the steel mill, because the plant the Chinese had just taken away was also called Phoenix, in commemoration of the way that Dortmund had risen from the ashes of bombing raids in 1944. Nobody could tell, however, whether the single pair of forgotten boots was an oversight or an intentional pun.

Eighteen months after the Phoenix's migration, I stood in the bar in Zum Brauhaus, a hostel on Alfred Trappen Street. It was a simple place with pine tables, upright chairs, photographs of local soccer teams on the wall, and a one-armed bandit in the corner that had attracted the attention of a stolid woman who mechanically shoved coins into its slot. At a table behind her, a teenage girl with a blank expression sipped a pint of lager. I stood by the bar, where the woman serving drinks introduced me to a man called John. He had been born and brought up in Britain, in the northern industrial town of Bolton, and had been posted to Germany with the British Army a few years after the war. He married a German girl and they moved to Dortmund, her hometown, after he left the army. He had worked in the steel mill for more than twenty years, but now that it had gone, he took a philosophical view of its departure. The Chinese economy was booming, whereas Germany's had reached a plateau. If the Chinese could put the Horde plant to profitable use, then maybe it was a good thing that they had bought it, he said.

But there was no denying that the Phoenix's loss was keenly felt. You could see the psychological displacement in a small park at the lower end of Alfred Trappen Street. There, around a monument to a synagogue that had been destroyed during the war, groups of unemployed steelworkers sat under spreading beech trees with their cans of lager in plastic bags. John held a thumb to his lip and made a sucking sound. A future without heavy industry was going to take some getting used to, he said. Nobody had a clear idea of what would take its place. The only thing that the local authorities had come up with so far was a plan to redevelop the area that the steelworks had occupied into a lake larger than the Binnenalster in Hamburg. It would feature four small islands and a tombolo. Around the shore there would be moorings for a marina, rows of upscale restaurants, and nearly five hundred acres of parkland. But so far the marina scheme had not received a positive reception.

As John was talking, another former steelworker, a large, powerfully built man in his forties, had joined the conversation.

"Let me ask you," he boomed. "Do we look like yachtsmen to you?"

The sea voyage of the Thyssen Krupp steel mill ended 5,600 miles away from Horde at a small, windswept port on the alluvial bed of the lower Yangtze River. The water, wide and sluggish, was deep enough for all but the largest sea vessels to dock. A few hundred yards inland from the riverbank, the plant had been reassembled. I recognized it immediately. It looked somehow cleaner than in the photographs I had seen of it in Germany, though that may merely have been an illusion created by the white sand and metallic gray sky that surrounded it.

The company that had bought it was called Shagang, or "sand steel," after the distinctive physical environment in which it had blossomed from humble beginnings as a village workshop in 1975. In that year, China's entire steel output had scarcely been greater than that of Dortmund alone. But in the intervening years business had taken off, and the workshop's expansion had first consumed the village that built it and then usurped the neighboring town. Now everyone in the area seemed in thrall both to steel and to the former peasant farmer with a rudimentary education who had turned a backyard furnace into one of the world's most efficient producers. His name was Shen Wenrong.

When I checked into the Steel Town Guest House, just down the street from the Sand Steel Hostel, the receptionist told me that everyone was thankful to Shen. Without him, she said, this place would be nothing. Now it was full of the incongruities of industrializing China. A five-star hotel with an outdoor mural of mythical goddesses in flowing gowns was under construction in the reed bed by the river. Its name, locals said, was to be the Heavy Industry Hotel. Not far away, a restaurant called Sweet Water stood beside mounds of stinking rubbish rotting in a canal. Wide new boulevards had been built in another part of town, but a dearth of manhole covers had turned driving into a slalom with consequences. And in front of a sports arena was a replica of the bronze charging bull that stands not far from the New York Stock Exchange. On its plinth, a poem written by Shen Wenrong had been carved into granite:

> The bull will rush forward without whipping,
> Once in flight it covers a thousand miles.
> We ask the golden bull: Why are you like this?
> But the bull can fly over oceans too—
> Only then should you call it a miracle.

The town's name was Jinfeng, and it had the air of a temporary encampment. Most of its inhabitants were migrant workers, peasant farmers who had flooded in from their villages to find work for the equivalent of around 40 cents an hour. There were about thirty thousand of them in Jinfeng, and shortly after dawn they tramped in long silent lines to the steel, cotton, and glass factories that held the promise of a future free from the thousand-year tyranny of their fields. At dusk the factories would disgorge them back to their dormitories—a sullen, twilight army. The local economy bore the imprint of their presence: shops selling hard hats, steel-toed boots, and lengths of rope lined their route to work. There was also a discount clothing shop for those who wanted to spruce up before triumphant trips home. A pair of leather shoes with a fashionable square toe was on sale for $4 and patterned T-shirts were going for 10 cents.

A bit farther on, I dropped into a liquor store and was attracted to the poetic names on several bottles of white spirits. One Drop Fragrant (90 cents), Cool River Destiny (75 cents), Eastern Crossing (95 cents), Boiling Ditch (60 cents), Drink Happy 100 Years ($1.10). The last one I looked at was called Ordinary, and it cost 20 cents, but just as I picked it up the shopkeeper called me over.

"Don't drink that. You couldn't stand it. It's for migrant workers," he said.

Later that afternoon, near the Steel Town Guest House, a white truck moving at the speed of a milk float came down the road playing a jingle and a recorded message from a speaker on its roof. "Jinfeng Cinema. Outstanding song and dance. Traveling performance. Five o'clock start. Don't miss it," the message said. In the passenger seat, a young woman with rouged cheeks and her hands interlaced in front of almost naked breasts was "casting the beautiful eye" to passersby. On the other side of the road, a truck carrying iron ore juddered to a halt as its driver and passengers jostled for space by the window to get a better view.

Before coming to Jinfeng, I had spent weeks trying to secure an invitation to Shagang to see Shen. But at every step I had been thwarted by a man called Wu. When I phoned him to request a visit, Wu suggested that I send a fax. I did. He told me it needed alterations. I made them. Then he told me I should send a list of the questions that I wanted to ask. I wrote them. When my documentation finally met Wu's specifications, the stalling took a different tack. Things were busy now, he said. Next year might be a better time to visit. Besides, Jinfeng had no good hotels, and traveling thereabouts was inconvenient.

In the end I just went, and one morning I made my way to the forbidding iron gate that stands at the plant's entrance. Three stern guards in uniforms and peaked hats stood in a pillbox. I told them I needed to find Shen's office. They smiled, pointed it out from the mass of long, low factory buildings, and allowed me to walk straight in. It was an open-plan, communal space, and as soon as I went through the building's main door, I found myself standing in the middle of it. I had not seen pictures of Shen, but I had been told that he was a big man with the ham hands of a farm laborer. Getting my bearings, I turned around a couple of times, taking in the rows of staff sitting in cubicles and staring at computer screens. Then I noticed that a couple of feet behind me, through a glass divider, was a big man poring over documents at a desk. A number of workers, all clutching papers, had formed a line next to him. As each person reached the front, the large man would grab his papers, study them intently for a minute, and issue orders in a low, growling voice.

It had to be Shen. I walked over to join the line, but just as I was nearing the front, a man came over to ask what I was doing. It was Wu. He smiled in a resigned way and said he was delighted to see me. However, he said, it was not clear if Shen would be working today. In any case, I had better go with him to a separate office and fill out forms, make a formal request. But by now I was standing three feet away from the man I had been hoping for months to meet. I was not going to be budged.

When Shen looked up and saw an unannounced foreigner at the front of his morning business line he seemed neither surprised nor pleased. He stared at me over the top of his reading glasses for some time and then, with an impatient wave of his hand, told me to sit on a low wooden stool by his side. His desk was no bigger than a schoolchild's, very different from the wide, polished, hardwood "boss's platforms" that Chinese corporate chieftains normally awarded themselves. Its glass surface was piled with two stacks of papers, and between them was a plastic holder containing a few cheap ballpoint pens. There was no photograph of his wife or children, no mementos of business success, and no computer. Shen seemed to prefer doing business in physical form, in the here and now. Many of the workers and managers who had stood in front of me had been clutching reports that were handwritten or typed on typewriters.

As I explained to him why I had come, he cut me off in midsentence and told me to wait in a back room. Half an hour later he reappeared. We sat at a conference table and he told me to dispense with formalities and just get on with asking whatever it was I wanted to know. I asked him why he had bought the Thyssen Krupp steel plant. "I needed a horse that would run fast and not eat much hay," he said. "When the next crash in world steel prices comes, and it will certainly come in the next few years, a lot of our competitors that have bought expensive new equipment from abroad will go bust or be so weighed down by debt that they will not be able to move. When that time comes, you will see that this purchase was good."

Shagang bought the steel mill by paying its price in scrap: $24 million. Its transportation by land and sea from Dortmund had cost $12 million, and its reconstruction (plus the purchase of nearly one square mile of land) cost another $1.2 billion.[3] All told, it came in at about 60 percent of the cost of buying a new plant, and, by reconfiguring it, Shen was confident he would be able to squeeze from it three million more tons of annual output than the Germans had managed in Dortmund. When the mill started producing at full tilt, it would more than double Shagang's current capacity, catapulting the company into the ranks of the world's top twenty producers.

If Shagang had decided to buy a new plant, not only would the cost have been far greater but also it would have taken about three years to make and one or two years to assemble. By comparison, Phoenix was indeed a fast, low-maintenance horse. Shen said he'd had the advantage during negotiations with Thyssen Krupp because, although steel prices worldwide were in a trough when he bought the mill in 2001, he knew demand in China was set to balloon over the following two to three years. The Germans, he said, were happy just to find a buyer. They could not have been expected to foresee that an extraordinary upsurge in Chinese demand in 2003 and 2004 would propel global steel prices to levels at which Phoenix, in its original Dortmund setting, would have made a handsome profit.

All in all, the Germans had been very cooperative, Shen said. Both he and Qi Guangnan, the chief engineer responsible for packing up the plant in Horde, had admired their technical knowledge and their trustworthiness. And clearly they had loved their factory, said Qi, who recounted how a big, middle-aged German who showed him around had started sobbing at the door of the sinter plant. "He had worked there for twenty years," Qi said. But the great thing about the Phoenix plant, as far as the Chinese were concerned, was that back in Germany it had supplied steel to Volkswagen, the car maker. In China, few firms as yet had the technology to make automobile-grade steel. There was a market to be had in substituting for the expensive imports of auto-grade steel, especially now that car sales nationwide were in an unprecedented boom. Volkswagen itself had a large plant in Shanghai, which was not far from Jinfeng. Shen's vision, then, was simple. Cars designed in Wolfsburg would still be built with steel made from Dortmund's fine technology, only the whole process would unfold within the span of the delta where the Yangtze meets the sea.

When I left, I was accompanied to the gate by Wu, whose resigned expression was accentuated by the weight of his bushy eyebrows. He had been with Shen since they grew up, and as we walked through the plant he spoke of the memories he was seeing in his mind's eye. The place where we stood in the factory forecourt had been a bed of reeds when he and Shen had first started out. And somewhere lost in the mass of buildings was the site of the farmer's shack where Shen had lived out a childhood as poor as it was possible to be in one of the world's most impoverished countries.

I thanked Wu for taking me around. He said it had been no problem. "Only next time," he said, "send a fax."

People I spoke to in Dortmund had assumed that their steel mill must have been bought by a Chinese state-owned enterprise or perhaps by some sinister arm of a totalitarian regime. This type of perception was widespread in Europe and the United States. The conventional wisdom seemed to be that the Chinese companies acquiring equipment or technology in the industrialized world were somehow agents of the Communist government, or at least were financed by state banks with loans they would never have to repay. Indeed, some of the corporations that sought to buy equipment, companies, and assets overseas did fall into this category. But in the case of Shagang and Shen Wenrong, such a characterization did not match reality. The story of Shen's rise belonged to a different tradition, one that was much more instructive about the forces transforming China.

To understand these forces better, it is necessary to delve into a crucial yet often misunderstood passage of history. In the popular imagination, the launch of China's economic reforms in 1978 was a planned, top-down affair managed by a man who is often called the architect of the country's emergence, Deng Xiaoping. According to this version of events, Beijing has all along been cleverly manipulating a master plan that has delivered structured, gradual free-market reforms. But the reality has not been so neat. Many of the key events and occurrences that propelled forward progress toward capitalism were, in fact, unplanned, unintended, or completely accidental. It is undeniable that the 1980s, the decade of Deng, brought genuine and deep-seated change that improved the lives of hundreds of millions of Chinese. But on closer inspection it turns out that much of the crucial impetus behind the creation of wealth during that period sprang not so much from the implementation as from the miscarriage of central government policies.

At the outset, the reforms were precipitated by a payments crisis.[4] The first thing Deng tried to do after winning his power struggle with Chairman Mao Zedong's successor, Hua Guofeng, was to try to carry out the priorities listed in the Ten-Year Plan for Economic Development. Deng had drawn up this document in 1975, but political infighting and the rise of the "Gang of Four," led by Mao's demonic wife, Jiang Qing, had stalled its passage through the bureaucracy. The plan boiled down to a huge shopping list: approval for the importation of twenty-two complete industrial production units, at an average cost of more than $500 million each, amounting to a total outlay of $12 billion — equivalent to the total annual income of roughly twenty-four million Chinese in those days. Deng gambled that these purchases could be funded by the discovery of big new oil deposits. Chinese companies, assisted by foreign engineers, were already feverishly at work sinking wells in promising locations all over the country. Unfortunately, little oil was found. Many of the purchases had to be postponed, but those that had already been paid for left a gaping hole in the state's finances.

Deng was forced to improvise to coax growth out of an economy that had only just started to recover from the Cultural Revolution, the decade of Maoist chaos that had officially ended in 1976. He brought in Chen Yun, an expert at defusing economic crises, to conceive of new strategies. Chen's view was that the initiative of farmers, who then comprised some 700 million of China's then population of 1.1 billion, had been suppressed for too long under the system of agricultural communes set up by Mao. From 1979 on, Deng instituted a new policy under which farmers could more directly reap the harvest of their labors rather than handing over their crops to the commune. To do this, they formed "work groups," with each group tilling its own designated strip of land and owning whatever it produced. However, a key tenet of the new policy made it clear that such groups could not be single families and that the land they worked would remain state-owned.

Nevertheless, in one of the first of several important acts of creative disobedience, farmers took the new policy as a license to cultivate family plots.[5] Local officials knew exactly what was going on, but they could also see that the enterprise of the peasant farmers had been unleashed, and it was consigning the lassitude of the communes to history. The impact was immediate. By 1984 the national grain harvest had risen to 448 million tons from 335 million in 1978, and meat became more widely available.[6]

Similar types of subterfuge attended China's prototype private businesses. In areas around the Pearl River Delta bordering Hong Kong, and in Zhejiang and Jiangsu provinces to the north and south of Shanghai, people began to form companies that were socialist and state-owned on paper but capitalist and privately owned in reality. The main ruse employed to conceal this disobedience was semantic acrobatics with the word "collective." When Mao had used it, the word meant that a company was wholly owned by the state but by more than one branch of it. In its new incarnation, "collective" could also mean a group of private, or partly private, owners. It was a fig leaf that came to be known as "donning the red hat," and it would not have fooled anyone had it not been for the complicity of local government officials. They were willing to allow such sophistry to flourish because they soon saw that "red hat" collectives could be the most dynamic job creators and taxpayers in their districts. Often, of course, they had the additional incentive to cooperate that came from direct shareholdings. Within a few years, an unsanctioned amalgam of "red hats," collectives, and "township and village enterprises" had become by far the fastest-growing sector in the national economy.

The willingness of local officials to disobey Beijing was therefore a crucial ingredient in the free-market reforms of the 1980s. And the artifice did not end with that decade. It was to continue well into the 1990s, notably with the establishment of thousands of unlicensed "development parks," to which local governments attracted corporate investors by offering a package of frequently illegal incentives.[7]

Taken together, then, these realities suggest that Deng was not so much the omniscient architect of free-market reform that he is often hailed to have been. A significant part of his success can be attributed to the disobedience of local officials, farmers, and entrepreneurs toward central government policies. Deng's contribution was not that he conceived of all the strategies that would lay the foundation for China's economic takeoff, but that he was willing to ride with whatever homespun formulas seemed to yield the growth that the country so desperately needed. This was no mean achievement; a phalanx of conservative ideologues in Beijing kept constant vigil from the wings, ready to convert the slightest mishap into an argument for revisionist measures.

Understanding the haphazard nature of much that happened in the 1980s helps in appreciating where men like Shen came from. Chaotic times throw forth heroes. Several of the entrepreneurs who by the late 1990s were driving Mercedes-Benzes, flying first class to the World Economic Forum in Davos, Switzerland, and sending their children to the best British public schools started at the bottom of the social pyramid in the early 1980s. In fact, at that time, misfortune—particularly if it came in the form of unemployment—could be the ultimate blessing. The payments crisis brought on partly by Deng's spending binge in the late 1970s was matched by an urban employment crunch. Some seven million educated young people who had been sent to the countryside to "learn from the peasants" during the Cultural Revolution were by the late seventies and early eighties flooding back to the cities. As they were assigned to work units, many of those with lesser educational achievements could not find a job. Beijing felt it had no choice but to allow them to indulge in minor private business.

Thus did the unemployed — and in some cases the unemployable — of the early 1980s get their foot onto an escalator that would within two decades deliver some of them to the highest echelon of wealth. Li Xiaohua, for example, started out selling watches out of a bag on the streets beneath the office block he now owns. There had been no job for him when he returned from a Cultural Revolution assignment to "repair the earth" in a frigid northeastern province near the Russian border. After hawking watches for a time, he took a train to the coastal resort of Beidaihe, sunk all of his savings into an American-made iced-drink dispenser, and prowled the beach for customers.[8] Another salesman's job and some canny property investments later, he found himself in 1994 as the number-two tycoon on a list of the richest people in the country. Since then he has slipped down in the rankings, but he does not lack for consolations. One of them was parked in a garage beneath his office: a red Ferrari with the license plate A 0001. "It was the first to be imported," he said.

Even richer than Li in the mid-1990s was Mou Qizhong, who had emerged from jail in 1979 without a job, a work unit, or any apparent prospects.[9] He took a loan to start a "suitcase company" selling ornate brass alarm clocks to shops in Shanghai and made a reasonable profit. Then came his pièce de résistance. He had heard that a regional air carrier, Sichuan Airlines, needed planes but had no cash to buy them. The Soviet Union, he knew, had planes but lacked manufactured products. So he brokered a deal: five hundred freight cars crammed full of instant noodles, shoes, garments, and other stuff in exchange for four Soviet passenger aircraft.

The audacity of the "socks for jets" transaction delighted Beijing, which hailed Mou as one of the country's "Ten Best Private
Entrepreneurs" and a "Reform Hero." But his star was burning
too brightly. Bearing an uncanny physical resemblance to Mao, he
cultivated the likeness by brushing his hair in the same manner as
the late Great Helmsman and by letting it be known that he did
not much mind being called "Chairman Mou." His ideas grew
delusional; he talked seriously about blasting a hole through the
Himalayas and using giant turbines to blow moist, rain-filled Indian air to parched parts of China. A scheme to launch satellites
on Russian rockets hemorrhaged cash, driving his firm toward
insolvency. Finally, the fraud inspectors closed in, and in 2000
Mou was sentenced to life imprisonment for a foreign-exchange
scam.

Mou and Li were the luminary agents of a broader trend. Deng
had said that some people should be allowed to "get rich first,"
but he left the question of who these people should be largely to
chance. For much of the 1980s those selected by the rounds of social roulette were mostly the *getihu* ("single body units"), or self-
employed. Many of them would turn up again two decades later
as the leaders of corporate China. Liu Chuanzhi, who as chairman
of Lenovo bought the personal-computer division of IBM in 2004,
was in the mid-1980s just starting out as a sales representative for
"Big Blue" in China.[10] He would later recall how in those days he
lived in a tiny communal space at the back of a bicycle shed and
had to dry his socks over a coal-burning stove in the middle of a
single room used by the whole family. When he attended his first
IBM sales meeting, he wore a suit borrowed from his father. (I tell
his story in detail in chapter 7.)

Other strivers included Liu Yonghao, who by 2005 was the
largest individual shareholder in the China Minsheng Bank, the
country's first private bank. Back in the mid-1980s he used a bit
of cash borrowed from relatives to start raising chickens on his
balcony.[11] Chickens had eggs that hatched more chickens, and
through various permutations Liu soon became head of New
Hope, the largest animal-feed group in China. He used money

earned from that business to buy his stake in Minsheng, which is now listed on the stock market. Lu Guanqiu, whose Wanxiang company had become so successful by 2005 that it was making auto parts for General Motors, was in the mid-eighties just starting to make gimbals in his small smithy.[12] Li Shufu, the founder of Geely, a private carmaker that by 2005 was outselling some of the world's best-known brands, was two decades ago piecing together refrigerators using parts bought with a 2,000 renminbi loan from his father.[13] Li Dongsheng, who in 2003 acquired Thomson, the French electronics company, for TCL, a private electronics and white-goods manufacturer, spent much of the 1980s producing magnetic tapes with a Hong Kong businessman in the back of an agricultural machinery warehouse.[14] Zong Qinghou, whose Wahaha group had by 2005 turned into a formidable competitor of Coca-Cola in China, was in the 1980s selling ice pops priced at less than a penny each on the street.[15]

The list goes on. Every rags-to-riches story is different, but risk and hardship are common denominators. In his village on the lower Yangtze, the particular hardship that Shen Wenrong had to endure was the death of his father when he was in his late teens. His mother was left with four boys and two girls to support in the aftermath of the twentieth century's worst famine, in which an estimated thirty million Chinese are thought to have starved to death in the early 1960s. Because Shen's family were peasants on a commune, and because the commune system rewarded labor with food, Shen, the second son, was put out to work. He was tall and physically strong and therefore of more use in the fields than in a classroom at school. People who knew him said that when he was assigned to a production brigade, he worked as if driven by the anguish of misfortune.[16] But with so many unproductive mouths, his family was always short of the food points that the commune awarded for hours of labor and often had enough for only one meal a day.

What Shen soon learned, though, was that the work points were a red herring. The people on the commune who ate well were not those who labored the hardest but those who had the coziest connections with the managers of the grain store. Acting on this insight, he cultivated Zhang Wenzhong, the head of a production brigade, and benefited in two crucial ways from this contact. The first was through the handouts of food that Zhang would sometimes give him. The second was a recommendation, when an opportunity opened up, for Shen to apply for a job in a cotton factory that had decided to hire "mud legs," as peasant farmers were known. The leap he subsequently made from field to factory was the biggest and most important of his career. People in factories earned cash, not points. They could save money and had prospects for promotion.

Initially, what marked Shen apart in the textile mill were the fruits of his agricultural toil: he could lift and carry heavy bales of cotton with ease. But as time passed it became clear to his superiors that he was much more than a workhorse. He had a quiet, determined temperament and a shrewd intelligence. By the mid-1970s, when his next big chance presented itself, he had risen to a senior position in a factory that had thousands of employees and was committed to expansion. But it could not expand without the steel that was needed to build new workshops, machinery, and housing. Steel was strictly rationed just after the Cultural Revolution and was in chronically short supply all over the country. So Shen, with others, decided to take matters into his own hands and build a secret backyard furnace.

Jinfeng was then a very small town, no more than a speck on the map north of Shanghai, that even Chinese would have been hard-pressed to find. It was inconceivable that so lowly a place would be able to win over the bureaucrats in distant Beijing to provide approval for a new steel plant. So the cotton factory bosses turned obscurity to their advantage. While Beijing was preoccupied with power struggles and the impending death of Chairman Mao, they conferred with local officials and made the calculation that if they just went ahead and built their small steel workshop, nobody in the capital would notice.

Their gamble paid off. The workshop they made was the crudest type imaginable. Technologically, it was on a par with the nineteenth-century British blast furnace that stood as a monument outside the Phoenix plant in Dortmund. It consumed scrap metal scavenged from the surrounding countryside and smelted it into iron bars that workers pulled by hand out of the furnace.

Shen spent much of his time there, fascinated by the process and trying to think of ways to make money out of the changes that were stirring throughout the country. The communes had by then been disbanded, and tens of millions of small entrepreneurs were taking their first steps. Demand for steel in the early 1980s was rising all along the eastern and southern coastal strips. Shen could see which way the wind was blowing, but he had to find a product that was simple to make and had an assured market. He noticed that when peasant farmers made money, the first thing they spent it on was a bigger house. He also knew that China's cramped cities, enduring the highest population densities in the world, would have to expand outward. He concluded that the future lay in window frames made not from wood but from iron. He sent engineers to Shanghai to tour around the window-frame industry leader, a state company called Xing Hu, with instructions to copy down as much of the fabrication technology as they could get away with.

Shen's old friend Wu, who accompanied the engineers on that trip, explained how it was done: "They prepared everything in advance so well that as soon as they saw part of the manufacturing process, they would understand quickly how it was done. Then they boiled down the things they did not know to one or two questions, because they knew that if they asked too much, the other side would get suspicious."

Within a few years, Shagang was the second-largest window-frame maker in the country, and its sales were starting to challenge those of Xing Hu itself. Shen, however, did not rest on his laurels. He heard from a Hong Kong businessman in 1987 that an 80-ton electric arc furnace, capable of producing 275,000 tons of reinforced steel bars a year, was up for sale in a town called Bidston, near Liverpool. The steel industry in Britain, squeezed by foreign competition and restrained by a mature home market, was already in decline. But a British industrial castoff was in those days a state-of-the-art facility in China.

Shen borrowed heavily to finance the purchase and had to sell equity in his company to a Hong Kong investor. But as he wrestled to raise funds, opposition to the plan was mounting among government officials and even within the ranks of his own workers. During one meeting in Jinfeng, a worker shouted out that the idea of buying the Bidston plant was "like putting the hens to flight and breaking all the eggs." The vice minister of metallurgy made a special trip all the way from Beijing to persuade Shen to change his mind. Even large state companies had not been daring enough to acquire untested foreign equipment and have it shipped back and reassembled in China. Operations like this, said the vice minister, were akin to "trying to eat the sky."

But Shen would not listen. If the equipment did not work, he told a mass meeting of workers in Jinfeng, they could put it in a museum. "You can hire me to stand outside and sell the tickets," he said at that time.[17]

His venture came to within an inch of failure. The plant was bought and reassembled back in China. But the whole operation took three years, during which time inflation had spiraled almost out of control, millions of antigovernment protesters had taken to the streets in large cities, and Deng had responded by ordering the People's Liberation Army to massacre the people in the streets around Tiananmen Square in central Beijing. The economic consequence of the 1989 crackdown was a state of nervous stagnation, and Shen, saddled with heavy interest payments on his loans, faced the prospect of selling steel at below cost into a glutted market.

Then, out of the blue in early 1992, Deng embarked on what became known as his famous "southern tour." Like emperors of old, he traveled with a retinue of mandarins to inspect the situation beyond his sequestered leadership compound in Beijing. He chose to visit the Pearl River Delta region bordering Hong Kong, and everywhere he went he was feted. At first, conservatives in the capital tried to suppress his message, but gradually the news leaked out that Deng was exhorting people to "be a little bolder, go a little faster." It was like a spark on a haystack. In a few brief weeks, the whole nation had caught fire and Shagang was perfectly positioned to ride the boom that followed.

That boom would carry Shagang along the path that eventually reached Dortmund. Chinese and foreign investors alike took Deng's message from the southern tour as a rallying cry for faster economic liberalization. Foreign direct investment began to flood into coastal areas; the Hong Kong stock and property markets rallied; China's own stock markets — one in Shanghai and the other in Shenzhen — were founded; Southeast Asian nations began to sell more resources to the emerging giant in their midst; and in 1995 China's economy grew at more than 14 percent in a single year. But all this would prove downright lackluster compared to the cyclonic forces that were unleashed in the first few years of the twenty-first century.

The appetite that was unleashed on the world from 2003 on was in its extent and nature utterly different from that which followed the southern tour. It emanated from nothing less than the full-bore transformation of a large continental economy, a transition through time, space, technology, culture, and ideology. China had for centuries been the world's biggest economy, and it was emerging once more, but along lines that were unprecedented. This cauldron of change, along with the combustions and eruptions that attended it, was set to fundamentally alter the globe in myriad ways. I set out in 2004 to look for a place that would encapsulate many of the changes taking place in China, somewhere that could serve as a symbolic epicenter of the energies remaking the country and, by extension, the world. Far up the Yangtze's turbulent course from the alluvial bed of Shagang, I felt I found it, a place that was largely unknown to the world that it was already helping to reshape: Chongqing.

2

The Future Is the Past
(Except When It Isn't)

Chungking, China's wartime capital, is marked on no-man's map. The place labelled Chungking is a sleepy town perched on a cliff that rises through the mists, above the Yangtze River to the sky; so long as the waters of the Yangtze flow down to the Pacific, that river town will remain. The Chungking of history was a point in time, a temporal bivouac with an extra-geographical meaning, like Munich or Versailles. It was an episode shared by hundreds of thousands of people who had gathered in the shadow of its walls out of a faith in China's greatness and an overwhelming passion to hold the land against the Japanese. Men great and small, noble and corrupt, brave and cowardly, convened there for a brief moment; they are all gone home now.[1]

THAT EXCERPT IS TAKEN from *Thunder Out of China*, the 1946 classic by Theodore H. White and Annalee Jacoby, two reporters for *Time* magazine who spent a few years in Chungking, or Chongqing as it is now called, during World War Two. The city they recall was for a while an American household name. It featured in Hollywood movies and romantic novels. Its fate was the focus of stormy congressional debates, and it was not unusual for the clocks above hotel reception desks in New York and Washington to show the time in London, Paris, and Chungking.

White and Jacoby traced the tribulations of General Joseph Stilwell, or "Vinegar Joe," who had been dispatched by Washing-

★

23

ton to aid the ailing forces of Chiang Kai-shek. Chiang, the leader
of the Kuomintang, or KMT, was later to lose a civil war against
Mao Zedong and flee in 1949 to set up a "free China" on the island of Taiwan, just off the mainland's southeast coast. But at the
time that Stilwell and America came to Chiang's assistance, his
energies were still fully absorbed fighting the Japanese, to whom
he had surrendered his capital, Nanking. From Nanking Chiang
retreated up the Yangtze River with a flotilla of junks carrying
dismantled factories and power plants, and did not call a halt until he was more than a thousand miles into the embrace of China's interior. The place where he unloaded his junks, where he set
up his "temporal bivouac," as White and Jacoby called it, was a
walled town of brick and bamboo dwellings that straggled down
to a river wharf.

The house that Chiang and Stilwell used to plan some of their
joint operations can still be seen in Chongqing today. A spartan,
solidly built place with wartime wooden floorboards, it stands
high on a cliff overlooking the misty river and is now a museum.
Photographs on the walls depict the tenor of that time. "Flying Tiger" American airmen who flew dangerous supply missions over
the Himalayas stand square to the camera, cigarettes lolling from
the corner of their mouths. The Chinese and American soldiers
who built the "Stilwell Road" into Burma are bathed in sweat as
they cut a trail through a thick, malarial jungle. Stilwell himself
looks thin, stooped, and almost kindly in his thick-rimmed spectacles, while Chiang is stern and immaculate in his generalissimo's
uniform. There are also views of Chongqing. The photographs
show a town reduced to rubble and charred remains by the repeated raids of Japanese bombers. So complete was the destruction that, peering into one of the grainy black-and-white prints,
it is difficult to spot more than a few buildings left standing on
the narrow littoral of the river. It is even more difficult, though, to
reconcile the scene in that wartime photograph with the vista of
the modern city visible from a museum window.

Chongqing's role as a footnote in world history is over. It is no
longer merely "a point in time," a focus for outside ambitions, or

a forward position in an international theater of events animated from Tokyo, Washington, and Nanking. It is now the center, at least symbolically, of a trend that is reshaping the world. The city is engaged in a revival more far-reaching than its wartime destruction. A tumult of construction is under way, an outpouring of energy that eclipses everything before it. The area that was a swath of rubble in a museum photograph is now a zone of highrise glass-and-concrete office buildings, neon-lit shopping malls, and restaurants selling hot pot, the spicy dish for which the city is famous.

The easiest way to describe the transformation under way in Chongqing is by comparing it with Chicago in the nineteenth century. The "city of the century" then was to the explosive growth of the American West what Chongqing, in many ways, is to the renaissance of China in the twenty-first century. Chicago was a gateway to vast and largely undeveloped lands, a hub where the traffic of roads, rail lines, and waterways converged, and a center for commerce where ambition eviscerated risk. Chongqing, also, is all of these things. The location of both cities was preordained by natural features, in Chicago's case by its proximity to Lake Michigan and the rivers that feed it, and in Chongqing's by its position at the confluence of the Yangtze and Jialing rivers. But the drive behind both places was and is the vitality of a population that migrated to live and work there.

Caught up in their booms, neither city could be described as aesthetically pleasing. H. G. Wells, who wrote *The Time Machine*, was appalled by the abattoirs in Chicago's northern suburbs, which slaughtered livestock from all over the Midwest. He wrote of an "unwholesome reek" as his train passed by the slaughterhouses and rail cars at sidings packed with "doomed cattle." Although some observers saw in Chicago "a concentrated essence of Americanism," Wells found it "one hoarse cry for discipline," and as he traveled through the final fathoms of smoke and grime into the "large emptiness of America," he described the city retreating into the distance as a "dark smear in the sky."

Chongqing presents a similar aspect today. As I approached it from the air, it was lost in its own pollution. The river mist that White and Jacoby remember creeping over their "sleepy town" has become a blanket of industrial smog, acrid to the taste, enveloping everything. I thought I could even discern the miasma curling into the corridors of my hotel. Beyond the hotel windows was a ceaseless clamor: the pounding of jackhammers, the churning of cement mixers, the impatient clarion of car horns, the cries of hawkers in back alleys, and the gurgle of pipes that spew a billion tons of untreated sewage into the Yangtze each year. Amid the hubbub, people were infused with purpose. Middle-class women in leotards pounded the treadmills in a fitness club visible from a main street through floor-to-ceiling windows. Around the corner, a group of businessmen, all dressed in black, disappeared into the faux-baroque doorway of an establishment called the Rich Club to have their drinks poured, vanities massaged, and passions quenched by country girls offering the "three accompaniments."

Nearby, in a hot-pot restaurant, an extended family celebrating a birthday party had grown red-faced on rice spirits. As the drink flowed, the singing began. The songs were high-pitched and nasal, and the tunes jaunty. I imagined that they were imports from villages in the mountains around the city. Outside the restaurant, on the roadside, as I stood taking notes, a high school student approached me, with her mother a couple of steps behind. In halting English she said she wanted me to get her out of this place. The pollution was lethal, she said, and everyone was being poisoned. Quiet tears started to roll down her cheeks. Her mother tugged at her arm, embarrassed at the display of emotion, but the girl persisted as the tears flowed more freely. I could see that the air was bad, but I was puzzled as to why this should cause grief. Then she told me: her father had died recently of throat cancer. Standing on the pavement next to a giant plastic-and-velvet Santa Claus, the teenager imitated the hoarse, barking way her father used to talk.

The raw human effort that girded nineteenth-century Chicago and propels Chongqing today underpins the two cities' most revealing similarity: the speed of their expansion. When Chicago was transforming the Midwest and helping to turn America from a coastal to a continental economy, the rapid pace of its physical and population growth became a much-mentioned phenomenon. Charles Dudley Warner, a contemporary travel writer, wrote: "There is in history no parallel to this [meteoric growth]. Not St. Petersburg rising out of the marshes at an imperial edict, nor Berlin, the magic creation of a consolidated empire and a Caesar's power."[2] Warner's friend Mark Twain, also a frequent visitor, recalled the city's changing visage in his book *Life on the Mississippi.* "We struck the home trail now," he wrote, "and in a few hours were in that astonishing Chicago — a city where they are always rubbing a lamp, and fetching up the genii, and contriving and achieving new impossibilities. It is hopeless for the occasional visitor to try to keep up with Chicago — she outgrows her prophecies faster than she can make them. She is always a novelty; for she is never the Chicago you saw when you passed through the last time."[3]

Impressive though Chicago's transformation must have seemed then, its dimensions pale when compared with those of present-day Chongqing. Herein lies the key to understanding why China's emergence is different and unprecedented. Although it is following a path of industrialization and urbanization blazed by the United States in the nineteenth century, Japan since the 1950s, and several other nations in more recent times, the sheer scale and speed of the renaissance puts it in a class of its own. The appetites that are correspondingly released are of a magnitude that is only just starting to be felt around the world, and yet they are already forceful enough to pluck a steel plant whole from the middle of the German city it used to nurture.

Chicago, then known as the fastest-growing city on earth, took fifty years, until 1900, to increase its population by 1.7 million people. Chongqing is growing at *eight times* that speed. In the six years beginning in 1998, it grew by 1.7 million, or an average of nearly 300,000 new inhabitants a year. Most of these people were migrants from the countryside who came to seek employment in factories, or as maids, laborers, and a thousand other jobs that hold the promise of an urban future and a new life for themselves and their children. To accommodate this human tide, the city proper has had to expand in size by at least a dozen square miles every year since 1998. In 2004, as the migration from rural areas accelerated, some fifteen square miles of new houses, factories, roads, railways, ports, and other infrastructure had to be built. The same again was happening in 2005. The result of this has been that since 1998, Chongqing has grown in population by the equivalent of three Dortmunds and a couple of Detroits. If the future bears out the conservative predictions of its urban planners, the city will leap from a current 4 million inhabitants to 6.6 million by 2010 — more than the combined population of the eleven cities that make up Germany's industrial Ruhr.

Chongqing city is the focal point of a larger area designated as a "municipality," and it may be that at some time in the future much of that municipality, which is now comprised mainly of towns, villages, and farmland that hold a total population of around 32 million, will agglomerate into a single conurbation. If it does so, it may lay claim to being the largest city on earth. But at the moment, the most extraordinary thing about Chongqing is that it is not necessarily exceptional. Urbanization on a massive scale is happening in towns and cities all over China, and the process is not expected to abate for the foreseeable future. This trend, taken in its entirety, is truly awe-inspiring. In 1949, the year of the revolution, the number of Chinese cities with a population of more than a million was only five, and those with between 500,000 and 1 million inhabitants numbered just eight. In 2000, the last year for which figures are available, those numbers had risen to forty and fifty-three, respectively.[4] Japan, by contrast, has only six cities with more than a million inhabitants.

Yet China's urbanization is still in its infancy. There are now roughly 400 million people living in towns and cities, but in 2050 that number is expected to have risen by between 600 and 700 million, to reach a total of 1 billion or 1.1 billion.[5] Even at that level, China may be only slightly more than 70 percent urbanized, compared with prevailing rates of around 90 percent for the United Kingdom and the United States, just over 80 percent for France and Germany, and 77 percent for Japan. The investment required to settle so many people in an urban environment is impossible to calculate with any accuracy, but it is clear that worldwide demand for steel, aluminum, copper, nickel, iron ore, oil, gas, coal, and many other basic metals and resources may remain strong for as long as cities in China expand at a rapid clip.

The momentum behind the process is animated by another of China's most salient characteristics, something I call the compression of developmental time. What this means, on a human level, is demonstrated by someone I met in Chongqing, a young woman called Huang. She had a dimpled smile, a face that betrayed her feelings, and a job selling low-end real estate to out-of-towners who wanted to move, as she had done, to the big metropolis. A miniature pink cell phone hung on a ribbon around her neck. But seventy miles away, in the village of her birth, Huang was the daughter of a farmer who fed plump white ducks on a small pond and tilled a half-acre plot of land. The family house was an old stone structure, and it was so typical of peasant dwellings that it was faithful to the very origin of the Chinese character for "home," which shows the symbol for "pig" beneath the symbol for "roof." In a back room beyond the kitchen, a pig sat in a sty beneath an open latrine. There was nothing unusual in this. Many of the farmhouses around Chongqing had a similar arrangement.

The point is that Huang's home and village had barely changed in hundreds of years. But the rise of modern cities like Chongqing had meant that in the two hours it took for Huang to travel between her old home and her new life, she traversed centuries of developmental time. This time-warp effect is a crucial propellant of China's economic rise. Back in the village, where land-to-population ratios are among the lowest in the world, families often have little more than a subsistence income. Around seven hundred million people are thought to get by on less than two dollars a day. That provides a huge pool of labor that is willing to work at preindustrial wages in factories capable of producing goods at a speed that is many times faster than was possible during the Industrial Revolution in England some 230 years ago. The productivity that results from this compression of developmental time is spectacular, and it guarantees that as long as there are factories being built in places such as Chongqing, there will be robust demand for the labor of farmers' children.

The wages of migrant workers have risen considerably since reforms began in 1978, especially for those who work in factories along the east and south coasts. But in historical terms they remain paltry. During the early stages of the Industrial Revolution, the British Parliament triggered riots by rejecting the Weavers' Minimum Wage Bill, legislation that would have lifted the wages of hand-loom operators above the prevailing 8 shillings for an eighty-four-hour week.[6] But in Chongqing today, offering such a wage might trigger a disturbance for the opposite reason. Adjusted for time and converted into renminbi, those 8 shillings would now be worth 1,300 a month, or about double what a semiskilled migrant worker could expect for a similar number of hours. Even in the booming factory towns in Guangdong province near Hong Kong and in the Yangtze basin, 1,300 renminbi a month is still an attractive salary. In nineteenth-century Chicago, too, workers were far better compensated than they are in China today. For instance, a worker in a lumberyard in Chicago in the late 1850s could expect to get between $10 and $15 a month in the dollars of the day.[7] Converted to current values, that is the equivalent of between $196 and $294 a month — or between one and a half and three times the current Chinese wage for a similar manual job. (As of this writing, $1 equals about 8 renminbi.)

The marriage of cheap labor and modern factories does much to make China competitive, and that competitiveness justifies the huge investments required to carry forward the expansion of cities. But those are not the only forces behind the country's burgeoning appetite. Another is that when it comes to infrastructure, China is remaking itself in the image of its superpower mentor, the United States — only often more quickly and on a larger scale. Sometimes the resemblances are uncanny. It turns out that it is no accident that Chongqing seems to mirror the Chicago of days gone by. Its city planners and transportation experts have spent months traveling the United States, absorbing the details of how efficiencies are created by modern cities and infrastructure. "The dream of becoming like Chicago is too delicious a dream," said Chen Zhigang, one of Chongqing's senior urban planners.

Chinese planners have ingested the American experience. They know that the interstate highway system is reckoned to have reduced the costs to American companies of producing goods and services by more than one trillion dollars in the first forty years of its operation, since 1956. So in the late 1990s, the Chinese started to build their own. The roads are numbered, as are those in the United States, and the highway signs have the same white letters on a green background. And just as in America, the new roads are spawning their own autocentric microeconomies. There are repair shops, car washes, gas stations, fast-food restaurants, and "leisure centers" that provide prostitutes for long-distance truck drivers.

In some places, the new expressways have opened up vast new markets. The city of Wuhu, a river port on the Yangtze's middle course, was a backwater as recently as 1998. When I first went there at that time, it took me six hours along a bone-jangling, pot-holed road to reach it from Hefei, the provincial capital. When I did the journey again in 2002, it took an hour and a half, and Wuhu had been transformed. In just four years, four expressways, a road-and-rail bridge over the Yangtze, and a river port had been built. It was now possible, the vice mayor told me, to reach 250 million people within eight hours of the city center. "That is the population of America," he said with a smile.

The only real difference between China's expressway system and U.S. interstates is that when it is done, China's road network will be longer. Although only around 18,500 miles have thus far been completed, Beijing plans by 2030 to have laid 53,000 miles, about ten thousand miles more than the existing U.S. system. At the same time as it builds its highways, China is also recreating an upscale version of America's great nineteenth-century railroad boom. It has plans for a high-speed track to link Beijing and Shanghai and is near to completing the Qinghai–Tibet railway, an engineering challenge that recalls the building of the U.S. transcontinental railroad through the Sierra Nevada. Nearly 800 miles of the Tibet railway run at more than 14,500 feet above sea level, and over 300 miles of track are laid on permanently frozen soil. Its longest tunnel, built through nearly four miles of rock, is longer than any carved through the Sierra Nevada by the thousands of Chinese "coolies" who had arrived in California after fleeing war and famine in China in the 1860s.

Of course, not all the feats of Chinese infrastructure have been inspired by American example. The dream of building a dam to span the Yangtze stretches back about eighty years, to Sun Yat-sen, the founder of the KMT and the first of several Chinese leaders to see the country's biggest river not as a flowing silken thread but as a powerful muscle that if flexed could lift the nation from poverty. Here is what Sun Yat-sen said in 1924 about the potential of China's rivers:

> If the water power of the Yangtze and Yellow rivers could be utilized by the newest methods to generate electrical power, about one hundred million horsepower might be obtained. Since one horsepower is equivalent to the power of eight strong men, one hundred million horsepower would be equivalent to the power of eight hundred million manpower . . . Manpower can be used only eight hours a day, but mechanical horsepower can be used all twenty-four hours . . . If we could utilize the water power in the Yangtze and Yellow rivers to generate one hundred million horsepower of electrical energy, we would be putting twenty-four hundred million men to work! When that time comes, we shall have enough power to supply railways, motor cars, fertilizer factories and all kinds of manufacturing establishments.[8]

In 2003 the Three Gorges Dam was built, and Sun's dream, if not his optimistic mathematical calculations, was realized. The Chinese project drew comparisons with the Hoover Dam — built in the 1930s across the Colorado River — which had helped create a new regional economy from nothing and raised a city, Boulder, out of an expanse of desert. The Hoover Dam was an engineering wonder of the world. But the Three Gorges, which spans the Yangtze River about two hundred miles east of Chongqing, is six times as long and eight times as powerful as the Hoover. And scores of dams larger or around the same size as the Hoover are planned for construction across the upper reaches of the Yangtze, the Mekong, and the Salween as the waters tumble down from the tablelands of Tibet. Each year since 2004, China has installed the equivalent of all the generating capacity of a country such as Spain, and it is expected to continue repeating that feat in the years to come.

The Three Gorges was to have spinoff benefits too. The lake it created is expected to stretch all the way upriver to Chongqing, eliminating the rapids and currents that made the KMT's retreat from Nanking so perilous. In 2006 the lake was filling up, and by 2009 oceangoing vessels will be able to travel all the way from the sea to Chongqing, a distance of 1,250 miles. The city is building two large container ports in anticipation of an upsurge in traffic.

When this happens, the changes it may bring could be similar to those wrought by the construction of the Erie Canal in 1825. The Erie was an essential foundation of American nationhood, opening up the western interior to commerce by reducing the cost of grain freight rates between the Atlantic Ocean and the Great Lakes by 90 percent from the very first day it started operating.[9] It is interesting to note, however, that the cost of shipping a ton of wheat one mile along the Erie in 1825 was around 120 times higher than the cost of transporting a ton of merchandise one mile down the Yangtze in 2005, calculated by adjusting dollar values over time. The reasons for this may include efficiency gains in ship technology as well as improvements in packaging, management, financing, labor organization, and the greater availability of alternatives to river transport.

Taken together, these advantages describe one aspect of China's supercharged emergence. Centuries of developmental time have coalesced into a concentrated vigor. The marriage of Industrial Revolution–era labor costs and twenty-first-century production technology is fueling a rural-to-urban migration on a scale that has never before been approached and facilitating a construction boom of unheard-of dimensions in cities linked increasingly by an infrastructure network that equals or surpasses America's. That, in one sentence, describes the source of some of China's world-shaping energies and appetites.

China is thus absorbed in laying the underpinnings of a future superpower. There is little doubt that Beijing would like one day to have the most powerful economy in Asia, and, probably, the world. Indeed, it is already commonplace for observers to extrapolate from current growth rates that China will surpass the United States as the world's largest economy sometime around 2040. This prediction assumes, of course, that the graphs tracing the country's current trajectory continue their unrelenting ascent. Those who make this assumption do so partly because of the long-range prospects for development that are evident in places such as Chongqing. Another common justification for predictions of greatness is historical determinism — the belief that because China had been the world's economic superpower for most of the past two millennia, it is destined to be so again.

It may transpire, however, that events do not conform to neat extrapolations. In the second half of this book, I try to show why linear predictions of a manifest Chinese destiny may be flawed. As for historical determinism, the facts are by no means as straightforward as they may seem. Leaving aside the broader philosophical question of whether history is hard-wired to repeat itself, the issue of whether China was *ever* truly an economic superpower is itself open to debate.

Certainly, its technological prowess has been awesome. Long before the dawn of recorded history, the Chinese appear to have mastered techniques that would not become known in Europe until thousands of years later. Silk fragments recently discovered in the province of Zhejiang near Shanghai have been carbon-dated to around four thousand years ago — two thousand years before sericulture spread to the Roman Empire. Another recent discovery, this time in the northern province of Henan, suggests that as early as the sixteenth century B.C.E., in a bronze foundry covering an area of more than 30,000 square feet, the Chinese may have used a prototype of the industrial process, complete with the division of labor, that would not become widespread in Europe until the Industrial Revolution. In addition, it is well known that although bronzes were made in the Near East earlier than in China, the single-casting techniques developed in settlements on the central plains of China and the sophistication of the finished items remained unrivaled for hundreds of years.

As in any country, China's technological development moved in fits and starts. Centuries went by during which little of worth appeared to have been invented, followed by an apparently sudden flowering of creative talent. Perhaps the greatest outpouring of such talent came from the tenth to the thirteenth century. The inventions of that period include several technologies that either remain in use today or have lapsed from modern life only relatively recently. The windmill, the lock gates that control the flow of water in canals, mechanical clockwork, power transmission by a drive belt, water-powered metallurgical blowing engines, hemp-spinning machines, gear wheels, stern-post rudders for ships, water-powered trip hammers for forges, all originated in China. Other inventions, such as gunpowder, printing, and various astrological devices, were also in evidence in China before they gained currency in the West.

In more modern times, the examples of ships and porcelain provide further evidence of China's technological superiority. Fifteenth-century shipyards in China made oceangoing wooden traders that were three times the size of anything that the British put in the water until the 1800s. The largest of these vessels, one of the treasure ships used by the Ming dynasty admiral Zheng He on his trading missions to Asia and Africa, weighed a staggering 8,500 tons. Nothing nearly that size was built anywhere else in the world until more than four hundred years later, when the British engineer Isambard Kingdom Brunel defied legions of skeptics by constructing his *Great* ships out of iron in the mid-nineteenth century.

The example of porcelain shows a similar, enviable precocity. The exact date of porcelain's invention in China is a subject of controversy, but it is clear that by the thirteenth century techniques were well advanced. By the sixteenth century, most of Europe's ruling classes were in thrall to this mysterious material, which combined a translucent luminosity with a hardness that allowed Chinese artisans to make ceramics that were almost eggshell-thin. So enraptured were some of Europe's princes, monarchs, and barons by porcelain that the flow of funds from aristocratic coffers to the pottery town of Jingdezhen, in central China, swelled over time into a flood. One nobleman, Augustus the Strong of Saxony, shelled out 100,000 thalers — enough to pay the annual salaries of a thousand skilled craftsmen — to buy porcelain in the first year of his reign alone.[10]

The economic impact of porcelain imports was such that many of the most powerful families in Europe threw themselves into a desperate quest to discover how the wonderful material was made. All they had to go on were vague secondhand accounts that had trickled back from China: a special clay was required, and it had to be fired at very high temperatures. More than that was guesswork. By 1705 a replica had been achieved in France, a so-called soft paste. But it was instantly recognizable as inferior to the real thing.

Augustus the Strong, however, was both resourceful and determined. He set up what would now be called a research and development program — though one with medieval characteristics — in his castle at Meissen. His researchers worked as captives, and his chief technician, Johann Bottger, may have been in fear of his life, having made the earlier blunder of promising his impatient patron that he could turn base metals into gold. Alchemy he never managed, but he did, through luck, stumble upon the right ingredients for porcelain. He mixed a certain type of fine clay found near Colditz with alabaster in 1708. It happened that Colditz clay was identical to Chinese kaolin, the hitherto secret ingredient that made porcelain so hard and glassy. Although it would be some years before Meissen porcelain could compete with the exquisite

artifacts of Jingdezhen, the discovery nevertheless helped alleviate Europe's first, but not its last, balance-of-payments crisis with
China.

In time, though, the creativity that led to innovations such as
porcelain seemed to dissipate. In the late eighteenth and early
nineteenth centuries China lost the technological lead that it arguably had held for millennia. This decline was partly relative; the
Industrial Revolution had thrown up a tumult of ingenuity that
spread across much of Europe. But it was also partly that China itself was growing stale. Theories as to why this happened abound.
One suggests that the rigidity of an imperial examination system
that channeled intellectual energy into literature and neglected the
sciences had an impact on technological inventiveness. Another
maintains that a sharp growth in population made it cheap to hire
workers, thereby inhibiting the development of labor-saving machinery. A third raises the possibility that deforestation deprived
China of adequate supplies of wood, its primary energy source. A
fourth suggests that the ceaseless military campaigns along China's northern and northwestern frontiers diverted funding and
focus away from peacetime pursuits. The Chinese government,
for its part, blames its slide from technological preeminence on
the rapaciousness of Western powers that attacked Chinese ports,
peddled opium to its people, and occupied parts of its territory.

All of these theories would seem to contain a measure of validity. However, the work of Angus Maddison, a leading economic
historian, shows that the decline, in terms of individual prosperity, started long before the eighteenth century.

A high point in Chinese prosperity was achieved in the Tang
dynasty (618–906), an era that is also regarded as a cultural golden
age. Some of the most moving poetry dates from that era, and the
ceramic likenesses of courtesans, horses, and camels fashioned
then remain unsurpassed in their beauty. In those days, the country had several cities with a population of more than half a million, whereas Europe's proudest urban centers could boast of only
tens of thousands of residents. The Tang was also an age of inter-
nationalism. The Silk Road ran from the central city of Chang'an,

or modern-day Xi'an, to the central Asian cities of Samarkand, Bukhara, and beyond. The ports of Quanzhou and Guangzhou on the south coast were heavily engaged in trade, mostly with Southeast Asia. Foreigners were present in numbers that were not to be equaled until the first half of the twentieth century. Not only did some 25,000 Turks, Afghans, Tajiks, Jews, Zoroastrians, and Christians reside in Chang'an, but non-Chinese occupied senior administrative, military, and commercial positions. In southern trading cities, foreigners may have been even more numerous than in Chang'an. Perhaps as many as 100,000 non-Chinese may have lived in them during the first half of the Tang, before xenophobic massacres in 760 and 879 drove numbers down.[11]

But a couple of hundred years later, according to Maddison's figures, things slowly started to deteriorate. By 1400 Chinese were still richer on average than Europeans, and their economy was also larger than that of western Europe. At that time, Chinese earned an average of $500 each (calculated at 1985 values), spread across a population of 74 million people, meaning that China's gross domestic product amounted to the equivalent of $37 billion. Western Europeans, by contrast, were earning $430 per head and had a population of 43 million, so their overall economic output was worth $18.4 billion. In 1820, however, China's per capita income remained at around $500, but Europeans were by then earning on average $1,034 each. By 1950 the difference was even more dramatic. The Chinese were by then earning around $454 per capita, less than they had done in the fifteenth century. Europeans, by contrast, were pulling in an average of $4,902 each.[12] Even though Europe's population was still smaller than China's, the value of its economic output was larger by several multiples.

These figures show why it might not be appropriate to regard China in history as an economic superpower, at least by contemporary standards. For hundreds of years the country was locked in a cycle of growth without development. Its people, on average, were living the same lives in 1950 as they had done a millennium earlier, in spite of obvious changes in technology, customs, and politics. The only impetus behind the expansion of the Chinese economy during those centuries seems to have been the increase in its population. But this did not bestow prosperity and vitality to the people; rather, it intensified competition for limited resources, inflated the death tolls from periodic famines and natural disasters, and forced the government to expend more and more energy on social control. In short, though China was certainly a large economy and often the largest economy on earth, the lives of the majority of its people rarely rose above the level of subsistence.

In other ways, too, China's realities were not consistent with the image or idea of an economic superpower. In common usage, the word "superpower" implies a projection of influence. But China, since the Tang dynasty, dwelt largely within itself. Although it traded with the outside world, the volume of this trade as a percentage of the size of its economy, or the economies of those it traded with, was tiny — no more in the nineteenth century, for instance, than around 1 percent of its GDP. Therefore, the effect China had on the world around it was mostly that of a big, brooding presence that fought protracted wars along its borders. Over the centuries, various Western commentators noticed this, but Adam Smith may have summed it up best in his 1776 masterwork, *The Wealth of Nations:*

> China seems to have been long stationary, and had probably long ago acquired that full complement of riches which is consistent with the nature of its laws and institutions. But this complement may be much inferior to what, with other laws and institutions, the nature of its soil, climate and situation might admit of. A country which neglects or despises foreign commerce, and which admits the vessels of foreign nations into one or two of its ports only, cannot transact the same quantity of business which it might do with different laws and institutions.[13]

It is neither a coincidence nor a surprise, therefore, that China's economic ascent since Deng Xiaoping started reforms in 1978 has been accompanied by a level of openness to foreign commerce that is reminiscent of the golden age of the Tang. The fruits of this policy are also visible in figures: in 1975, the nadir in well over a thousand years of economic history, Chinese earned on average just 7.5 percent of the income of western Europeans. But by 2000 there had been a startling turnaround, and incomes were up to about 20 percent of European levels.[14] Which, to put it another way, means that Beijing had succeeded in turning the clock back to around 1850, the last time the wealth gap was so narrow.

The process by which China is turning back the clock and joining the world is not pretty or forgiving. It is full of human suffering, alienation, and longing. And it starts with men like Wang Qiling, the head of a family of migrant workers. Wang, a slight, wiry man with eyebrows set in a frown, works as a caretaker at a weekend cottage rented by Westerners in a beautiful village on the outskirts of Beijing. The village grew up in the Ming dynasty (1386–1644), when its inhabitants were charged with guarding and tending the tombs of the emperors' favorite concubines. But after the Ming succumbed to an invasion of Manchu nomads from the northern steppe, the tombs fell into disrepair. Bricks from their perimeter walls were pillaged to build houses, and the land inside them was used to plant fruit trees or crops. In recent years, one large, intricately carved marble slab that was an offertory platform to a concubine's spirit has become a makeshift ping-pong table for village boys.

Wang's home is far from Beijing, in a part of China that is so different it could be another world. He comes from the village of White Horse, in a rural county several hours' drive from Chongqing, which is famous for *hua jiao*, the peppers that make Palace Treasure Chicken and other dishes that scorch and numb the tongue. His birthplace is hot and humid, full of shade from broadleaf trees and loud choruses of insects. On the outskirts of Beijing, though, the air is dry, the winters long, the food strange, and the locals mostly unfriendly. In particular, the couple who own the cottage next door to the one Wang tends are unpleasant simply, it seems, because they can be. They tell him to his face that his thick southern accent, which mixes up the tones that are essential to understanding Chinese, hurts their ears. They tell him he speaks worse than the foreigners he works for and that he should go back home, leaving the concubine tomb village to the people for whom it was intended.

When a macaque that the couple kept tethered to a tree by their cottage broke free one day and bit Wang seven times, they saw no reason to apologize. They, after all, were successful people with a 100-milliliter motorbike who had given up working in the fields, borrowed some money, and bought a sauna business in the nearby town of Changping. To them, Wang represented the life they had left behind. He was a person of no consequence, a peasant. In his own way, however, Wang was engaged in the same project as his neighbors. He had walked out of his home village for the same reason that all of the 120 million people who make up the "blind tide" of migrant workers did. To escape. He had left his home, his wife, and his teenage son for seven straight years because his job as a caretaker offered some hope of finding a path out of the myriad humiliations of poverty. Whatever the drawbacks of his current work—the loneliness, the way he missed seeing his son grow up, and the strangeness of watching weekend guests spend the equivalent of several months of his salary on an afternoon barbecue—they were not so bad as the memories of a childhood without enough food.

The escape that Wang was plotting was not his own but his son's. Without an education or skills beyond farming, his own life was already set in its trammels. But his son had a chance at a future. Ever since he was born, he had been costing his father extra. He was named Sifa, a play on the words for "four fine," because, being the third child, he had exceeded the quota of two offspring that farming families were limited to in the mid-1980s, when he was born. The fine for breaking the quota in those days was 400 renminbi, the equivalent of about a year's income and an amount that Wang had been proud to fork out. Sifa had repaid the investment, excelling at school and becoming the first person from White Horse village ever to make it to a university. He did not go to a prestigious campus like Peking or Tsinghua University in the capital, but his enrollment at college represented a first step on the single-plank bridge over the chasm that separates those who work with their brains and those who use their hands. All in all, though, it cost around 10,000 renminbi a year to keep Sifa at college — more than Wang's annual salary.[15]

Fortunately, he could call on assistance from his daughters to help pay the bills. One daughter, Qining, had joined the army of more than twenty million other migrant workers who had found employment in one of the new cities clustered along the waterways and highways of the Pearl River Delta near Hong Kong. The other daughter, Qiping, had been a nanny to an English family, first in Beijing and then for a few years in London. She had gone to the capital in the mid-1990s, several years before the "blind tide" had reached its high-water mark. It was a daring move, one that her mother at the time had resisted on the grounds that it was not safe for a country girl barely out of her teens to try to make a living in an unfamiliar metropolis. But Qiping had insisted, and things had gone her way. The family she worked for was kind to her, and she loved the children she looked after. In London they all lived in a nice house next to a park. Looking out over the park's well-tended lawns and arbors, she sometimes wondered why so much good agricultural land was being allowed to go to waste.

The most difficult thing about living in London was the cost. Although Qiping was lonely, she avoided making friends because of the outlay that it entailed. A cup of coffee could set you back the equivalent of a week or more of spending money back in White Horse. She saved everything she earned, and in the four years that she lived in London, she did not buy one article of clothing. Even though she had a husband in China, a young man who had pursued her for more than a year, she never phoned him. When he called her long distance, she would berate him. "Why do I have to endure loneliness here, away from my family and everything? To make money! But you are wasting our precious money on phone calls," she remembers telling him on the phone. He would counter that he was using Internet calling cards because they were cheaper than the usual rates. He had to hear her voice, he would say.

"I am keeping these cards as a token of our love," he told her once.

The money she was earning was worth much more than the objects it could buy. Young women in rural China have to contend not only with the privations of widespread poverty but also with an entrenched patriarchal system. When a woman marries, she leaves her parents behind and becomes the property of her husband's family. "A woman marries outward," as an old saying puts it, "the way wastewater is thrown from the house." The wife is expected to work for and obey everyone in the male line—her husband, his father, and his brothers. Her only hope of changing this disenfranchised state is to give birth to her own power base, a son. But even if she manages this, she has to maintain vigilance toward her mother-in-law, who is often wary of her daughter-in-law's growing influence. The mother-in-law–daughter-in-law relationship is a staple of literary tragedy, and for good reason. Although family hierarchies have loosened up in the cities, the countryside remains a cruel place for young women joining society.

Suicides among young rural women rank as one of China's greatest social ills. The number of women who commit suicide —about five hundred a day on average—is much higher, in both absolute and relative terms, than in any other country. Some 56 percent of the world's female suicides occur in China, according to a study by the World Bank, Harvard University, and the World Health Organization.[16] This figure does not, of course, include the very large number who try to kill themselves but fail. Swallowing pesticide, which is readily available, is the most common means employed. It yields a quick and intensely painful death, which can be averted if the woman's stomach is pumped in time. Although the general cause of suicide is a feeling of hopelessness and rejection, the trigger is often physical abuse. The newspapers are full of stories of gruesome matrimonial violence.

What women lack most in rural China is status, and the prevalence of suicide shows that the lack of status can be fatal. The money that they earn, therefore — in factories on the coast, as housemaids and nannies in the large cities, or as prostitutes in bars, "leisure centers," and motels all over the country — is often spent when they return home, to compensate for this stifling deficiency. They buy things that confer an aura of importance. When Qiping got back from London with the fruits of her youthful labor, about $10,000, she spent it on a house. Not just any house but a four-story, white-tiled building with about four hundred square feet of space on each floor. She could have fitted her London bedroom inside one of its bathrooms. She put a large flat-screen TV in one room, complete with a DVD player and high-end sound system. She bought other gadgets that she never used. The house had drained all of her savings; she borrowed about $5,000 besides. But to her it was definitely worth it. Everyone knew she was a woman of substance, not a person to be trifled with. It was surely no accident that the home of her brother-in-law, just across the road from her own, was a full story shorter than hers.

The story of Qiping is not quite typical. Most migrant workers are not nannies and they do not usually go abroad. They toil in factories in the Pearl and Yangtze River deltas, or in steel towns such as Jinfeng, making heavy industrial goods or the things that fill the shelves in Wal-Marts, Targets, and Home Depots. Few of them get health benefits, many work shifts of twelve, fourteen, or even eighteen hours a day, and most of them earn Industrial Revolution–era wages. But there are still millions upon millions of people who are willing to do such work, not because they are attracted to it but because they are driven to it by the material and social privations bequeathed by Chinese history. Centuries of poverty and oppression have made village life in China anything but a rural idyll. People such as Qiping, her sister, and her father in the concubine tomb village near Beijing are, in some sense, not so much economic migrants as émigrés from a cruel past.

3

The Population Paradox:
Innovation, Piracy, and the
Grail of Market Share

T HE TRAIN SAT in the station for a long time, and when it finally departed it seemed to creep, so the moment of movement was all but imperceptible. My first inkling that the journey from Chongqing had started came when the play of platform shadows on the net curtains of my "soft sleeper" compartment slipped slightly in their frame. Then the indistinct outlines of people hawking chicken legs and tea eggs from carts slid slowly out of view. Other, more fleeting images took their place: underwear flapping on a suburban clothesline, a man shoveling coal, and farther down the track a donkey standing by stones in a quarry. As the train quickened, the snapshots blurred and the rhythm of the rolling stock grew louder. And then, after a certain time, that rhythm no longer registered in consciousness and the compartment seemed to fall still. Only the tremor of water in teacups on the table by the window supplied a sensation of flux. As on all long journeys in China, an air of suspended time seeped through the car, lending candor to conversations between travelers whose destinations would mark the end of their acquaintance. I sat, as so often before, looking out the window and thinking about the sheer size and complexity of the country parading past.

Out of Chongqing, the track quickly runs into mountains and through an impressive series of tunnels. Later, it travels into a landscape that opens out onto the floodplains of the Yangtze. The

★

natural scenery changes but in every direction throughout the journey one thing is constant. People. The weight of their presence is everywhere. Even in the spaces between the factories, towns, and villages, people could be seen moving to and fro on bicycles, tractors, carts, buses, and cars.

The vista from the train window was rarely uncluttered by development. The pressure of population was such that the smallest parcels of cultivatable land, high on mountain ledges and on the verges of roads, had been put to agricultural use. On this journey, as on many others over the years, I wondered how the pervasive presence of people has shaped China's experience and molded the national consciousness. I remembered a young woman I knew some eighteen years earlier in Tokyo. The daughter of a high-ranking cadre in Beijing, she had been sent to Japan for language study. We met at a night school crammer. One evening after classes, our conversation turned to the Great Leap Forward, the three years of Mao-inspired chaos that resulted in a famine in which at least thirty million people are thought to have died. "It was a good thing that they died," she said. "There are just too many people in China."

It is difficult to separate individuals from the influence of the population that surrounds them. And yet the urge is insistent. How does a national populace of 1.3 billion, the largest in the world, affect politics, economics, and society? What of the psychological impact, accumulated over centuries, of living as a single unit among a multitude so forbiddingly huge? Most of the Chinese to whom I have addressed these questions have shrugged, as if they were futile or the answers blatantly obvious. Nevertheless, intimations of a profound legacy are everywhere, embedded in human behavior, in the attitude of the state toward order, on every page of a turbulent history, and in the governing relationships of commerce.

Numbers possess a power that transcends the mechanics of mathematics. In the distant past, *wu ren chu* ("no-people places") denoted the boundaries of the Chinese world: the grasslands, steppe, mountains, and desert to the north and west, beyond which everything was alien and hostile. By contrast, the world within the central plains was ordered by numbers and remains so. Almost every phenomenon, principle, policy, and directive is broken down into constituent parts. Babies are said to "roll over at three [months], sit up at six, and crawl at eight." The link between nature and human activity is also numerically expressed. The following rhyme, conjured in the mists of history but still recited in Beijing today, calibrates the interaction of humans and climate in nine-day periods around the time of the lunar new year:

First ninth, second ninth, don't let your hands show;
Third ninth, fourth ninth, people are walking on ice;
Fifth ninth, sixth ninth, stand on riverbanks and watch the
    willow [buds];
Seventh ninth, the river ice splits;
Eighth ninth, geese arrive;
Ninth ninth and add one ninth, plowing oxen are everywhere
    on the land.

Human affairs are also arithmetically ordered. The "one China principle," "two whatevers," "three-character classic," "four modernizations," "five elements," "six desires," "seven emotions," "eight immortals," and the "stinking ninth category" are all terms in common usage. And as issues evolve, it is often the content rather than the matrix that alters. When the Communist Party decided that the "dictatorship of the proletariat" should no longer be one of the "four cardinal principles" of its ideology, the Party replaced it with something else rather than upset symmetry by reducing four principles to three. Officials are captivated by numbers because their career achievements are assessed by statistics, a reality reflected in the adage "Statistics make officials, and officials make [up] statistics."

The ability to memorize and regurgitate numbers and numerical sequences is another staple of successful officialdom. I remember one quarterly briefing of economic results held by Li Deshui, a senior staffer in the National Bureau of Statistics. Staring straight ahead and without any apparent notes, he threw out hundreds of figures, all quoted to at least one decimal place, in response to an avalanche of unscripted questions. Later, when official printouts of the statistics came through, I checked them against the notes I had taken during Li's performance. He had been 100 percent accurate.

The awe reserved for numbers is quickened when it comes to mathematical relationships, and of these, none is more alluring than multiplication. Always somewhere in the love affairs of foreigners with China down the ages there is the promise of the quantum leap. It was there when the Jesuits in the sixteenth century planned to convert 150 million souls — an opportunity bigger by multiples than any that existed in Europe. It was also evident in the fever of foreign traders in the mid-nineteenth century, when one English merchant observed, "If we could only persuade every person in China to lengthen his shirttail by a foot, we could keep the mills of Lancashire working around the clock." In a similar vein, William Howard Taft, who served as secretary of state and later as president, said in 1905 that "one of the greatest commercial prizes of the world is the trade with the 400,000,000 Chinese."[1] In the modern era, since the process of "reform and opening" began in 1978, some $550 billion of foreign direct investment has flowed in, a lot of it accompanied by dreams of exponential growth. "I can envision the day when over half the automobiles sold in the world are sold in Asia and perhaps even in China," said Joseph Gorman, the former CEO of TRW, America's largest manufacturer of car parts, in one typical comment. "If China were by the year 2010 or 2020 to have as many autos as the current per capita auto population of Germany today, there would be 500 million autos."[2]

Chinese officials, cognizant of the enchantment of numbers, like to boggle the mind on overseas trips. Bo Xilai, the minister of commerce, told a European audience in 2005: "China is a big family. We have 200 million middle school students. Every day 22,000 girls get married; 44,000 babies are born. We eat better since we opened China's door. Every day we eat 1.6 million pigs and 24 million chickens. Our premier not only wants young people to have a chance to study and grown-ups to have jobs, he also has to take care of 20 million kids in kindergarten and 12 million people aged 80."

But if foreign businessmen arrive in China transfixed by size and scale, many of them depart haunted by the concept of share. They envisage being able to sell their products to a multitude of Chinese and then watch as the hoped-for multitude is sliced and diced into morsels. Only certain sections of society are willing buyers of most products, and reaching them is made difficult by layers of local protectionism. When a market is finally found, aggressive domestic competitors have usually got there first. The fabled billion-person market is frequently reduced to a fraction in the figment of a dream.

It has been ever thus. Chinese history is much less the story of multiplication than of long division. The experience of having to share scarce resources among so many people has at times been inconvenient and at times traumatic. It has left an imprint not only on people like the young woman I met in Tokyo, but also on the language. The counting word for people, for instance, is "mouth." Rather than ask someone "How many people are there in your family?" you would say, "How many mouth-people do you have?" The low ratio of land to people has made the adequate provision of food a pressure felt by every dynastic ruler.

For emperors, famines were not only disasters that could, and frequently did, cause rebellion; they were also the ultimate insult. Emperors were *tian zi*, the sons of heaven, and as such they were the link between the earth and the celestial authorities that controlled the rain, wind, and temperature. Thus droughts, floods, famines, and other natural disasters were often seen by the people as evidence that heaven had withdrawn its favor from its son — that the emperor had lost *tian li*, heaven's mandate. For example, according to one legend the emperor Shangtang, of the Shang dynasty (1766–1122 B.C.E.), decided to sacrifice himself after the country had suffered seven years of drought. He chose self-immolation on a pyre as the preferred manner of his death, but at the very instant the wood was lit, the celestial powers took pity and caused rain to fall, thereby putting out the fire and ending the drought with one stroke. Although the story of Shangtang is a myth, there is nothing fanciful about the crucial relationship among land, population, and power over the past three or four thousand years. The perceived loss of heaven's mandate was seen as legitimizing revolt, and many a rebel leader, including Mao Zedong, had been swept into power at the head of a peasant army galvanized by hunger and the promise of handouts of land.

The key decisions made by such rebels after they took power always involved how much land to redistribute from the landlords to the peasant farmers and what level of agricultural tax to levy. These simple choices did much to determine the economic future and social structure of the empire, as well as the nature of the ruler's power base. If land was parceled out too liberally, the emperor risked losing the allegiance of the elite. But if not enough was doled out, the peasants would remain impoverished and were liable to rise up again. If taxes were too light, the imperial coffers would be strained and the emperor's authority weakened. But if they were too heavy, the masses could grow disgruntled and threaten the survival of the dynasty. Faced with the need to strike such a delicate balance between available food and demanding mouths, most new rulers made only cosmetic changes.

But Mao, the founder of the modern era, was different. His approach was not only revolutionary but unprecedented. He identified his power base as the rural peasantry and urban masses, and he ordered the persecution of landowners, capitalists, and anyone else with a bad "class background." No quarter was given, no balance struck; within three years of assuming power, he had decapitated the rural elite and presided over the murder of an estimated two million landowners. Mao did not recognize any authority greater than his own, so the tempering tradition of "heaven's mandate" had no truck with him. But most decisively of all for the future of China's economy, he scorned the notion that the scarcity of land was a restraint on population growth. Every mouth, he said, was attached to two arms. People could always produce more than they consumed.

The population explosion that Mao encouraged has had far-reaching consequences. The number of people living on the mainland shot up from an estimated 582.6 million at the time of the 1953 census to an official estimate of 1.295 billion now. (The real number is almost certainly higher, but nobody knows by how much.) Anyone who had the temerity to warn the Great Helmsman of his folly, such as the chancellor of Peking University, Ma Yinchu, was summarily dealt with. Ma's "new population theory," which warned of catastrophe, was denounced and the professor himself was purged. Only after Mao had died and the Communist Party had changed its mind on population did the politburo see fit to rehabilitate Ma, who by this time was nearly one hundred years old. In the twenty-two years that his advice had gone unheeded, China's population had grown by 325 million.[3]

It was not Mao who had to pay for his excesses but the masses he claimed to have liberated. In the 1980s the state intruded into the most private realm of human behavior, decreeing that urban families could have no more than one child, while those in the countryside were restricted to two or, in some cases, more. Female infanticide, long a gruesome outcome of the fierce competition for resources, became more widespread. More common, however, was the abortion of female fetuses following ultrasound scans. One result of this has been a startling imbalance in some demographic segments of society between boys and girls, and a thriving illegal trade in brides.

Economically, population forms China's most basic paradox. It is at once the country's greatest strength and its gravest frailty. An unparalleled stock of human capital allows China to assume the characteristics of several countries at once. Its huge pool of low-cost, diligent factory workers arouses envy across the developing world, and yet China is not merely a giant sweatshop. Mainland universities produce more graduates each year than those in the United States. Though only a fraction of the population could currently be called consumers, the promise of a vast domestic market grows more real as the middle class (estimated at between 100 million and 150 million people in 2004) expands. In any case, recent history has proven that it is the prospect of a large market, rather than its actual existence, that is the key to luring foreign investors.

Nevertheless, these strengths are offset to a considerable degree by the old oppression of numbers. Although China is poised to overtake the United Kingdom to become the world's fourth-largest economy, on a per capita basis it ranks barely above the world's poorest nations, with an average income of just over $1,000 a year. Even if the country's gross domestic product one day becomes as large as that of the United States, simple mathematics ordains that its people at that time will on average be only one-sixth as wealthy as Americans. At current relative rates of growth, the size of the Chinese economy will match that of the United States a few years before 2040. But by that time, too, the children of Mao's population explosion in the 1960s, 1970s, and early 1980s will have entered their retirement years. In fact, by 2040 around one-third of the projected population—some four hundred million people—will be over the age of sixty. It may be that China will grow old before it becomes rich.

The most important impediment of population, however, is a variant of the challenge that emperors since ancient times had to deal with (and Mao so singularly failed to do). In the past, the balance each dynasty strove for was that between food and mouths, but the last quarter century of development may have banished this concern forever. The crucial equilibrium now is that between people and jobs, and so far it has proven elusive. Even when the economy grows at 9 or 10 percent, it fails by a margin of several million to create the twenty-four million new jobs required each year. So while China appears to the rest of the world to be enjoying an amazing growth bonanza, the officials working behind the high walls of their leadership compound in Beijing feel trapped in an endless employment crisis.

This creates an unyielding pressure for growth that influences every economic plan and strategy, and can leave Beijing with little room for compromise in its deliberations with trade partners. Barely a week goes by without some incident of labor or social unrest somewhere in the country, and some of these flare-ups are serious. If the growth rate were to drop dramatically, these convulsions would be almost certain to intensify. As economists in Beijing are fond of saying, China is like an elephant riding a bicycle. If it slows down, it could fall off, and then the earth might quake.

The pressure of population combines with other features of life to create the salient characteristics of corporate China. Chief among these is a tendency among companies to carry on producing, or even expand production, long after any discernible profit margin has vanished. This behavior can be ascribed to the mesmerizing attraction of trying ever harder to win a bigger share of the "billion consumer" market, but it is by no means as simple as that. The issue is of critical importance, though, because it helps demonstrate why it is that most manufactured products in China are in chronic oversupply — and, by extension, why so many of them are extraordinarily cheap. Virtually any manufacturer selected at random might illuminate the causes behind these various phenomena, but before I left Chongqing I reconnected with Lifan Motorcycle, a company I had been following for some years. The more I learned about it and the exploits of its remarkable founder, Yin Mingshan, the more I came to see it as a case study of how Chinese manufacturers often manage to undercut the prices of overseas competitors by a third or more.

Yin's career, like that of many self-made entrepreneurs, has been far from orthodox. It started when he emerged from prison, feeling, as he put it, like Sun Wu Kong, the Monkey King. In the classic sixteenth-century novel *Journey to the West*, by Wu Chengen, the Monkey King is flung into a furnace by his enemies, but instead of dying an agonizing death he emerges burnished like metal, his eyes blazing and his muscles as strong as hawsers. "It was as if the thing that I feared most was behind me. My patience had been trained and my judgment was clear, just like Sun Wu Kong," Yin said the first time I met him.[4]

We sat on hard-backed wooden chairs at a circular table in a glassed-in office at Lifan's corporate headquarters. There was an empty chair between us. Yin leaned back and stretched his legs out as if he found the hours immediately after lunch a little wea-rying. Visible through the windows were motivational slogans, painted in red on the white walls of his factory. "He who does not feel hardship and fatigue is not a Lifan person," said one. "If you do not work hard today, you will search hard for a job tomorrow," warned another.

Yin does not look like an ex-convict or, for that matter, like the Monkey King. He is tall, a little stooped, and has an avuncular bearing. A pair of large, black-rimmed spectacles dominates his face, giving him a professorial air. He was locked up in 1961 for "counter-revolutionary" activities, one of the most vaguely de-fined and yet most serious crimes. His parents had come from landowning capitalist families, so Yin was considered a member of the "black five categories": people from whom no good could be expected. So when a twenty-one-year-old girlfriend of his who had an uncle in the United States applied to leave China, the vengeful Communist officials of the day were incensed. "America was the enemy. I was twenty-three and the girl and I were good friends. That meant she was a traitor and I was part of an escap-ing-to-the-enemy traitorous clique," he remembered.

Yet in prison Yin did not harbor a grudge. His recurrent thought was that he had wronged Chairman Mao and he wanted the Party to forgive him. When the prisoners were ordered to feed the swine, he would grab the biggest bucket of swill. When they had to empty the public toilets, he would strive to fill up his nightsoil cart quicker than his peers. "I only dreamed of being a person again," he said. But class enemies and traitors were not shown leniency, no matter how they behaved, and Yin stayed be-hind bars for nearly twenty years. When he was released in 1979, it had nothing to do with his good behavior. One day a letter ar-rived explaining that there had been a mistake. The Party was rehabilitating him. And that was it—no apology, no compensa-tion. But to Yin it was a miracle. Deng Xiaoping had seized power and started to put right some of the worst excesses of Mao's rule.

Some twenty years later, Yin had become one of China's most successful private entrepreneurs, but he still shook his head at the memory of how audacious Deng had been in overhauling Mao's legacy. "There were still plenty of officials in those days who believed that everything Mao did was correct," he said.

It had not been easy, however, for an ex-con in his forties with no work experience to find a job, even if he did feel like Sun Wu Kong. But as with so many entrepreneurs of the 1980s, Yin's poor employment prospects turned out to be a blessing. He was allowed to start up a private business selling books, and he made a tidy profit. By the end of the decade, his personal wealth was far greater than that of those who had remained on the state payroll. What was more, he had an eye to the main chance. He'd noticed that people doted on their bicycles, delighting in the smallest differences: a seat that had a tartan cover, a new type of bell, or a bob of rabbit fur on the keyring of a bike lock. He perceived that the whole of society was straining at the moorings of enforced egalitarianism. Motorbikes would be the next big thing, just as they had been in the early days of Japan's industrial takeoff. In 1992 Yin sold off his warehouse of books and raised $15,000 to set up the Chongqing Hongda Motorcycle Fitting Research Institute, a company of eight people, including his wife and son.

The word "Hongda" in the company name was not a mistake. It was a statement of intent. Yin yearned to build a world-beating company. He wanted to imitate the success of the great Japanese corporations Honda and Yamaha by driving them out of the Chinese market. When he had done that, he would take them on in the wider world. But somehow he had to get from his oil-slicked workshop in a suburb of a rundown secondary city to a point where he could challenge motorbikes bearing brands recognized around the globe.

There was little time to spare. Both Honda and Yamaha were selling well in China, building their reputations and status. Yin took what he saw as the only feasible route: he copied designs and stole technology. Yamaha engines had recently become available locally, following a licensing deal the Japanese company had forged with Jianshe Industrial, an old armaments firm that only forty years earlier had made the machine guns and cannons used to resist Japan's wartime encroachment. As part of the deal, local shops were set up that had access to a full range of Yamaha spare parts and the know-how to make repairs. Yin went to these shops, bought their parts, and picked up tips from the mechanics who worked there. Within a few months of reverse engineering he had built a replica Yamaha engine. "To start with, we completely copied other people's stuff," he said. "In 1994 we made our own engine for the first time. It was not a copy. In 1995 we did three of our own engines. The Japanese never imagined that the traditional Chinese manufacturers would develop so quickly. They were quite aloof and condescending, like the Americans before Pearl Harbor."

But in reality there was little the Japanese could do. Chinese government restrictions meant that Yamaha, Mitsubishi, and Honda were not free to set up their own factories where they wanted; they had to form joint ventures with state-owned partners who were chosen for them by the government. They were also told they had to transfer technology to their partners as an entrance fee into a vast potential market. In addition, they were allowed to exercise only loose control over their marketing and a network of suppliers. But the lure of a billion Chinese swapping their bicycles for motorbikes seemed to override their misgivings. Yamaha got fully into bed, creating a fifty-fifty joint venture with Jianshe, a typical offspring of socialist planning that had eighteen thousand workers on the payroll and another thirty-five thousand either on pensions or in some other way dependent on the factory. All of the dependents had to be paid for out of current revenues because the concept of pension funds did not exist in China in the early 1990s. Decision-making at the plant was diffuse and sluggish, and every initiative was costly. However, these problems, thorny though they were, paled next to the issue of intellectual property.

The factory leaked its technological secrets like a sieve. Components suppliers who were supposed to be discreet and loyal were actually engaged in a roaring trade selling parts out the back door to counterfeiters. Yamaha found it hard to get a grip on how serious the problem was until it brought out its flagship model, the 100-milliliter four-stroke Jinbao, in 1995 after years of preparation. Then the full horror was revealed. Within months of its launch, exact replicas were being made in thirty-six factories throughout the country. The worst of it was that even though the copies were nearly identical, they were sold for around 6,000 renminbi each, compared with the 18,000 rmb that Jianshe-Yamaha was charging for the Jinbao.

By the mid-1990s, piracy was becoming an all-too-common phenomenon. Once it had infected an industry, it spread like a virus up the value chain and leapt from company to company. By the early years of this century it was endemic, no longer a peripheral handicap to doing business but a fact of life that almost every company in virtually every sector was forced to consider or confront. Various estimates had it that American, Japanese, and European companies may have been losing more than $60 billion a year through Chinese piracy of one sort or another.[5] By necessity such estimates were rough, but if they were anywhere near accurate, it meant that the loss to Western companies through intellectual property theft was far in excess of the total flow of foreign direct investment into China. In 2004, for example, foreign investment amounted to $56 billion.

Some rip-offs were systematic. Almost every time a Hollywood blockbuster was cut, it would appear on DVD in China before it had been released in the same format in America. To accomplish this, pirate networks had to have operatives under cover in the film companies that they were ripping off. DVD copies seen in Beijing often bore intermittent warnings saying "Studio screening only. Copying strictly forbidden." Another victim of chutzpah has been the book publishing industry. A sixth volume in the series of Harry Potter novels appeared in China months before J. K. Rowling had written it. When the real version did appear in English, several pirate firms competed to translate and sell it online.

A number of translators, unhappy with the way the book ended, wrote their own denouements.

Similarly, a series of how-to business books written by Paul Thomas, a Harvard Business School professor, became a mini publishing sensation in Beijing in 2004.[6] As Thomas's fame grew, he lent his reputation to other books by writing prefaces, and everyone seemed to be winning. Then it emerged that there was no professor at Harvard that fitted his description, and the books bearing his illustrious name had been written by students paid the equivalent of one-third of a cent per word to make it all up. Fake books, it turns out, are big business. Several publishers, including state-owned houses, had more than a hundred bogus titles on the market in early 2005.

Other counterfeits are either tragic or comic, or both. Golf clubs have been widely pirated, but with varying degrees of success. A set of impressive-looking clubs can cost less than one-tenth of their price in the United States or Europe, but some snap in mid-shot, releasing the head of the club to chase the ball down the fairway. Other fakes are even more dangerous. Kettles blow up, electrical transformers short-circuit, medicines have no effect, brake pads fail, alcoholic beverages poison those who drink them, and the use of inferior milk powder has caused several babies to starve to death.

For many foreign companies, however, the problem is not substandard knockoffs so much as fakes that faithfully replicate the quality of the original. Motorbikes aside, the car industry has provided a prominent case study for this kind of abuse. Chery Automobile did not exist when Volkswagen, the market leader, launched its popular Jetta model in the late 1990s. But thirty-three months after starting from zero with a new company in the city of Wuhu, on the banks of the Yangtze River, Chery had made its first car, a four-door sedan called the Chery, which bore more than a passing resemblance to the Jetta, at that time China's best-selling car. Suspicions were immediately raised, partly because Chery's main investor, SAIC, was a joint-venture partner of Volkswagen's and partly because one of Chery's top executives used to make the Jetta in China for Volkswagen's subsidiary Audi. Volkswagen investigated and found their own original parts inside the Chery. They wrote and spoke to executives at Chery, which is owned by the Wuhu city government, and eventually the Chinese company agreed not to use any more original parts.

But Chery's intellectual property tangles were not over. General Motors, which is also a partner of SAIC's, is suing Chery for $80 million for piracy following Chery's launch of a compact car, the QQ, that GM claims is a dead ringer for the Spark, a popular model produced by GM's subsidiary Daewoo. Chery denies all wrongdoing and says officially that it welcomes the case, which is to be tried in a Beijing court. And while both sides wait for their day in court, the QQ — which has a price tag of $3,600 — is selling like hotcakes and the Spark, costing twice as much, has yet to win much of a following.

Whatever the interplay of right and wrong, the commercial result of piracy is always the same: rapid value destruction across a wide range of manufactured products. This is true not only for established goods but also for new technologies, and evidence of an unremitting downward pull can be found both in individual examples and in aggregate prices of manufactured items since 1998. Regardless of the breakneck growth in the wider economy or the prevailing inflation as measured by broad indices such as the consumer price index, the average prices of manufactured products have fallen each year. In some cases the declines have been significant. A 29-inch flat-panel television that cost 6,000 renminbi in 1998 was going for just under 2,000 rmb in late 2004. Color-screen cell phones were a new, trendy product in 2001 and were priced accordingly, at around 6,500 rmb; by late 2004 they too were trading at under 2,000 rmb. Domestic brands of DVD players, all configured to play counterfeit DVDs, hit the market in 1998 at 3,000 rmb but cost around 500 rmb by late 2004. Set-top boxes, which allow viewers to receive satellite television signals, started selling for around 2,300 rmb in 2000 but were going for around 700

rmb in late 2004.[7] Each of these products represented a new foreign technology that, once introduced to China, suffered a swift
destruction of value, due in part to piracy.

The problem, though, as Yin Mingshan was starting to discover
in the late 1990s, was that piracy had a way of returning to haunt
those who had once thrived on it. With the technological barriers
to entry nonexistent and capital freely available, more and more
motorbike manufacturers were springing up, each of them following the trail that Yin had blazed to prominence. By 1998 there
were more than a thousand motorbike factories in China producing some fifteen million units a year — five million more than
were sold. As unsold bikes filled warehouses, vicious price wars
erupted until profit margins were completely obliterated. But the
big players, still transfixed by a vast potential market, refused to
alter their strategy. Liang Xueben, the general manager at Jianshe-Yamaha, told me in 1999 that he was committed to maintaining market share.[8] Only 3 percent of Chinese owned motorbikes,
he said. One day the market would take off and amazing profits
would be had. Yamaha could not afford to cede ground to upstart
domestic competitors now.

Seven years later, the hoped-for boom in sales had not materi-
alized and the problem of oversupply was more acute than ever.
Yin was disillusioned. Almost all of the value had been stripped
out of the industry, and he had begun telling people — only half
in jest — that he would soon start selling his motorbikes by the ki-
logram, like pigs. "The ex factory price of our cheapest model is
twenty-five renminbi per kilo. That is a bit more than a kilo of live
pig," said one of his deputies, Yang Zhou, during another of my
visits to the plant. A more pertinent comparison, however, might
be with the cost of the metal and other components that go into
building a motorcycle. At a sale price of around 2,500 rmb, a motorbike costs only a shade more than its scrap value; its other components, such as engineering, labor, development costs, brand,
distribution, and the experience and vision of the company's ex-

ecutives, are rated as valueless. "Clearly, this is not healthy. It is malignant competition," Yang said.

In a normal market economy companies cannot go on selling at below cost for years. Banks start to worry about their clients' ability to repay their debts and eventually call in loans. But China is not a normal market economy. It does not have a well-functioning bankruptcy law, so the liquidation of insolvent companies is difficult. In addition, banks are awash with liquidity; Chinese people save an average of around 40 percent of their income, and the supply of money in the economy is well over double the annual gross domestic product. This means that banks often have more deposits than they can find borrowers to lend to, and are therefore less than vigilant about calling in suspect loans.

Aside from this, there are other concerns. A senior provincial banker with the Industrial and Commercial Bank of China, the country's largest bank, told me that precipitating a bankruptcy by recalling loans from an insolvent company was inimical to the interests of the bank. The domino effect would be palpable as that company's suppliers were also pushed under, he said. Unemployment would rise, potentially causing a decline in consumer spending and endangering social stability. "It is much better to wait for the next upturn in the market rather than cause a slump across the board," the banker said. The extremely low number of Chinese corporate bankruptcies, by international standards, illustrates how ubiquitous this attitude is.

This peculiarity leads to another, one that is shaped partly by the ever-present lure of selling to the mythical "billion." Under market economy conditions, when a company encounters an oversupply of the product it makes, it generally pulls in its horns. But in China this happens only rarely. A more common response is to continue producing at the same rate while looking around for another industry sector to diversify into. On one trip to the Pearl River Delta, I visited the world's largest maker of microwave ovens, a company called Galanz. From there, I went a few miles up the road to Midea, one of the world's biggest manufacturers of air conditioners. Both companies were classic examples of their type. Each had started off as a humble workshop in the early 1980s, making products that looked like prototypes from the Industrial Revolution. In Midea's case, these were small electric fans with blades beaten into shape with a hammer on a wooden bench by the company chairman (one such fan now sits as an artifact in a glass cabinet in the company museum). But when I visited in 2001, the glory days of patriarchal leadership were over and both companies had run into a quagmire of oversupply. Their margins were sinking fast, and executives from each reckoned the other was operating at a loss. But their response to this predicament surprised me. Galanz, the microwave maker, decided to expand into air conditioners, and Midea, the air-conditioner maker, was moving into microwaves. Never mind that nationwide demand for air conditioners lagged supply by ten million units that year and microwaves were similarly overproduced.

I asked Yu Yaochang, vice president of Galanz, how come the banks were willing to support such a diversification. "The banks only care if your company is getting bigger and stronger. If you expand production, you are increasing scale and reducing unit cost. That is bigger and stronger. And anyway, we are the biggest local company. If they don't lend to us, who are they going to lend to?" Such reasoning helps to create the salient characteristic of the Chinese economy: almost all (around 90 percent in late 2005) manufactured products are in chronic oversupply. Midea, for example, in addition to its core product of air conditioners, was also making coffee pots, refrigerators, dishwashers, breadmakers, air purifiers, and microwave ovens. Haier, one of the country's best-known consumer electronics companies, counts insurance, pharmaceuticals, personal computers, mobile phones, and a chain of noodle restaurants among the eighty-six products with which it is involved. D'Long, a scandal-tainted company listed on the Shanghai Stock Exchange, makes everything from ketchup to car parts.

So when the profit margins of Lifan's motorbike business were squeezed, Yin's response was not to retreat but to attack. He branched out into buses, mineral water, paint thinner, imported wine, newspapers, duck-down jackets, and a successful Chinese football team that bore his company's name. He had been reading management books by Jack Welch, the then CEO of General Electric, whose photograph appeared on the cover of pirated translations of his books selling all over China.

Diversification, Yin said, helps a company weather downturns in the business cycle. Nevertheless, it was clear that if his core motorbike business was to survive, he would need to find a new source of revenue and sales growth. The answer was obvious: exports. Any company that could survive in the cauldron of Chinese competition surely had a chance overseas. His selected battleground was Vietnam, where Lifan came face-to-face with Honda. The Japanese company's market share was around 70 percent in Vietnam when Lifan made its first forays, but Yin had the obvious advantage of price. His opening salvo was to offer bikes that looked virtually identical to those of Honda but cost one-third as much. It proved a powerful lure, and within three years Lifan had outstripped its old rival.

Yin's early childhood was spent listening to the percussion of Japanese bombing raids on Chongqing and watching the smoke rise from fires that raged through the back alleys. Yet his rivalry with Honda and Yamaha appears devoid of nationalistic sentiment or any trace of revenge. In fact, he expresses admiration for Honda, in particular. "As Isaac Newton said, I stand on the shoulders of giants," he commented without irony. In fact, I developed a sense during our meetings over the years that Yin sees himself and Soichiro Honda, the late founder of the Japanese company, as kindred spirits. Both started their careers by tinkering with engines in oil-slicked garages. Neither had much of a formal education, and both knew well the sting of ostracism from the establishment. (Honda's career was all the more remarkable because he operated outside, and sometimes in opposition to, the tight nexus between the Japanese government and large corporations.)

The irony was, though, that while Lifan started by copying Honda, the Japanese company ended by imitating its Chinese rival. The loss of market share in Vietnam had rattled Honda, which hastily established a production base on Hainan Island, Chinese territory just across the sea from Vietnam. There it used an almost exclusively Chinese business model; it benefited from cheap Chinese labor and got its parts almost exclusively from mainland suppliers, many of which were churning out the third- or fourth-generation descendants of copies of original Japanese parts. But it did the trick. Honda was able to slash prices in Vietnam by about half and claw back some market share because of the superior cachet of its brand. The company also won success on another front. A long-standing lawsuit against Lifan for using the name Hongda bore fruit, and Lifan had to pay out 98,000 renminbi.

The battles are far from over. Japanese companies are known for financing their forays into export markets by charging more for their products at home than they do abroad. Chinese corporations do just the opposite. Many of them, Lifan included, export as a means of staying afloat at home. Yang Zhou, Yin's deputy, says the profit margins on bikes sold in Africa, Iran, and Latin America can be as high as 10 percent in some cases, whereas margins in China are wafer-thin or negative. In Nigeria, for instance, the company can sell for 6,000 rmb a bike that goes for half that in China.

Although his sales in the United Kingdom are minuscule, Yin was wondering how to build his brand among the British public. Unexpectedly, he started talking about soccer, tossing out the names of almost the entire England squad, followed by each player's transfer fee (the price paid to buy out a player's contract so he can play for another team). Then he asked me whether I thought he should buy a British club as a means to increase brand recognition. I asked him which one he was thinking of. *"Lan-che-si-te,"* he said, but the name was unfamiliar to me. It was not Manchester United, because that is *Man-lian* in Chinese, and anyway, he had heard that Rupert Murdoch was once prevented from buying Man U, so Yin was sure he would also be barred from snapping up a British "national treasure." Unwilling to reveal my ignorance of a club he may have taken a shine to, I asked whether he reckoned the players were good enough to carry the Lifan name.

"Well, they might not be very good, but they are quite cheap," he said. "Ten million, maybe. Twenty, max."

My journey from Chongqing ended at a terminus of China's industrial revolution, a place where the hundreds of thousands of products made in factories like Yin's ended up. It was called Yiwu. Only fifteen years ago, this small town in the middle of Zhejiang province, on China's eastern seaboard, had been distinguished by little but its unusual name. *Yiwu* means "loyal crow," but when you ask local people why, you get a range of answers. Nobody seemed to care much anyway; there is too much going on. In less than two decades, it has transformed itself from a sleepy backwater into one of the busiest places in the country. Even though it remains little known outside China, Yiwu has become the largest wholesale market in the world.

The scale of the place is dizzying. Some 34,000 stallholders sit in one vast exhibition hall after another, selling around 320,000 different products. Almost every category of manufactured item made in the factories of the Pearl and Yangtze River deltas is on sale in hangars covering 3,700 acres. I had been urged by Chinese friends to visit Yiwu in order to marvel at the prices. They had told me that if you took the price of the best bargains in the cheapest market in Beijing and then halved it, you would be getting close to the cost of buying the same things in Yiwu.

On my way to the exhibition hangars in the morning, I passed the Hiyat Hotel. It had a dusty glass façade in bluebottle blue, a golden laughing Buddha by the front door, and a plastic Santa Claus in the lobby that looked as if it was about to topple over. I wondered why the hotel company that owns China's tallest and grandest hotel, the eighty-eight-story Jingmao Tower in Shanghai, had bothered to invest in a tacky two-star establishment in Yiwu. Then I noticed the spelling. The Hiyat, of course, had nothing to do with the Hyatt.

I walked on until I came to a shopping mall selling fashion accessories. The first shop was advertising leather bags, "made in Italy" by that renowned brand Gussi. They cost $11 each, but, the shopkeeper said, you could always bargain a bit. Nearby were three stores in a row. One was called VSL, another LYS, and the third SYL. They all had on their walls a large photograph of a youthful Yves Saint-Laurent with his trademark thick-rimmed spectacles.

In another corner there were Lacoste rip-off shops, again close to each other. One was called New Crocodile, another Crocodile of the Yangtze, a third Crocokids, and the last Croc Croc. I walked into one of the shops and asked the clerk whether the real Lacoste-branded products were being sold in her shop or in France. "The French crocodile and the Chinese crocodile are the same brand. They have merged," she said. Then she waved dismissively at the rival shops nearby. "They are all fakes, those ones. You can easily tell."

A bit farther on, three shops had signs with the same distinctive tall and thin lettering that Dunhill uses. One was called Denghaoli, another Dunbaolu, and another Doctortoh. It was relatively easy to figure out that they were all trying to be like Dunhill. But others in a different corner presented a puzzle. I had to think for a while about Woershaqi before I assumed it must have been a derivative of Versace. Wearesaatchi, the next shop, was easier. Another outlet had come up with the idea of using an ice cream brand to sell haute couture. The shop sign read "Haagendess," but there was not an ice cream in sight. Only leather bags.

As I left the shopping mall, I bumped into a group of policemen. I asked them how so many fake brands could be allowed to do business so openly. China had agreed when it joined the World Trade Organization in 2001 to stamp out piracy. They looked at one another and then looked back at me. One of them took the cigarette out of his mouth and used it to point at the wall a few feet away from Crocodile of the Yangtze. "See that plaque? There is a number on there. You can try calling that if you have a complaint," he said.

The plaque read "Smashing Fakes Hotline. Call: 32157." I called the number and a woman answered. She told me that I had the wrong city. This was Jinghua and I needed Yiwu, she said. "Try 5558853," she added. I did, and a man answered, but he told me that the hotline I had reached was not for reporting fakes but for consumer issues. I needed to speak to the fakes inspection brigade, he said. "Try 5324716." He said the number quickly and then hung up. I had my cell phone wedged between one hunched shoulder and my ear, with my notebook resting on a raised knee. I just got the number down before I lost my balance. When I called, a man answered. He acknowledged that I had got through to the fakes hotline but added that he was too busy to talk. "I am writing a report," he said. I told him I wanted to inform him of brand copyright violations, but he repeated that he was busy. "Try 32157," he said, referring me back to the number I had started with.

I had no desire to go around in circles again so I left the mall and walked the rest of the way to the main wholesale-market exhibition hall. In the foyer, I was immediately confronted by a large sign near the escalators. "Value Quality. Honor Credibility," it said in giant gold characters on a red velvet background. It was signed by the Yiwu municipal government, the same people who were supposed to be running the antifakes hotline.

Inside the exhibition hall, it was just as my friends had foretold. The prices were unbelievable. The same kind of tea mug I used at home, which you could find in Ikea and other stores for at least a dollar, was on sale in Yiwu for 5 cents. A graphite-titanium tennis racket that appeared to be of medium to good quality was going for roughly what a tube of tennis balls would cost in the United States — $7.80. The famously cheap toasters Wal-Mart sells for $11 each would have seemed outrageously overpriced in Yiwu, where they could be bought for half that sum. A Chinese-made DVD player that had caused a minor sensation in America when it was put on sale at $29 was effortlessly undercut in Yiwu. An unbranded electric drill, the spitting image of a Black & Decker product, cost $12, with a full set of drill bits thrown in. A sledgehammer was going for $1.40, an ax for chopping wood for $1.20. And so it was across the board. Almost every product was on sale for about one-half, one-third, or one-tenth of the lowest price available in the cheapest discount stores of Europe and America. What's more, the quality of these items seemed in no way inferior to the products on sale in stores around the world. In many cases, in fact, they were the same goods.

Yiwu offered a glimpse of the source of the discount store phenomenon sweeping the developed world. Half an hour's walking around its cavernous exhibition halls was enough to destroy any mystery about how Wal-Mart, Target, Home Depot, Lowe's, Best Buy, and other discount retailers are able to offer goods so cheaply. In fact, I began to be impressed not by their capacity to discount but their ability to get away with charging hefty markups without incurring a consumer backlash. All of the large discount stores bought their merchandise in China, and they all owed their rankings in the upper echelon of the world's 500 largest corporations in part to the fat margins they earned from procurement in China. Total procurement of wholesale goods by foreign retailers was expected to reach $60 billion in 2005, according to official Chinese estimates. If you make the highly conservative assumption that these goods are sold in the developed world for double the wholesale price, then it appears that at least a staggering $120 billion worth of merchandise sold in European and American discount stores comes from China.

The big discount houses are not the only ones getting in on the act. Yiwu was full of freelancers. Individual traders from all corners of the globe were strolling from one booth to another placing bulk orders of buttons, jewelry, holiday ornaments, kitchen appliances, electronics, cutlery, crockery, sports equipment, car parts, agricultural machinery, and hundreds of thousands of other products. A few years ago, the number of foreign traders resident in Yiwu was in the low hundreds, but now there were more than five thousand of them. Business had boomed after the quality of the stuff on offer had improved. I met Barry Beaumont from New Zealand at a stall selling oil paintings. His friend was lifting one canvas after another from a stack of hundreds on the floor, looking at it for a second or two and then tossing it aside, either on a pile to be bought or on a stack of rejects. Sometimes he would ask Beaumont for his opinion of an artwork before deciding on which pile to put it. Most of the paintings were copies of famous originals by van Gogh, Constable, Dalí, Chagall, and Monet. Beaumont and his friend had no illusions that they were buying anything other than "good crap, the type of thing you might find hanging near the loo in a coffee shop."

"They are painted by the locals around here for twenty [renminbi] each, so you buy them from the stallholder for twenty-five," Beaumont said. "To start with, they will ask you for one hundred and forty each, so you need to bargain them down. It takes time and they are tough, so generally I leave the bargaining to one of the girls." He pointed to three heavily made-up, middle-aged Chinese women standing nearby, his purchasing agents. "They are much tougher than us," he added. "The Chinese don't mind selling cheap to Chinese, but they will never give a foreigner the same price."

Beaumont had started coming to Yiwu seven years earlier, after a business he had in New Zealand failed. To begin with he bought agricultural machinery, metalworking equipment, and industrial tools for cutting and working plastics. At first he did not want to risk anything but small orders. But things went well and now he did not bother with consignments of less than $10,000 in value. If you bought a hundred of anything in Yiwu, you could get the price down by a reasonable margin, but if you bought a lot of a thousand, you might be able to get as much as 50 percent off, he said. The Chinese manufacturers expected to make only a 2 or 3 percent margin on what they sold, and the export agents rarely tried to make money off the clients. The main reason the agents were in business was to reclaim a government value-added-tax rebate of up to 17 percent of a product's value.

The real profits, Beaumont said, were earned by those who knew how to distribute and sell the goods once they had been shipped to their target markets. Some people took profits of 100 percent, but Beaumont contented himself with a 30 to 40 percent markup in order to build a reputation with his customers. Still, things were getting more competitive now as people from all over the world began to discover Yiwu and places like it across China. Over time, this would mean that the hefty profits that discount stores derive from China will start to shrink, as will the commissions and markups of middlemen in places such as Hong Kong, where agents add nearly 30 percent to the cost of every mainland product that passes through the territory.

But while such things may change on the periphery, the world's cheapest market is set to endure. Yiwu is the point at which the collective energies of China's industrial transformation converge. Its low prices are the final expression of a hundred different realities, reforms, and trends that underpin the prowess of a rising giant. The presence China projects to the world originates primarily from the strengths that Yiwu symbolizes. This is because throughout history, the big shifts in the global power balance and in the hierarchy of nations have all been accompanied — or, often, preceded — by a whole set of new price signals.

In many of its conditions, China's ascent mirrors that of the United States in the second half of the nineteenth century. Not only does Chongqing's transformation resemble that of a youthful Chicago, and the construction of China's infrastructure replicate America's both in conception and even in specific details, but also the movement of the sons and daughters of farmers to factories along the coast echoes the mass migration of young people from Europe to the New World 150 years ago. New technologies — in the United States a century and a half ago it was railways, in today's China it is the Internet and other digital media — are creating quantum leaps in productivity. International flows of capital and expertise from Great Britain to the United States in the nineteenth century, and in modern times from the industrialized nations to China, are lubricating the process of change.

In those days — as today — price shifts were a harbinger of the economic, political, and social changes to come. The period from 1873 to 1900 is known as the era of "deflationary boom" because prices of agricultural and manufactured items fell almost across the board in the United States.[9] The opening of the prairies to agriculture sent the price of grain plummeting throughout the developed world, causing rural unrest in Europe, the depopulation of the countryside, and a crisis among the British landowning classes that was to reverberate in the increasingly egalitarian twentieth century.

Similar changes hit industry. Andrew Carnegie, the Scottish-born industrial baron, took a new steel technology, called the Bessemer converter, from Britain to the United States in much the same way that Shen Wenrong transported the Phoenix plant to China from Germany. From 1872 to 1898, Bessemer steel prices fell 80 percent in the United States, and Carnegie commented prophetically, "The nation that makes the cheapest steel has other nations at its feet."

Indeed, British industry found it hard to adjust to the relentless cycles of deflation in manufactured products, and many companies went bust. From 1875 to 1896, British prices fell by an average of .8 percent every year. Nevertheless, living standards improved for most British people because of the sharp increase in the number of inexpensive imported goods. By the end of the century, the situation was so pronounced that President Theodore Roosevelt was able to comment:

> Even if the United States were not so blessed with raw materials, the excellence of her manufactured products guaranteed her dominance of world markets. Current advertisements in British magazines gave the impression that the typical Englishman woke to the ring of an Ingersoll alarm, shaved with a Gillette razor, combed his hair with Vaseline tonic, buttoned his Arrow shirt, hurried downstairs for Quaker Oats, California figs and Maxwell House coffee, commuted in a Westinghouse tram, body by Fisher, rose to his office in an Otis elevator, and worked all day with his Walden pen under the efficient glare of Edison light bulbs.[10]

A century later, it is China that is exporting deflation in manu-factured products, and it is Americans and Europeans who are in-creasingly living out their lives assisted by a cornucopia of prod-ucts made in China. As an early signal of a shift in the distribution of geopolitical power, it seems unmistakable.

4

The Ties That Bind:
China Goes to Europe

YIWU AND MARKETS LIKE IT are just specks on the map of China, but they represent the sources of a global economic phenomenon. Nobody can look at the prices there, and the range of goods on sale, and fail to wonder what will happen to manufacturers in the rest of the world when the full force of China's industrial revolution hits their factories and shopping malls. Or maybe this is merely alarmism. Perhaps Europe and the United States will weather the oncoming Chinese typhoon with no more discomfort than they betrayed when the Japanese economic miracle went global in the 1970s and 1980s. I decided to take my own soundings on the contours of things to come by visiting one of the oldest manufacturing towns in Europe, Prato, in Italy, not far from the historic city of Florence.

Prato had every appearance of a typical Tuscan market town. In the stillness of early evening, shadows swept across the russet roofs of the old town and onto the rough-hewn stones of the central piazza. Flocks of doves swooped and wheeled around marble statues of founding fathers and flew off to low green hills in the distance. Church bells chimed with a measured, funereal rhythm, drawing a stream of mourners for Pope John Paul II, who had died a day earlier in Rome, toward the Cathedral of Santo Stefano. The men were in blazers and the women in long dresses, and when they reached the cathedral's flagstone steps, they stopped to greet friends or relatives with a word or a kiss on each cheek. Children with their hair damped and neatly parted waited for their parents and then accompanied them through the heavy wooden doors. Inside, candles illuminated the main points of piety: the alcoves of saints, the choristers in their lace ruffs, and, by the altar, a life-size photograph of the pope in his later years gripping a staff with both hands. It was several degrees cooler inside than out, and some of the women in thin blouses shivered and hugged their arms as they made their way up the aisle.

Everything, in fact, was how it should have been in a well-to-do, self-respecting town in northern Italy. Except for one feature. Walking in the opposite direction from the Catholic faithful — toward the western suburbs — were people set apart by their bearing and appearance. They strode purposefully through the crowds, singly or in twos, keeping their gaze downcast in the manner of locals who have no need to navigate through familiar surroundings. It was clear they were not tourists; they had no cameras or bags and they wore simple clothes. They were, it turned out, members of a large immigrant population of Chinese. Since they started to arrive in Prato around fifteen years earlier, they had transformed the destiny of one of Italy's oldest industrial towns and changed the lives of its indigenous population.

I walked along behind one man. As we moved, the surroundings altered. We passed a hairdresser's shop with a Chinese sign in the window, a supermarket with trays of fungi and litchis out front, several stores offering cheap overseas phone calls, an apothecary selling ginseng and other herbal remedies, a health club with flashing neon lights, a bookshop stacked with martial arts comics, and a restaurant called Golden Sea. I began to feel as if I had returned to China, perhaps to a place like Qingdao or Weihai, which had been foreign treaty ports in the early twentieth century and still combined European architecture with Chinese life. Prato had a population of 180,000, and of these, around 20,000 were Chinese.[1] They lived according to their native culture in an enclave the locals seemed to have vacated. The only obvious concession to their adopted country I could detect was a shelf full of books in a supermarket promising shortcuts to fluency in Italian.

The man I followed stopped outside a supermarket called Xiaolin. He joined a knot of other men who stood peering intently at a wall on which various notices, all in Chinese, flapped in a light evening breeze. The wall held the reason for their presence. Printed or handwritten on the notices were advertisements for jobs. A car mechanic was needed in a nearby town, a restaurant down the street was seeking a waiter, and a shop required a cashier. Most of the ads, though, were for *buyigong,* or "cloth garment workers." Each notice had telephone numbers written on strips that hung from the bottom of the paper like a fringe. The men stared at each one in turn, but none of them ripped off a number. *Buyigong* was not for them, one said. You had to have skills. You had to be able to cut cloth accurately according to a pattern, and you could be fired for the smallest mistake. The men standing outside Xiaolin were looking for something more menial: general work such as sweeping floors, hauling garbage, cleaning machinery, and stacking finished garments into piles.

One man from Shenyang, in the northeast of China, started to speak. He had grown vegetables in a greenhouse on the outskirts of his home city, but since arriving in Italy he had gone from one low-level job to the next. His previous job had required him to work eighteen hours a day, he said. Overhearing him say this, his friend, a heavy man who had been slumped over a railing nearby, jerked upright with indignation. He was wearing dark trousers, a black jacket, and a white shirt. His face was crumpled into folds beneath the eyes, as if weathered by interlocking rivulets of fatigue. "Eighteen hours?" he asked. "More like twenty. Then four hours' sleep, then twenty hours again, and then again. It is like that month after month. We get six hundred euros a month. That is about what you need to survive here. If you can really cut down on food, maybe you can save about fifty to one hundred euros a month on that wage. But it is exhausting. Mostly what you dream of all day is being able to sleep."

There was a pause while the others in the group took in the big man's outburst. Some nodded their heads. Others went on staring at the wall. Then one, a small man with a southern accent, said something in an almost inaudible voice: "People from the north-east are lazy."

The heavy man glared at him. He made a fist and took a step forward. But everyone else was laughing, and suddenly he soft-ened. Instead of fighting, he said: "The northeast used to be the industrial base of all China. We used to lead the whole country making military equipment when you bastards from the south had your backs toward heaven in the paddies."

"If that's the case," said the southerner, "why don't you go back and start making tanks again?"

"If I did," the heavy man said, "you'd be the first to be marched in front of them."

By this time a woman had joined the group. She was also from the northeast and had held a lowly position in a local gov-ernment. She had an open, cheerful face and a way of speaking that sounded as if she was making intellectual observations. "You know, it is generally thought that people from northeastern cities such as Shenyang are better educated than those from the south," she said to nobody in particular. But those words seemed sage enough to end the altercation.

The men and women outside Xiaolin that April morning were illegals. They had come to Prato as part of "snakebodies," led by "snakeheads" to Europe. In other words, they had made the peril-ous journey from China by train, truck, on foot, and by sea as part of a small, terrified group that had entrusted its fate to the Chi-nese gangs who run the world's largest people-smuggling net-works. Back at the places where their journeys had begun, there were children, parents, wives, and others who were depending on them to send money home. At their destinations there were walls plastered with tatty job ads representing hope for a better life.

I asked one of the men by the wall to tell me what his jour-ney had been like. He demurred. Members of the snakebody are sworn to secrecy by the snakeheads who arrange their trips. I had to persuade him by agreeing to use a false name and to camou-flage other aspects of his journey. After a series of meetings and interviews, for which I paid him some money, the story of how Huang came to be in Prato slowly emerged.

In the mid-1990s, Japanese demand for soft-shell turtles was surging, and farmers in Fuqing, a county in the southeastern province of Fujian, were well placed to benefit from the new culinary craze. Much of the county was too waterlogged for agriculture, but turtles could be raised in freshwater pools excavated out of the marshes. Huang's father duly invested, and everything was going fine until late 1997, when the Asian financial crisis struck. Turtles are a luxury, the type of thing businessmen eat when they are trying to impress someone. So the price plummeted as the whole of Southeast Asia tightened its belt and Japanese demand eased. Huang's father's business unraveled. By late 1999 he was bankrupt, and his creditors in the underground banks that service a thriving gray economy in southern China were getting restless. These banks, though illegal, were actually run by the local government, so when Huang's father could not pay up, the officials threw him into the basement of a local government building that doubled as a jail.

There he had to stay, like Mr. Micawber, until someone could pay his debts. There was no chance of legal redress because his loans had been illegal in the first place, so Huang began to consider his last option. Going abroad would mean having to leave behind a wife and a ten-year-old son. But there were plenty of precedents in Fuqing that suggested the perilous journey to a foreign shore could pay off handsomely. You could tell at a glance which households had a son or daughter earning good money in Europe or America: their houses were the tallest in the neighborhood, and the construction of extra stories sped up or slowed down in tandem with the ebb and flow of remittances from overseas. So Huang went to the moneylender to whom his father was in hock, who agreed to make another loan with the understanding that if his trip overseas failed to yield the necessary funds, the lender would seize all of the property of Huang's extended family. Then, after some discussions between the moneylender and a local snakehead, it was settled: Huang would leave a few months later for England.

As he told me these things, we sat in the corner of a café looking out on the tiled roofs of old Prato. Life in Fuqing, with its unofficial prisons and soft-shell-turtle farms, seemed so far away as to be barely imaginable. But every time Huang mentioned the moneylenders, his face tightened. "They are not like the state banks. They know everything about you. You can never escape from them," he said. "They know how many beers you have in your fridge and how many of those bottles are half full."

By June 2000 he was ready to leave. But news of a tragedy spread through the community. Fifty-eight Chinese had been found suffocated to death in the back of a tomato van as it tried to cross into Britain through Dover. The Dutch driver had closed the air vents to prevent any sound of his human cargo from being heard outside.

The crackdown that followed in Fuqing made everyone nervous. Police inspectors from Beijing went from house to house, interviewing people and trying to find the snakeheads who were responsible for arranging the passage of the young men and women to Europe. Strangely, though, the Dover tragedy did not dampen the desire among people to try for a new future abroad. Consequently, the price of passage went up. The snakeheads demanded that Huang pay another $3,000 on top of the $12,000 he had already handed over. He had no choice but to borrow more, this time from his father's elder brother, so by the time he finally set off, in September 2000, he was carrying with him the hopes of an imprisoned father, a mortgage on two houses, and the goodwill of his uncle.

A snakehead supplied Huang with a passport and a Chinese exit stamp and told him that it was now too risky to attempt a trip to northern Europe; the police had clamped down since the Dover tragedy. He would be heading to the south—maybe to Italy, maybe to Spain—with several traveling companions also driven by a mixture of obligation and misfortune. One woman among them was four months pregnant, and none of them were over thirty years old. In Beijing they were told they would take the Trans-Siberian Railway, crossing into Russia at Blagoveshchensk, a busy town on the Chinese border. They had no Russian visas so they were packed into crates as freight. The box that Huang was told to slither into was half full of blue parkas, so it made a fairly comfortable bed. The gaps between the wooden panels allowed him ample air to breathe, and when the temperature plunged as the train thundered through the Russian night, Huang burrowed deeper into the parkas.

Several hours later a snakehead who spoke Russian and had a relationship with the train's guards helped Huang get out of the crate. He and his fellow stowaways then spent a few more days sitting amid the freight. Sometime before they reached Moscow, the snakehead got a call on his mobile phone. He turned to the group and told them that getting off at Moscow would be too risky. They would have to jump off the train while it was still moving and head across country. Huang looked at the pregnant woman, fearing for her safety, but there was nothing to be done. The snakehead waited until the train slowed down near a level crossing and then slid open the door. They leapt onto a grassy verge next to the tracks and everyone survived the jump, though the pregnant woman was weeping silently by the time they re-grouped in a ditch. The snakehead worked his mobile phone, and within a few hours a white van arrived to pick them up. They drove for days, stopping at night in nondescript houses by the side of the road.

Suddenly, without warning, the snakehead told them to get out and walk. Dusk was falling and there was a mountain range ahead of them. Huang thought it might have been the border of the former Yugoslavia. They were about to cross into a war zone on foot. They walked all night; a local man guided them, first through forests and then through mountain passes, in silence. Once, one of the snakebody asked where they were, and the snakehead snapped: "We haven't come to see cultural relics.

What are you asking for?" On the other side of the mountains, they rested in a white house on a hillside that had mattresses on the floor but no other furniture.

A truck came to pick them up that evening, and they drove again all day. The house they were lodged in this time was more comfortable. It had running water, furniture, a kitchen, and a room with bunk beds. The group stayed there for a week before being packed off for the last leg of their journey — a trip in the hold of a cargo ship from a small port somewhere on the Adriatic, bound for Sicily.

Such sea voyages were among the most dangerous parts of the whole ordeal. During the week I was in Prato, the local Chinese newspapers gave front-page coverage to one operation that had gone wrong. The Italian coast guard had intercepted a ship sailing from Malta to Sicily, and the snakehead, desperate not to be caught, had forced his charges at gunpoint to jump into the sea. According to the testimony of some of the survivors, several members of the snakebody told the snakehead they could not swim. But he made them jump anyway, and some are thought to have drowned.

Huang's sea crossing was uneventful and at last his ship docked. In the back of the van that drove them to Milan, he was too tired for emotion and still too scared to relax. From there he spent the next four years in Bologna, Rome, and, recently, Prato, always doing menial jobs, sweeping, stacking, washing, and lifting. When the authorities in Fuqing noticed that he had begun settling his father's debts in regular installments, they freed his father from the makeshift prison. He and his father then set about paying off the debt to the father's elder brother. By the time I met Huang, in April 2005, he was almost debt-free, but he could not go back home. His son was fifteen years old and his school fees were too expensive. Huang had not seen him since he left China, and when he spoke of him, his voice cracked. "Everything is for my son," he said.

• • •

I was not surprised to find Chinese people in Prato. In fact, they were part of the reason I had come. It struck me that their presence might offer a telling insight into the competitiveness of European manufacturing in general. Prato had been the center of European textiles for more than seven hundred years, and its reputation for high quality was enriched by a history that no advertising could buy.

Centuries of Florentine courtiers, including Machiavelli—the most sharply dressed of them all—had swathed themselves in its cloth. Prato also had designers who were second to none in the industry, and a glamorous list of clients: Armani, Prada, Ferré, Gucci, Max Mara, Patrizia, Pepe, Banana Republic, Valentino, and Versace had all done their shopping here. Now, with the presence of the Chinese, it had another enviable advantage—access to probably the cheapest and most determined labor force in the world. Men such as those outside the Xiaolin supermarket, for example, were willing to work nearly double the hours of their Italian counterparts for about half the compensation. A Chinese cloth and garment cutter, for instance, could expect to take home about 1,000 euros for a month of six-day weeks at fifteen hours a day, without any pension or health benefits.

So here was my question: if, blessed by this confluence of good fortune and hard-earned expertise, Prato could not compete with textile towns in China, then what hope, ultimately, was there for the rest of the European industry, which employed around 2.7 million people in twenty-five countries and had a turnover of 225 billion euros a year?[2] And, by extension, what would the outlook be for the rest of European manufacturing?

Prato's early experiences, I learned, had been positive. The first illegal immigrants began to arrive in the mid- to late 1980s, and, according to an artist who was among the first to arrive, children on the streets would look at them as if they were extraterrestrials. The numbers then were relatively small, and they were absorbed naturally by the town's textile factories. But by the early 1990s they had become a potent economic force of some ten thousand cheap and often skilled workers. The combination of Italian flair and Chinese labor fostered a miniboom, and the number of textile companies rose to around six thousand in the mid-1990s from some four thousand at the start of the decade. But the local Italian bosses had no way of knowing at the outset quite what they had let themselves in for. It would not have seemed worthy of note to them then that most of the people they employed to sweep floors, cut cloth, and sew on labels came from Wenzhou, probably the most entrepreneurial place in all China.

Wenzhou, in the province of Zhejiang, is a port city south of Shanghai. A ring of high mountains that stand between Wenzhou and the rest of China has bred in its people something of an enclave mentality. For centuries they have been more likely to look outward than inland for their opportunities, rather in the same manner as people from Goa, Malacca, or Djibouti. Free trade has been their lifeline, and the city was one of the last places to submit to Communist rule after the 1949 revolution.

Indeed, communism always seemed an alien contrivance. During the Cultural Revolution, when merely talking about private enterprise could land you in a labor camp, some Wenzhou families owned their own farm animals, traded on the black market, or provided services for a fee. With the advent of free-market reforms, the city was among the first to blossom, and today it is a national center for several industries, including shoes, agricultural valves, lighters, eyeglasses, and clothing, for which it seems to have no comparative advantage aside from the sheer force of will. Its businessmen are daring, diligent, and sometimes ruthless. But what makes them unusual is the degree to which they work together. So if a Wenzhou businessman in some far-flung corner of China or elsewhere in the world has an idea that he thinks will fly, he can usually call upon quick, concessionary financing from an informal network of relatives and business associates.

This is what happened in Prato. After a few years of working on the factory floor, one after another of the Wenzhou workers decided to set up businesses on their own. The number of Chinese-run firms registered at the House of Commerce in Prato rose from

212 in 1992 to 1,753 in 2003. Indeed, the same thing was happening elsewhere too. In Empoli, a Tuscan town that makes leather goods and garments, several hundred Wenzhou businesses also sprang up, and in the Emilia-Romagna region, embracing Bologna, Modena, and Reggio Emilia, the number of Chinese-run factories also proliferated.[3]

Stories of how immigrant laborers in threadbare clothes walked off the factory floor one week and set up in competition with their former bosses the next began to fill the business pages of local newspapers. Of course there were ups and downs, and success did not always come easily to Prato's newest type of entrepreneur. Wang Liping, for example, raised money from associates and relatives in Wenzhou to finance the purchase of a $35,000 shipping container of thread. But when the thread arrived in Prato, he discovered it was too thick for Italian spinning machines. "I lost every cent I invested," Wang Liping said. But six months later he tried again, this time borrowing from different associates. Now he runs a business selling thread and sewing machine accessories with annual revenues of around $1 million.

Another entrepreneur, Wang Yihua, a young woman with a company called Great Fashion, came to Italy in 1989 after a journey organized by snakeheads. On her first attempt to leave China, she had been caught hiding in one of the train's toilets in Erlian, a town on the border of Mongolia, and police sent her home with a severe warning. A few months later, still only nineteen, she tried the same journey again and was successful. Now she drives a Volkswagen convertible with fuzzy dice dangling from the mirror, wears designer sunglasses, and speaks fluent Italian. In addition to the Chinese workers in her factory, she has also employed an Italian designer.

For a while, everyone seemed to benefit from Prato's growing associations with China. The cheap thread and cloth that were coming out of Wenzhou, Nantong, Hangzhou, Suzhou, and other textile towns were available not only to start-ups like Great Fashion but also to the long-established companies of the Pratese. As costs went down, business flourished, and it seemed that this midsize town in Tuscany had found an elusive formula, a way of harnessing the energy of a rising China to serve its ends. The local government embraced its unexpected good fortune. It set up an immigrant service center to help those who arrived — illegally or otherwise — with their first few steps in Italy. It recognized the Wenzhou Chamber of Commerce in Prato as a local organization and cemented a sister-city pact with Wenzhou in China. As a demonstration of sincerity, Prato even funded the restoration of a Ming dynasty temple in Wenzhou by craftsmen sent over from Italy.[4]

But the bonhomie was not sustainable. The illegal-immigrants-turned-entrepreneurs began to put their former Italian bosses out of business. Of the six thousand or so textile companies that existed in 2000, fewer than half remained in mid-2005. Several Italian companies with more than a hundred years of history are barely hanging on. The main reason for this is that whereas in the past only one part of the process of making a garment was outsourced to China, now almost every step of production is being shifted offshore. As spinning, weaving, cutting, and sewing move to Wenzhou, the Chinese factory bosses in Prato become better suited to the transition than their Italian counterparts.

The typical Prato textile business resembles Wang Yihua's Great Fashion. She produces ready-to-wear garments for an Italian brand holder, but the only functions performed in Italy are the design and the sewing of the brand holder's label onto finished garments that return from China. The factories back in Wenzhou are so large and efficient that they need only a week from the time they receive a new design by e-mail from Prato to the time they dispatch the shipment of the finished clothing to Italy. Even allowing for Prato's unusual source of cheap immigrant labor, the cost differentials between China and Italy remain huge. "The euro is so strong these days," said Wang. "Chinese workers in Prato are earning about ten times what they would back in Wenzhou."

The municipal authorities in Prato seem unsure of what to do. The boom that Chinese labor had helped to create is turning to bust. Seven hundred years of textile tradition are in danger of extinction, and along with them Prato's links with its past. The meaning of this realization came to me as I sat in the office of Francesco Delfino, general manager of the province of Prato, in the Palazzo Banci Buonamici. It struck me that everything around us had been founded on cloth. Outside the window was a statue of Francesco di Marco Datini, a fourteenth-century cloth merchant and philanthropist. The building in which we were seated was an old textile palace with trussed ceilings and alabaster statues of Roman emperors looking out from alcoves in the main hall. Delfino was philosophical about his town's visitation from China. He could see the diligence and agility of the people from Wenzhou, but he could also see, first in their arrival and now apparently in their gradual departure, that they threatened an indigenous culture. He did not know what the future held, but he was sure that somehow the Pratese would find a way through.

Prato's predicament is common throughout the European textile trade and in all of Italy's artisan industries. In Biella, a wool town near Piedmont, Chinese competition is forcing closures of factories that have lined the river there since the thirteenth century. Other companies, among them the cashmere garment firm Fratelli Piacenza, have moved production to lower-cost countries. In Montebelluna, a cluster of companies that produced sports shoes have shifted production to an industrial park in Romania. And in the south of the country, the footwear center of Barletta, home to some 2,300 shoe companies, is reeling from stiff foreign competition.

Towns and industries such as these have faced competitive threats from overseas on several occasions before, and on each occasion they have found ways to outmaneuver their rivals, by moving into higher-end markets or by emphasizing the excellence of their brands or by concentrating on new designs. But this time there is no obvious refuge. China is competing in every area of textiles, as well as other manufacturing and artisan industries. At the low-cost end, huge Chinese factories are widely acknowledged to enjoy unassailable advantages. But even in haute couture — the preserve of brands like Givenchy, Yves Saint-Laurent, Versace, Valentino, Ungaro, and Chanel—the influence of China is palpable. It is not that Chinese brands have begun to compete in these areas; that may not happen for many years to come. Rather, it is that several brand owners have undertaken large-scale outsourcing to China in an effort to offer good-quality fashion at more affordable prices. The result has been a narrowing of margins at the high end of the fashion industry and a Europe-wide dilemma over whether to follow the outsourcing trend at the risk of diluting brand values.

Some brand owners may think they can hold on to both the outsourcing and the brand. At least one gentlemen's tailor on Savile Row in London, for example, measures clients in his premises on the famous street and then promptly outsources the actual tailoring to China. When the customer returns to pick up his new suit a couple of weeks later, he may have no inkling that it was stitched together in a basement somewhere in Wenzhou by a seamstress earning Industrial Revolution–era wages. For obvious reasons, the Savile Row tailor may decide to keep this aspect of his operation quiet. But eventually the word will get out, and Savile Row may lose a little of its aura.

A similar process is under way within many of the big haute couture houses, and the logic behind it is inescapable. If most of the cloth available these days in Prato comes originally from China, why would a fashion house not go directly to China to buy the same thing for less money? One problem they face, however, is that in the eyes of most of their customers, a large part of a brand's appeal lies in the knowledge that what they are wearing was made in the traditional way by companies with hundreds of years of history. The other problem with outsourcing is that when work is sent to China, some key technology and know-how usually follow so that quality can be assured. But, as we have seen, to transfer technology is to nurture competitors, and when those competitors reach a critical scale, the pressure for the whole industry to relocate to the cheapest, most efficient production center becomes intense.[5]

Such are the dynamics of global capitalism; the story is the same whether the industry in question is textiles or automobiles or shipbuilding or almost anything else. Only reactions to it vary. Some people are unsentimental about the social capital that is lost when a whole industry shuts down or moves away, but others feel they have lost part of themselves when a community to which they have given their life packs up and disappears.

The beautiful lake town of Como, in northern Italy, is a case in point. Since Roman times, Como has been a locus of the silk industry. The sensual cloth that flows in liquid harmony with the body's movements was a favorite of Cleopatra, the mistress of Julius Caesar and Mark Antony. The material she wore, which Pliny the Elder, the scholar, believed came from the "hair of sea sheep," was imported from China both overland and by ship. By the fourth century C.E. it had become a common accoutrement in all civilized outposts of the Western world, and the money spent on it was draining the wealth of a declining empire. In one of the first examples of industrial espionage, the emperor Justinian is said to have commissioned Persian holy men to smuggle the eggs of *Bombyx mori*, the silkworm, and mulberry seeds into Constantinople in 550. By the end of the sixth century, the enigma of sericulture was being unraveled in many parts of Europe, and Como flourished as a place that produced silkworm cocoons, spun silk, and created finished garments. By 1840 the countryside around the town was given over to more than three million mulberry trees, the leaves of which supply the silkworm's only food.

When, about two decades ago, it became obvious that the silk material harvested and spun from Chinese silkworms was cheaper and of similar quality to that made in Como, the first thing to be outsourced to China was the spinning and weaving work. Then much of the garment-making went too, and later some companies in the small town of Shengzhou, in Zhejiang province, got hold of the same computer-controlled looms that gave Como an edge in quality control. Within a few years the Chinese, who run their looms all day and all night, were putting Como companies out of business, and in the space of just seven years the number of computer-controlled looms in Shengzhou has jumped from 8 to 670. The Chinese town single-handedly produces almost half of the world's silk neckties, while Como's industry appears to be in terminal decline. The change has been that swift. To many in the Italian town it seems like only yesterday that Bill Clinton was seen on television taking the oath of the presidency in a Como silk tie.

In one sense, there is a historical symmetry to the rise of Shengzhou and the concurrent decline of Como; it is as if the moth of *Bombyx mori* has decided, after a 1,500-year sojourn in Europe, finally to fly back home. But for Moritz Mantero, whose company makes silk for ties sold by Ralph Lauren, Brooks Brothers, and similar brands, such observations are abhorrent. He has been to Shengzhou and found the smokestacks, concrete-block buildings, and pollution of the place "horrible." At home, he has watched as some twenty thousand silk-industry jobs have disappeared since 2001 and dozens of long-established firms have gone under. His company, he is confident, can survive by concentrating on precision manufacturing and excellent design. Walking around the stone mansion that has been the company headquarters since his grandfather's day, Mantero pointed out a room that holds the key to the firm's future. Inside were ten thousand volumes of old design samples, many of them purchased from failed textile mills.[6] He grasped one leather-bound volume, the 1893 spring collection of a defunct French garment maker. The patterns inside still seemed fresh: one design, a geometric sequence of ellipses, was at once reiterative and mystical.

But even in design the Chinese are catching up. When a Como corporate customer of Babei, the largest of Shengzhou's 1,100 tie makers, encountered difficulties in paying for the silk he had imported from China, Jin Yao, Babei's president, took his compensation in the form of the Italian company's design shop. In so doing, he bought access to the only segment of the industry in which the Chinese are not yet dominant. Now, back in Shengzhou, he will be able to marry designs from hundreds of years of Italian creative tradition to his factory's ability to churn out twenty million ties a year. That is a combination that might just finish off Como.

I went by train from Prato to Chiasso, a town just over the Italian border in Switzerland. By chance I found myself sitting next to two Chinese, one older, thickset man in casual clothes and his young, keen colleague in a suit. The older man was the boss of a textile company based in Zhejiang, and his associate was the company's representative in France, where they had recently acquired a linen manufacturer, Terre de Lin.

The young man had taken it upon himself to be his boss's eyes, ears, and cultural compass among the alien corn, offering up an effusion of unsolicited observations in a cloying voice. So when the boss asked him why he had been unable to arrange any business meetings for the next day, the young man went into a discourse on the laziness of Italians. They never want to meet because they take so much time off. They always play golf or sit in cafés and leave their businesses unattended. Had the boss noticed, the young man wanted to know, how many barbershops are closed on Mondays? Imagine that: closed on Monday. In fact, the whole of Europe is similarly afflicted with sloth, which only goes to show that when people have money, they lose enthusiasm for work. "Their lives are just too comfortable," said the young man, screwing up his mouth as if the thought tasted bitter. The boss nodded silently as he stared out at the Tuscan countryside.

Both men seemed interested by this theme. A while later the boss remarked that they had been traveling for an hour and a half and had hardly seen a single factory. "Foreigners like looking at scenery," the young man offered. The boss paused for thought, then asked, "Scenery or production, which is more important?" He began to leaf through a stack of faxes. Looking up with his reading glasses still on, he asked his employee to make a call to schedule a meeting at some future point in their itinerary. The young man stood up and excused himself with a little bow and the explanation that in Europe only people of "low quality" used their phone in a train car. The boss mumbled an objection, but the young man continued to move to the space between the cars to make his call.

Sometime after he had returned, my cell phone rang and I answered it.

"You see, some foreigners can be quite low-quality too," the young man said to his boss. "And look at his phone. So old. Yours is so much better than his."

It was true. My phone, with its scuffed corners and dull gray display, was certainly inferior to the boss's all-beeping, all-flashing, full-color model. Nevertheless, I found myself unable to resist letting them know that I could understand what had just been said. "Is that so?" I asked in Chinese.

To my disappointment, the young man did not skip a beat. "Yes. I was just telling my boss that your phone does not match up to his. How much did you pay for it?" he asked.

As the journey went on, we struck up a lively conversation. The boss's curiosity ranged over many subjects, some familiar, some surprising. Why were foreigners lazy? What was Europe going to do when it did not have much industry left? Could you really run an economy on services alone? Did European cows really consume two dollars a day in farm subsidies? Was there any reason for the European Union to exist? Hadn't it come into being because a few French and German politicians had wanted to play political games?

In among the questions, there were pronouncements. China, the boss said, would be finished if it took its eye off economic development and started to play politics again. Playing politics was the worst thing that could happen to a country. During the Cultural Revolution, playing politics had cost the formal education of millions of people, and the boss had been one of them. Making money was the only objective truth, he said. But foreigners already had enough money, so now they were playing games with politics.

To start with, I was not sure what he meant by the word "foreigners." We were traveling through Italy, after all, so by most reckonings the boss and his associate would count as foreigners and the Italians would be locals. But then I remembered an article in the newspaper of the Chinese community in Prato. One front-page story involved "three foreign thieves" stealing something from Chinatown. It was not until the end of the article that the thieves were identified as having Italian names. I called the news-paper's editor to ask if this had not in fact been an error, a mis-print, perhaps. She answered that the misapprehension was mine: anyone who was not Chinese was foreign, wherever they were. The same rule seemed to apply in all the Chinese-language news-papers I found: Italians were invariably referred to as foreigners. With this in mind, I asked the boss how he found doing business in an alien culture such as Europe's. "It is better than before. Five years ago hardly anyone in the textile industry would meet us. Some would not even take our calls," he said. "Now, wherever we go, we meet the CEOs. You know what the difference is? Money. It is the only thing that foreigners respect."

When the train pulled in at Chiasso, I said goodbye to the boss and his assistant, got off, and started walking. At the end of a long, empty platform and past some sleepy border guards stood Emilio Camponovo, the person I had come to meet.

The last time we had seen each other was in Shanghai, at a large conference on precious metals in a five-star hotel. The audi-ence had just been treated to a bullish forecast by a Chinese offi-cial on the podium; the lines on his PowerPoint graph all aimed skyward, demand was set to soar, and China would soon be the largest market for precious metals on earth. Then everyone re-paired for lunch. I found Emilio studying his food near a self-service tureen of rice, which had drawn a long line of diners.

He looked tired. Chinese officials could say what they liked, he said, but the fact was that per capita expenditure on gold in China was a fraction of that in the developed world. Even in India, peo-ple spent far more on gold ornaments than the Chinese. It was true that Chinese had a preference for platinum, but that was not much use to Emilio. He was the founder and part owner of one of the largest gold refineries in Europe. "All we need is for every Chinese to buy a gold chain," he said, rolling back his cuff to reveal a chain with the heaviest, thickest links I had ever seen. I had the sense that he was joking, but when I did not laugh, his eyes lit up. "You think it is possible? One day they might?" I said I could not tell. "No, probably not, I suppose," he said.

At the end of the platform in Chiasso, Emilio looked happier and more relaxed. He was a large man in his sixties, wearing a sports jacket made of silk and an open-necked shirt. The fibers of the jacket scintillated in the sunlight. As we walked to lunch, he told me some local history. The border ran slap through the middle of what was really one town; the southern part was Como in Italy and the northern part was Chiasso in Switzerland, but the dominant ethnicity on both sides was Italian. The separation had made for some interesting arbitrage opportunities, he said. In the 1970s, the Italian government subsidized gasoline but sugar was difficult to get hold of. In Switzerland, by contrast, gas was expensive and sugar plentiful. "So every day here," he said, pointing at an empty car lot next to the border post, "you would have a big trading. Sugar that way. Petrol this way. That was how it went."

At lunch the conversation was somewhat somber. The gold business was in trouble. Northern Italy was home to more than ten thousand jewelry manufacturers, most of them small-scale artisan outfits that, taken together, made up the largest gold jewelry industry in the world. But competition from China and Turkey was threatening to wipe them out. You could see the changes already in Italy's demand for refined gold: in the past four or five years it had slumped from more than 600 to around 350 metric tons annually. Camponovo saw little prospect for improvement. Every year, he said, Chinese entrepreneurs and designers descended on the big jewelry fairs in northern Italian towns such as Vicenza to buy specimens to take home and reproduce at less than one-tenth of the Italian price.

Camponovo appeared resigned that this practice would continue and that Italy's jewelry industry might be heading for collapse. He did not blame the Chinese, he said. They were willing to work hard and they were smart. What really exercised him during our lunch and later, talking in his office, was how ignorant the Italian and Swiss governments seemed to be of the nature of Chinese competition. From his perspective, the threat came less from China's rise than from the failure of European governments to understand it and formulate policies to deal with it. For instance, he said, corporate tax rates in his canton of Switzerland were effectively more than 50 percent of profits. But in spite of this heavy burden, the canton had announced larger budget deficits year after year. The reason for these deficits was not any significant increase in spending on essential infrastructure; Chiasso is one of the wealthiest places in Europe, and the roads, railways, schools, and hospitals are already excellent. The main cause of the deepening deficit was state payments to individuals for medical treatment. Of some 300,000 people living in the canton, around 90,000 qualified through various loopholes for help in paying their health care costs. "We are killing ourselves with comfort," he said.

Health care was one cost. Unions were another: there were ten different unions represented among the staff who worked in Camponovo's gold refinery. The red tape and the various benefits were suffocating, he said. In every company and profession it was the same story: the socialist welfare state had turned from a boon to a burden. A couple of years ago, he said, there had been a move to increase the twenty-five-hour work week of schoolteachers in the canton by one full hour. But many teachers opposed this, so a public, canton-wide referendum had to be held to resolve the issue. Camponovo shook his head at the memory of it.

I thought of the boss and his assistant on the train and wondered what they would make of a canton-wide referendum on a twenty-five-hour week for teachers.

It is said that in state-to-state diplomacy there is no such thing as friendship, only periods when mutual interests coalesce. So when

Jacques Chirac, the French president, struck up a friendship with his Chinese counterpart, Jiang Zemin, that was so attentive it bordered on courtship, some people found it hard to know where to look. The two leaders found time in their schedules to keep up a correspondence on the subjects of art, poetry, and culture. Jiang had heard that Chirac admired the poetry of Li Bai, a Tang poet, and he sent his own ink-brush calligraphy to the French leader. Chirac repaid the courtesy by showing the Jiang calligraphy scroll to honored guests and praising the fairness of the Chinese president's hand. Jiang later commended Chirac's knowledge of Chinese culture, remarking once that "he is more of an expert than me. In Shanghai, he even correctly dated a bronze statue."[7]

When Jiang and his wife, Wang Yeping, visited France, Chirac invited them for a weekend at Château Bity, the sixteenth-century home in the Corrèze region of central France that Chirac and his wife, Bernadette, usually keep sequestered from their political commitments. Indeed, when Hillary Clinton visited the local town of Sarran, of which Bernadette was deputy mayor, she was given a tour of favorite Chirac haunts in the town but never made it as far as the family château. The special treatment for the Jiangs was extended later to the whole concept of China. The Eiffel Tower was illuminated in the red of the Chinese flag to mark a "Year of China" in France, and, as part of a reciprocal "French Culture Year" in China, eight jets from the French air force swooped over the Great Wall, leaving tricolor contrails behind them. Chirac maintained in a speech at Jiang's alma mater in Shanghai that things were getting so close between the two nations that a state of "brotherly love" had developed.[8]

Was all this merely politics as usual, or did Chirac really harbor special feelings for Jiang and the Chinese people? Certainly, he cannot have been oblivious of the commercial utility of friendship with Beijing; in late 2004 the French companies that went along on his visit to China garnered contracts for Airbus planes, Alstom trains, water treatment plants, hydroelectric equipment, and wheat that were valued at 5 billion euros.[9]

But from another perspective, Chirac's overtures to Beijing

were far from universally popular at home. Alain Madelin, the president of the Liberal Democratic Party, likened Jiang to the former Chilean dictator Augusto Pinochet and said there should be a limit to the red-carpet treatment he received in France.[10] Similarly, Wei Jingsheng, China's most famous exiled dissident, poured scorn on Chirac's appreciation of Jiang's calligraphy. "Everyone in China knows that Jiang writes like a child," he said. "Chirac is making a fool of himself."[11] Perhaps, after all, Chirac's willingness to suffer the slings and arrows of domestic criticism proved that his ardor was genuine.

Then again, perhaps not. Only a few months after he assured Beijing that China's rise was a wonderful thing that offered rare opportunities for French growth and job creation, the French president completely changed his tune. Sitting next to Gerhard Schröder, the then German chancellor, at a meeting to discuss the future of Europe, Chirac said: "We have a real problem in Europe. The considerable increase in Chinese textile exports to our countries calls into question the jobs of thousands of workers. We cannot accept a death blow to the jobs of a significant number of workers in our countries."[12] So why the volte-face? The commercial relationship between France and China had not objectively changed, and the "friendship" between the two countries was still nominally intact. What was different was Chirac's perception of his political interests. France was about to vote in a referendum, and the issues of jobs and competitiveness were paramount.

Ostensibly, the subject of that referendum was whether to approve a new European constitution that would open the way for an expansion of the European Union beyond its twenty-five member states. But in reality the vote in France was generally about whether people were satisfied with their lot and, more particularly, whether they felt that the previous EU expansion from fifteen to twenty-five members had benefited them. The answer to these questions, first in France and then in the Netherlands, turned out after the vote to be an emphatic no. Various theories have been advanced as to why both countries voted against adoption of the European constitution and the further enlargement of the Union. But the dominant concern appears to have been unemployment, and especially the migration of jobs to the new EU members in eastern Europe. The referendum result was fundamentally a conservative cry against the loss of social benefits and a decline in the prevailing quality of life.

The referendum's rejection was a painful political blow for Chirac, and it threw the whole European project into crisis. Several politicians have since tried to reignite the cause of greater European unity and to point to ways out of the current malaise. British prime minister Tony Blair, for instance, warned of "failure on a grand, strategic scale" if EU member nations were to drift apart, turn their backs on globalization, or ignore the need for reform of Europe's institutions.[13] The way to inject new growth and energy into Europe, Blair said, included investment in knowledge, in active labor market policies, in science parks and innovation, in higher education, in urban regeneration, and in help for small businesses. In a speech to mark the United Kingdom's presidency of the EU, he added that the Union's social model needed to be modernized and a system of farm subsidies that claims 40 percent of EU budget revenues had to be gradually overhauled.

But Blair, in common with other establishment EU politicians who have addressed the subject, has failed to give an accurate accounting of the competitive threat Europe faces. The impact of China's rise is not something that can be mitigated by a few incremental reforms, some reallocation of budgetary resources, and the launch of several initiatives to spur innovation. It is a challenge unprecedented in the annals of global capitalism, the product of epoch-making changes under harsh conditions in the world's most populous country. The events unfolding in Prato and Como are merely early soundings of things to come. One early example of trade friction was the "bra wars" spat over the entry of supercompetitive Chinese textiles to Europe. Tomorrow it will be electronics, motorbikes, steel, chemicals, cars, and cartoon animation. The simple, unpalatable truth is that in many areas of manufacturing, European companies cannot compete in the long run, no matter what countermeasures they or the EU may take.

Some examples illustrate this point. An Italian company, Seves SpA, had two factories making heavy glass insulators in Europe, one in Italy and one in St. Yorre, France. It had to decide which one to close after competition from China convinced the management that manufacturing in Europe was not sustainable. It chose to close the French factory because its workers were 57 percent more expensive than those in Italy and worked 19 percent fewer hours.[14] What surprised the management was the savings they gained when they built a new plant near Shanghai. The starting salary for a production-line worker was 2,600 euros a year, compared with 17,000 euros in St. Yorre. The company offered to rehire any of its French workers willing to make the trip to Shanghai, but none volunteered.

Schiess, a 140-year-old maker of heavy-duty lathes and boring machines based in the German town of Aschersleben, typifies the *Mittelstand*, or midsize, machine-tool makers that are the backbone of the German economy. Even though Schiess is in the former East Germany, where wages are lower than in western Germany, the differential between Germany and China is still large. A skilled worker in Aschersleben makes $2,000 to $2,600 a month, while in China a worker of similar ability gets $400 or less. That is why Shenyang Machine Tool decided to shift many of Schiess's jobs to China after it bought the company in early 2005.[15]

ABB, the Swiss engineering giant, plans to hire five thousand new employees in China by 2008, and more than half of these will be engineers. They would be in addition to the seven thousand employees currently working for the company in different divisions in thirty large Chinese cities. During the same time, there are no explicit plans to hire any workers in Europe. "Our feeling is that we are overinvested in Europe and underinvested in low-cost countries like China," Jürgen Dormann, ABB's chief executive, said. "We have too many factories in Europe and buy too many of our raw materials in high-cost countries."[16] Similarly, IBM has announced a plan to lay off its thirteen thousand workers in Europe.

There is no end in sight to the trend that these examples illuminate. Faced with Chinese competition, companies either shift production to places such as the Pearl River and Yangtze deltas or move to one of the new members of the EU in eastern Europe — Poland, Hungary, or the Czech Republic. The deepening of the employment crisis in "core" European countries that results from these actions represented one of the biggest electoral challenges facing several European politicians, Schröder and Chirac among them. Germany is in the grip of its worst employment crisis since before World War Two, with more than 12 percent of its workforce, or around five million people, without a job. Throughout the EU, the unemployment rate is around 9 percent, and real wages in sectors such as manufacturing are falling. A further complication is the relatively low number of those laid off who are able to find new jobs in the service sector. This is partly because jobs in accounting, law, financial and risk management, health care, information technology, and several other service areas are also in the process of migrating to India and China.

As people fear for their jobs, understandable conservative reflexes — such as those displayed in the French and Dutch referendum votes — can fuel protectionism and resentment. At this point, it may take all the energy and determination of political leaders to prevent a general regression into chauvinism. The pain inflicted by the type of deep and structural reform that Europe needs can make such reform difficult to sell to the electorate. The nature of the European malaise so harshly exposed by China's emerging prowess is that the working populations of "core" Europe are — by many multiples — compensated too generously for producing too little. But for politicians it can be tough to sell a promise of downsizing, offshoring, outsourcing, and falling real wages to European electorates already saddled with twenty million unemployed. Intellectually, many in Europe may find it distasteful that the EU runs a subsidy under which cows get more than two dollars a day — more than the average daily income of seven hundred million Chinese. But when Europeans contemplate the consequences of any rapid unraveling of the agricultural subsidy system — the mass bankruptcy of small farms, the decline in land values, and the distress of rural communities—the appetite for change may wither.

China was able, in the five years from the onset of the Asian financial crisis in 1997, to lay off more than 25 million workers from its inefficient and heavily subsidized state-owned enterprises.[17] The fruits of that stern therapy are now evident in the competitive shock that is hitting Europe and America. But China is not a democracy. The state did not have to seek the permission of its people to "smash the iron rice bowl" of socialist welfare or turn its back on the ideology of communism. When workers rioted, protested, petitioned, or dissented, it answered with well-honed authoritarian tactics. The result has been that state-financed social welfare has in the space of less than a decade ceased to be a millstone for the corporate sector. The housing, schooling, health care, and pension obligations that more than 300,000 state companies used to meet on behalf of their workers have been eliminated, reduced, or privatized. China today is a great deal less socialist than any country in Europe; the 120 million or so migrant workers, for instance, receive no benefits at all.

Not only is the cost of employing a Chinese worker a fraction of that in Germany, France, and Italy—and roughly between one-sixth and one-quarter of the going rates in eastern Europe's EU member nations—but also state expenditures in China are lower as a proportion of gross domestic product than in the countries of western Europe. That means the taxes the government levies on its corporations and its people can also be lower. In Germany, for instance, state expenditures came to 47.8 percent of GDP in 2004. An accurate figure for China is more difficult to calculate because of various categories of quasi-governmental financing, such as funding by state banks for state infrastructure projects, which is not normally included in the official figures. Nevertheless, narrowly defined Chinese state expenditures, as a percentage of gross domestic product, come to less than half of German levels.[18]

These discrepancies define the challenge China presents to the social democratic model that Europe so painstakingly constructed from the ruins of World War Two. But it is far from clear whether, faced with this challenge, Germany and France—and to a lesser extent the other countries of western Europe—possess the will or ability to smash their own "iron rice bowl."

Sometimes the rhetoric seems to be moving in the opposite direction. Just as Marx and Engels are losing their Far Eastern constituency of 1.3 billion, they may be gaining ground back in their ancestral homeland. Franz Müntefering, chairman of the ruling Social Democratic Party, told listeners in Berlin in 2005 that "the growing power of international capital" with its "unbridled greed for profit" represented a "threat to democracy."[19] This was followed a few days later by Chancellor Schröder's taking issue with the evils of an "unrestrained neo-liberal system." Other politicians warned of "predator capitalists," while Müntefering later lambasted faceless foreign investors who were descending on Germany like "swarms of locusts."

From the context of his remarks, he appeared to be pointing the finger at the United Kingdom and the United States, but he could just as easily have been talking about China.

5

America Bought and Sold:
Acquiring Technology
for a Great Leap Forward

ROCKFORD, ILLINOIS, is a low-rise midwestern town surrounded by undulating farmland and horizons that, though generally flat, are more eventful than in the prairie country farther to the south and west. The straight lines that form where the cornfields and dairy pastures meet the sky are broken by a grain silo here, a clump of trees there, and the odd immaculately painted farmhouse. I arrived there from Chicago in late February, when the snow was still in drifts around the curb at the Greyhound bus stop. A taxi took me down East State Street to the Alpine Inn Motel. My first impressions were of churches, fast-food outlets, and waitresses with open faces who said an encouraging "Mmm, mmm" as they put your food down. Signposts visible from the road offered a flavor of Rockford's character: the Westminster Presbyterian Church, Home Town Buffet, the Church of Christian Fellowship, Pot Bellies Drive Thru Sandwich Works, the Blackhawk Baptist Association, Don Pablo's Mexican Kitchen, Lutheran Church, Tom and Jerry's Fast Food. Interspersed with these places were shops advertising that everything inside was going for less than a dollar, and glass-fronted booths offering to lend people their monthly income in advance.

Outwardly, it looked like the last place you might expect to uncover evidence of China's global presence. There were no Chinese here that I could see, aside from those working in restaurants such

as the Great Wall, and they had been in Rockford for so long that
they remembered a visit, back in the 1980s, by George H. W. Bush
when he was a mere vice president. Neither was there any hazy
historical connection, unlike in the nearby town of Pekin, Illinois, a place that had long ago borrowed the name of the Chinese
capital for reasons that were now forgotten. Rockford appeared
to be quintessential Middle America, full of practical folk raising
wholesome families without too much concern for the world beyond the wheat belt. And yet, through circumstance rather than
design, this appearance was somewhat misleading. Though outwardly invisible, the imprint of China was almost everywhere,
embedded in the town's past, looming over its future, and etched
into the contours of its geography.

On the day I arrived, there was a modest traffic jam leading
out of town along East State Street to the suburbs. Strangely, almost nothing was traveling in the other direction, toward the center of town. I asked the receptionist at the Alpine Inn where everyone was going. "Wal-Mart," he said. I went against the crowd,
into the town, and when I got there I found it was virtually de-
serted. Only the library, a movie theater, and a rundown Greek
restaurant were open. Where was everyone? I asked a librarian.
Several years ago, she replied, the downtown had been a focal
point. But it had started to die as companies folded and workers
moved away. Then, a few years later, Wal-Mart had set up a vast
discount store out in the eastern suburbs, inducing a cluster of
restaurants, fast-food outlets, and other hypermarkets to follow.
Soon Rockford's center of gravity had shifted.

Behind each stage in the metamorphosis was China's persis-
tent influence. China had accelerated the loss of manufacturing
jobs and then propelled the rise of Wal-Mart, which bought more
and more of its products from Chinese suppliers. Now, the librarian said, the local economy was enmeshed in a kind of Chinese
puzzle. Local jobs went off to China and returned in the form of
cheap manufactured goods, which were bought by the very people who had paid with their jobs in the first place.

Rockford had only recently been laid low. It had in better days

risen to considerable prominence from small beginnings as an encampment at the end of the Galena and Chicago Union Railroad.
Many of the early settlers were Swedes, hard-working people on
the run from pasteurization. Louis Pasteur's benign discovery of
a way to kill the bacteria in milk had had unforeseen side effects:
as fathers lived longer, sons despaired of ever being able to take
over the family farm and migrated in search of new lives. Like
many early immigrants, they had little inkling of where they were
heading; they just rode the railroads west from New York until
the track ran out in Illinois. When they got there, they were re-
minded of home. The area around the beautiful Rock River was
heavily forested, and the trees were being felled to feed a construction frenzy in Chicago. The great fire that devastated Chicago in 1871 injected impetus into the lumber trade and generated a huge demand for furniture, which the Swedes, along with
other immigrants from Italy and Germany, moved quickly to fill.

Making furniture required precision tools, and those tools had
to be made by someone. The local carpenters proved more than
equal to the task, shifting from woodworking to metalworking
and machine-tool making. One craftsman, doodling in his spare
time, even invented the jigsaw. But Rockford's real rise to prominence in the industry that was to define its development came
after an entrepreneur called Winthrop Ingersoll moved his small
machine-tool factory to Rockford from Cleveland in 1891. Records from those days describe his new plant as 150 feet long and
50 feet wide with 19 men on the payroll. The town that it inhab-
ited had 27 churches, 8 banks, 174 industrial companies, and "six
costly bridges" spanning the Rock River.

To start with, business was quiet, but in the early years of the
twentieth century the automobile industry started to flourish, and
Ingersoll's reputation for building precision tooling and milling
machines spread fast. Walter Chrysler, the master mechanic at
Buick, bought a complete line of machines for milling aluminum
crankcases. Henry Ford was also a customer; the key production
machinery that made the Model T was manufactured at Ingersoll.
The expertise gleaned from contracts such as these would later

help the company develop ways to machine parts for nuclear reactors, Boeing aircraft, and several generations of military warplanes.

One success built on another, and by the middle of the last century, Rockford had become a leader in the American machine-tool industry. Although this did not make the town a household name in America, its contributions to the military-industrial complex won it an unenviable fame in the Kremlin. During the Cold War, this wholesome midwestern community was near the top of a list of places that the Soviet Union had selected as targets for a nuclear strike. In the event of a showdown, Moscow was set to unleash its intercontinental ballistic missiles on Washington, New York, Los Angeles, and . . . Rockford. Apparently, the motivation for this was similar to that which led to the bombing of Schweinfurt, an unremarkable German town where in World War Two ball bearings were made, without which the Luftwaffe's planes and the tanks of the panzer divisions would have ground to a halt.

Residents of Rockford now laugh at the air raid drills, the fallout shelters, and the radios that were tuned to 640 and 1040 on the AM dial, the frequencies used for emergency broadcasts in the event of nuclear attack. But in those days all of it was serious. Not only was Ingersoll engaged in making equipment crucial to the U.S. military, but Sundstrand, a company on Eleventh Street, was the sole source of an electrical system without which most military aircraft could not fly. At one point of high Cold War tension, the Pentagon grew so concerned at this glaring vulnerability that it ordered Sundstrand to set up a second factory, independent in every aspect—engineering, administration, testing, and production—far away in Denver.

As things turned out, of course, the Soviet Union was to have no more than a psychological impact on Rockford. It was China, the other Communist behemoth, that was destined to leave a lasting imprint. For about two years before I got there, the city had been caught in a quiet crisis of manufacturing that had stolen across the American Midwest, sweeping away scores of small and medium-size businesses. Many of those that had gone under were long-established family firms that had weathered wars and economic recessions as well as the rise of Japan and South Korea.

I wanted to acquire an overall reckoning of how many such companies had gone out of business, but comprehensive figures proved difficult to obtain. Many of the closures involved businesses employing tens rather than hundreds of people in towns that rarely made the national newspapers. And yet unofficial surveys offered sobering revelations. In one, Bruce Cain, president of Xcel Mold and Machine, in Canton, Ohio, collected the advertisements for equipment sales that followed the closure of companies in the metalworking industry in ten states in the general area of Ohio. Cain testified before a hearing conducted by the U.S. Congress that between May 2003 and September 2004 he had collected 180 auction fliers — one, on average, every three days.[1] Behind almost every closure or downsizing was a watershed moment when, apparently out of the blue, a new Chinese competitor had emerged offering prices that were a third or less of the best price the American company could manage.

One industry that was particularly hard hit was machine tools, the bedrock of the manufacturing sector and Rockford's specialty. Without the machine tools to make the components of a car engine, there would be no engine; without precision instruments, there would be no high-technology products. The Chinese government, which is overwhelmingly composed of engineering graduates, realized long ago the pivotal role that machine tools play in building a strong industrial base. It made the industry a strategic priority and urged its state-owned companies to scour the world for technologies they could acquire or absorb. At almost all of the closing-down auctions across the Midwest, Chinese buyers were out trying to snap up amortized machinery, technical blueprints, and operational know-how. In Rockford, too, the footprints of acquisitive Chinese corporations were everywhere.

I had come to Rockford for a dinner. Not just any dinner, but the Rockford Regional Chamber of Commerce's event of the year. Around six hundred of the region's leading businesspeople would sit around big tables at a restaurant called Cliffbreakers. The guest of honor was to be Al Frink, the newly appointed "manufacturing czar" in George W. Bush's administration, the person charged with resuscitating a manufacturing sector that had hemorrhaged nearly three million jobs since Bush took his seat in the Oval Office. Don Manzullo, the congressman from the Sixteenth District of Illinois, which includes Rockford, and a campaigner on Capitol Hill for the development of small businesses, would also be there. The official topic of the evening was some anodyne catchall like "The State of Manufacturing in America." But what everyone really wanted to know was how Washington was going to deal with the challenge from China and, more specifically, whether Rockford was doomed to die.

Cliffbreakers looked a little out of keeping with the strait-laced, God-fearing community in which I had spent a week before the night of the dinner. There was more than a touch of Las Vegas about it: rhinestone chandeliers, a fountain in the foyer, Greco-Roman plaster work, and a corridor lined with photographs of famous guests — including Frank Sinatra — who had once performed there. I wondered at first if I had come to the right place, but then I began to see familiar faces. There was a man I had met earlier whose factories had produced a special gear wheel for the space probe that had gone to Mars. Near him was the young engineer who had made a cog so small that it could fit in Lincoln's nose on a penny. Talking to him was a woman in whose factory I had seen workers welding filaments of wire so fine that they could only be seen under a microscope.

The first person to greet me was Tom McDunn. He was in the same three-piece black suit he had been wearing at his brother-in-law's fiftieth birthday party a few nights earlier. It had been a pleasant, sober evening. We sat at a long table eating slabs of pizza and drinking lemonade. The conversation had been cheery and polite. China was not a topic for a happy gathering, and the only time I remember it being mentioned was when the man next to me leaned over and confided that the appetite of Chinese steel mills for scrap was so voracious that some of the manhole covers in his neighborhood had disappeared. "Fancy that," he said.

"They tell me that local boys lever them up to sell them for scrap. We can sell scrap metal and waste cardboard to China, but our good stuff they can make cheaper than we do."

McDunn had been a senior executive at Ingersoll before it ended its illustrious history in bankruptcy in 2003. Even before it went under, Chinese buyers had started to circle. The first part of the venerable old company to be sold off, the auto machine-tool business, called Ingersoll Production Systems, was bought by a state-run Chinese giant, Dalian Machine Tool. As soon as the Chinese took over, McDunn said, the stacks of blueprints and engineering specifications from decades of cutting-edge automotive innovation were dispatched to the head office in China. Dalian, after all, was one of several Chinese companies seized with climbing the next big technological hurdle: how to build a homegrown high-performance automobile engine.

Having bought Ingersoll Production Systems, Dalian decided to use the American company as a stalking horse for the main prize: Ingersoll Milling Machine. Not only had Ingersoll Milling been an important U.S. military contractor since before World War One, but it was also at the time of its insolvency working on highly sensitive projects. It made the machinery that honed the wings of America's fighter aircraft and had developed a technology that ensured more reliable performance from the fuel tanks in rockets. It also produced the equipment that fashions the turbine parts used in nuclear power plants and the machines that coat B-2 stealth bombers with the material that makes them invisible to radar. Such secrets would have been invaluable to Beijing, and Dalian came within a hairbreadth of obtaining them. Nobody from the Pentagon, the Department of Defense, the Central Intelligence Agency, or the other security arms of the U.S. government had noticed that the Chinese company was bidding for Ingersoll Milling through Ingersoll Production Systems. On paper, such a bid must have appeared a mere family affair. However, some local entrepreneurs tipped off Congressman Manzullo, who alerted Lisa Bronson, deputy undersecretary of defense for technology, security policy, and counter-proliferation.[2] The attempted acquisition was blocked, and Ingersoll Milling ended up being bought by an Italian company, Camozzi.

McDunn never said so outright, but I sensed that he thought China was a threat. Not everyone in Rockford was ambiguous on that point, however. Shortly before the banquet started, I met Dean Olson, a genial man with gray hair who had taken me around his auto parts factory earlier in the week. His big shock had come a couple of years earlier when Chinese parts at unbelievably low prices started to eat away his market share. "So," he said, "if you can't beat 'em, join 'em." He began to import some Chinese parts and distribute them to his network of customers along with the relatively high-tech parts that he made himself. The quality of the Chinese goods was fine, he said, and business was OK. But he was always waiting for the moment when the Chinese would climb farther up the technology ladder and produce the high-end products that kept his machinists employed. When this happened, Olson knew, their price would almost certainly be a fraction of what he charged. Under those circumstances, his only remaining business asset would be his distribution network. I asked him if it was possible that one day he might end up just distributing Chinese products. He looked a little offended. "That is a big question," he said.

The last person I met before the speeches started was Eric Anderberg, of Dial Machine, a fair-haired man in his thirties with an open face and a quick intellect. He had been to China on a trip led by Manzullo and Dennis Hastert, the Speaker of the House of Representatives, also from Illinois. Anderberg sat on a committee in Chicago that provided the Federal Reserve Board with feedback on the state of American industry. He saw Rockford's predicament from both a micro and a macro perspective. Dial Machine had had to let go thirty of its seventy workers in the past couple of years, and Anderberg seemed deeply affected by the experience.

"How do you tell people who have worked for you for all of their life, people whose families you know, that they no longer have a job? Everyone knows that a skilled, qualified machinist earning sixteen to seventeen dollars an hour will not find another factory job in Rockford now," he said. The place his former workers were most likely to end up was behind a counter at the discount end of East State Street, working in Lowe's, Home Depot, Target, Sam's Club, Men's Wearhouse, or Wal-Mart itself for seven dollars an hour without a pension. "The government says that it is creating jobs for those people leaving the manufacturing sector. But I say what kind of jobs? No wonder real wages were falling across the economy," Anderberg said.

His view of free trade was that it was fine as long as it was fair. But competition with China was structurally and qualitatively unequal. The Chinese fixed the value of their currency against the U.S. dollar, keeping it undervalued so as to give their exports greater competitiveness. They provided little or no benefits for their workers, so their costs were artificially low. There were no independent unions in China, so the safety standards he had seen in Chinese factories would have been illegal in America. The state banking system provided cheap credit to state companies that could default without consequences. The central government gave generous value-added-tax rebates to exporters that were not available to U.S. companies. Restrictions on emissions in China were lax, so factories had to pay relatively little to keep the environment clean. Chinese companies routinely stole foreign intellectual property, but it was difficult to prosecute them because their courts were either corrupt or under government control. Finally, the state kept the price of various utilities, such as electricity and water, artificially low, thereby subsidizing industry.

In contrast with all these cost advantages, Anderberg said, U.S. companies struggled with a welter of bureaucratic red tape and legislation that, according to official calculations, increased the cost of doing business by more than 20 percent.[3] To Anderberg and many others who had turned up to hear Frink speak, the time had come for America to get tough in its defense of the small and midsize enterprises that form the backbone of the economy and provide around 70 percent of America's employment. The U.S. manufacturing sector, though declining, was still so large that, taken by itself, it would rank as the sixth- or seventh-largest economy in the world. In other words, the value created by U.S. manufacturing firms was now only slightly lower than that created by the entire Chinese economy. This, then, was Frink's constituency.

As the main course of the dinner arrived, Frink got up to speak. From the start, he was at pains to identify himself with his audience rather than with the bureaucrats he worked for. He began with a brief joke about how he had a full head of hair when he had taken up his Washington job a few months back. But that, as was clear under the stage lights, was no longer the case. "GTMY," he said. "GTMY . . . Well, that is government-speak for 'Great to meet you.' Because everything in government is an acronym."

He gave a brief self-introduction. He had been born south of the border in Mexico, had come to the United States at the age of four and a half, and was raised in California. He started a company from nothing, and by the time he sold it off, it had won a national award for industry and employed four hundred people. He explained that his position had been created in response to criticism from small and medium-size manufacturers toward the policies and efficiency of the U.S. Department of Commerce. He did not know why the government had not seen fit to appoint a lead advocate for manufacturing before. After all, agriculture had its own cabinet secretary even though it contributed only about 2 percent to GDP. Manufacturing made up 15 percent of GDP, and with multiplying factors added in, its influence spread to 30 or 40 percent of the economy. But now, at last, America had its manufacturing czar. "That is what the papers refer to me as. I am kind of beginning to like that term. I don't know why, but . . . you know, 'czar,' it does have a ring to it after a while," he said.

Anyway, manufacturing now had one of its own in the White House. Someone who could feel its pain. Someone who had "stared at the ceiling at night wondering how he was going to make that payroll." Someone who, as the owner of a carpet company, had made paychecks even in the welfare-obsessed "People's Republic of California." Not someone who would be seduced by all the protocol and paraphernalia of Washington, but a man who could look political power in the face and tell it like it is.

Until that point, he had the audience in the palm of his hand. There were deep nods, eruptions of laughter, and amused smiles. His "champion of the little guy" buildup had raised hopes for a piece of good news — a promise, a pledge, or a projection that everything was going to be OK. But none came. In fact, he seemed to switch sides. It turned out that he thought outsourcing, a prime cause of Rockford's malaise, was a good thing. "Eighty years ago, when companies were on the East Coast and they moved to California, that looked like outsourcing. Maybe a hundred years from now we will be in an intergalactic community where we are outsourcing to other planets," he said. "Who knows where it will lead. But we can't be protectionist."

He did acknowledge that Washington was too bureaucratic, and he promised to reduce legal and procedural red tape for businesses. But when it came to China, the audience began to get restless. China was merely a low-cost producer, he claimed. It had no brands. American companies could compete by leveraging the value of their brands, just as he had when he was running his California carpet company. He had managed to sell carpets to one of the most "significant buildings" in China on the strength of the fact that he had carpeted the White House. The Chinese had paid more for that carpet per square foot, he said, than they had for the land the building stood on.

The administration, he said, was working on getting the Chinese to move toward a more flexible exchange rate system. But he could not promise the big revaluation of the renminbi that American manufacturers had been demanding. Yes, he did recognize that intellectual property abuses in China were a problem, but the White House was doing what it could. It had appointed an excellent team of antipiracy specialists in the U.S. embassy in Beijing, and Frink himself had been to Beijing to reinforce the message. He could not tell if his visit had borne concrete results, but judging by the reaction of his Chinese interlocutors, they had appreciated his candid approach. "The Chinese told me, 'You speak with straight tongue, white man,'" he said.

This time the laughter was hesitant, muted. And as people filed out of the hall after the dinner was over, there was disappointed muttering and complaints. How could the so-called champion of U.S. manufacturing support the wave of outsourcing that had decimated small and midsize enterprises nationwide and thrown three million onto the job market? Congressman Manzullo helped me to understand. Missing from the Rockford dinner were representatives of the Fortune 500. America's big multinationals were the ones who benefited from outsourcing, and they were also the ones who controlled U.S. political attitudes toward the manufacturing sector. They financed the campaigns of most of the congressmen on Capitol Hill. If the multinationals said outsourcing was good for America, it was good for America, until such time as ordinary voters could convince congressmen otherwise at the ballot box. "We have lost a lot of market share to China, and a lot of guys here have gone out of business because of that," Manzullo said. "Nevertheless, Boeing has about a two-hundred-fifty-million-dollar presence in northern Illinois, and the largest purchaser of Boeing aircraft is China. You gotta fight this thing and yet you gotta do it correctly, because their economy has to be robust enough to buy the stuff that [companies such as Boeing] are manufacturing."

The problem was that Boeing, like most multinationals, had worked out that it could save a lot of money by sending some of its manufacturing functions to China and other low-cost countries. It needed to do this to maximize the returns of its shareholders. But in doing so, it threatened to put out of business many of its small, long-term suppliers, such as those at the Rockford dinner. The process was self-reinforcing. The more Boeing outsourced, the quicker the machine-tool companies that supplied it went bust, providing opportunities for Chinese competitors to buy the technology they needed, the better to supply companies like Boeing. Boeing makes money, but ultimately at the expense of the industries and jobs that sustain Middle America. In the opinion of

Eric Anderberg, capitalism had lapsed into cannibalism. "Lenin said that America would tear itself apart from the inside through greed," he said. "And you know what? He was right."

Throughout the 1980s, one of the urban myths about China involved the proverbial state-owned company with more money than sense that had bought a big, sophisticated piece of machinery from an American, Japanese, or European company. The prized machine was then put in a corner and never used. The reason for this varied. Sometimes, the story had it, the Chinese were unable to read or understand the instructions. Sometimes it was that the wrong machine had been bought, and sometimes it was merely that the machine was too advanced for China's backward state. Yet on the many occasions that I heard this story, two things were always constant: the glee on the face of the engineer or technician who told it, and the message that the Chinese somehow just did not "get" technology.

These days, that story is no longer heard. It has been replaced by a new conventional wisdom that states that although China has made giant strides since the 1980s, it is destined to remain nothing more than a mid-technology power. This belief is more sophisticated than the 1980s urban myth, and the arguments that support it are reasonable.

One argument has it that China's abundance of cheap labor reduces the pressure on companies to climb the technology ladder, because employing extra workers often costs less than buying new machinery. This, in theory at least, is valid. Another argument points to the large gap in spending on research and development that exists between China and its developed-nation competitors. This is also factually correct. Total spending on R & D in the United States amounts to 2.7 percent of gross domestic product, but less than 1 percent of China's much smaller GDP is spent in this way. In addition, U.S. spending on R & D is more effective than that in China, adding 22 percent to the value of the product under development compared with less than 5 percent in China.[4] A third rationale in support of the mid-technology argument is that the paucity of protection for intellectual property saps the innovative verve of scientists. This too seems to be borne out anecdotally and by the low number of patents per head of population. In the industrialized countries that form the membership of the Organization for Economic Cooperation and Development, there are on average 150 patents per capita. In China there are only 5.

The problem with these arguments is not that they lack merit but that they miss the point. The observable reality is that China is climbing the technology ladder at a rapid pace, and its ascent is neither localized nor specialized, but identifiable almost across the board. The difference between China's technological emergence and that of developed countries previously is that China is driven not so much by research as by commerce. Chinese companies, by and large, derive their technologies by buying them, copying them, or encouraging a foreign partner to transfer them as part of the price of access to a large potential market. In this context, it is globalization rather than R & D that is the main catalyst behind China's reemergence as a technology power.

The potent lure of the 1.3-billion-person market, no matter how illusory it may be, has helped China to leapfrog some of the technology barriers that had stymied several of the Southeast Asian "tiger" economies in the 1980s and 1990s. Malaysia, for instance, was unable to build its own car engines, meaning that its national car, the Proton, was never more than a composite of parts imported at considerable cost from Japan and other countries. Neither did Kuala Lumpur, in spite of strenuous efforts, manage to develop a viable industry to fabricate the wafers that go into computer chips. As countries, Malaysia, Thailand, Singapore, Indonesia, and the Philippines got stuck trying to clamber over landmark technological barriers, allowing Paul Krugman, the U.S. economist, to remark that the success of the "tigers" had been driven more by "perspiration than inspiration." China, by contrast, is experiencing little difficulty in transcending these problems and is already more advanced in almost every field of technological endeavor than its Southeast Asian counterparts, in spite of being much poorer on a per capita basis. Chinese companies, spurred

on by Beijing's policies, are not so much vaulting over the technological hurdles in their path as going around them. The technology of car engines provides a case in point.

The ability to make a high-performance car engine has long
been seen as one of the crown jewels of industrial attainment.
The state-owned companies that formed joint ventures with GM,
Volkswagen, Nissan, Toyota, and others have been applying pressure on their partners for years to transfer enough technology to
allow the Chinese side to build its own top-class auto engine. But
the foreign partners have refused to budge, knowing that when
they lose this technology, they lose not only the product of generations of in-house R & D but also their attractiveness to their Chinese joint-venture partner. But while these big Chinese companies
chafed, a smaller upstart, based in the inland province of Anhui,
was formulating a new approach.

Chery, which had encountered piracy allegations from Volkswagen and GM almost since its inception in 1997, decided it had
no time to develop its own engine. Equally, the profit margins on
selling cars were too thin to justify the purchase of expensive engines from foreign manufacturers. The only way, according to Yin
Tongyao, Chery's president, was to buy engine-building technological expertise. When I visited the company in 2002, Yin had
just been to Britain, where he talked to Lotus, the auto engineering firm, about a possible deal. In the end, however, Chery went
with AVL, an Austrian engineering specialist that it hired to transfer the technology of engine design and the know-how to build
one. In March 2005, Chery unveiled a new engine plant that cost
$370 million and will manufacture 150,000 engines a year to start
with. Within five years, it hopes the engines will reach the highest
European and American environmental standards and production will increase to 500,000 units a year.[5]

The dynamics that drove Chery's technological leap owed
little to R & D and much to economies of scale. The reason why
Chery, which currently sells cheap cars at a low margin, was able
to afford the expensive engine technology was that the banks
were willing to finance it. The reason why banks were willing

to finance it (aside from some government support) was that the number of people wealthy enough to buy a car in China was due to grow from roughly 60 million in 2005 to an estimated 160 million in 2010. In other words, China was set to be by far the fastest-growing auto market in the world. Having made its technological leap, Chery is starting to export to the United States. It has forged an alliance with Malcolm Bricklin, the New Yorker who brought the Subaru minicars from Japan to the United States in the 1960s and the ill-fated Yugo from Yugoslavia in the 1980s.

But Chery's ambitions are much larger than those of either of these predecessors. It wants to be the next Toyota, exporting one million cars by 2012, all of them priced at a 30 percent discount to their nearest competitor, Yin said.[6] With the savings that Chinese manufacturers derive from low labor costs, an integrated supply chain, and other benefits, Chery is aiming to do for cars what others have done for textiles, shoes, and consumer electronics — blow away the competition with prices that can hardly be believed. Already, as we have seen, the company sells a compact car, the QQ, for around $3,600 in China.

Another big hurdle in the industrial coming-of-age is in the area of semiconductors and computer chips. China has had the ability, through purchases of foreign machinery, to make chips for about two decades. In the early days, the technology of whatever was being made in China was at least ten years behind the industry leaders. But in recent years, the establishment of a company called Semiconductor Manufacturing International Corporation (SMIC), by Richard Chang in Shanghai, has brought China-made chips into closer contention with industry leaders.

As with car engines, this achievement has been procured not by research but by the pull of a burgeoning market. The story of SMIC, one of the most advanced wafer "fabs" in China, reveals how technology in the global economy cannot but follow the market, no matter how many obstacles governments try to put in the way. The story starts in Taiwan, the breakaway island off China's southeast coast that Beijing insists is part of its territory. By the year 2000, Taiwan had become a world leader, along with the

United States, in the semiconductor industry. By 2001 it was earning $15.6 billion selling semiconductors to customers all over the world. But with China booming across the Taiwan Strait, the government in Taipei was facing a considerable dilemma. If it let Taiwanese companies go to the mainland — with its thriving market, cheap building costs, and inexpensive engineers — it risked losing one of the island's top industries to its outsize neighbor. But refusing to let them go would mean that competitors, perhaps from Japan, the United States, or elsewhere, might steal a march on the big Taiwan semiconductor companies, imperiling their prospects in the longer term.[7]

In 2002 Yu Shyi-kun, the Taiwanese premier, announced a compromise: Taiwan chip companies could invest in the mainland, but only under strict conditions. The most important of these was that the wafers and chips manufactured could be no larger than 8 inches and no smaller than .25 microns, respectively — in other words, at least two generations behind the cutting edge of technology. Such rules, however, were like grass before the wind. Richard Chang, for instance, simply registered his company in the Cayman Islands so he could circumvent Taiwanese restrictions and build up SMIC. When the U.S. government, which also enforces strict rules on the export of high-technology items to China, blocked a purchase of chip-making equipment from Applied Materials, Chang merely looked elsewhere. He got hold of an advanced .18-micron process technology from Japan and Singapore and is currently trying to close the gap with Intel's cutting-edge .09-micron chips with the help of equipment bought from Europe.

Having cleared these hurdles, SMIC has a firm lead over its competitors in China and plans to build at least six more "fabs" in the country, some of which will make state-of-the-art 12-inch wafers. Within a few years, the gap between Chinese and American technology in semiconductors may have closed, the only difference being that in China it costs about 15 percent less to make them than in the United States, Chang said.[8]

In other industries, the government has made a strenuous policy out of awarding sales to those multinationals that transfer technology while cold-shouldering those that do not. This trade-off is not unprecedented; postwar Japan demanded the same concessions from U.S. companies, which then watched with deepening alarm as their Japanese students metamorphosed first into rivals and then into industry leaders. The size of the Chinese market, however, gives Beijing special leverage. The most prominent example so far of the pressures at work has been in the rivalry for power equipment contracts in a country that builds enough power stations in a single year to keep a midsize European nation's economy supplied with all of its electricity needs. Large companies such as General Electric, Alstom of France, Mitsubishi of Japan, Siemens of Germany, and other competitors are all in the race, providing Beijing's industrial planners with ample scope to play one bidder against another. The stakes are raised still higher for the foreign companies because their home markets are already mature, meaning that a successful bid in China can make the difference between a good or bad year worldwide.

An early goal of the transfer strategy was to wrest from foreign companies the know-how to build coal-fired generators, a natural target given the relative simplicity of the technology and China's overwhelming reliance on coal as a source of power. By 2004, less than a decade after Chinese companies developed the first "homegrown" 300-megawatt coal-fired generator, Alstom was cooperating with Harbin Power, one of the largest local electricity companies, to make a state-of-the-art 1,000-megawatt machine. Although that was a significant technological achievement, it paled beside Beijing's next ambition, to manufacture top-of-the-range gas-fired generators. Beijing let it be known that any foreign company hoping to win contracts in the gas-fired-turbine market had to get serious about transferring technology by forming joint ventures with state companies and handing over the advanced manufacturing specifications.

This presented the multinationals with an agonizing decision. The technology embedded in gas turbines is close to that of the engines that power commercial airliners. But for the sake of the market, GE decided to play ball. It would hand over some of the details of how to make its 9F gas turbine, one of a series of generators that had been created by its aircraft engine and power systems divisions in conjunction with the U.S. Department of Energy. The 9F alone had cost around half a billion dollars to develop. In the three months of negotiations with potential Chinese partners, GE's approach, as always, was to offer just enough technology to win the contract but not enough to allow the Chinese side to build a rival turbine immediately. The Chinese, for their part, wanted the drawings for the entire turbine: the modeling and mathematics behind the shape of the turbine's blades, how the blades were cooled while rotating, and the chemistry of the blades' makeup.[9] A spokesman for GE declined to comment on the details of the deal it had reached, but it did eventually win an order for thirteen of its 9F turbines, worth some $900 million. Nobody is under any illusions, however, that when the next big contract is up for grabs, the Chinese will be driving an even harder bargain.

In other industries, market penetration is linked in a less direct fashion to technology transfer, but the two are nevertheless connected. Most large technology companies have been prevailed upon to set up R & D centers in Beijing, Shanghai, or elsewhere as a precondition, either explicit or implicit, for the award of contracts from state companies. Motorola has poured more than $300 million into nineteen technology research centers in the country. A Microsoft facility in Beijing employs well over two hundred researchers. Siemens says it has spent more than $200 million since 1998 working with a Chinese scientific institute to develop a third-generation mobile phone standard, TD-SCDMA, to challenge two competing standards being promoted by European and U.S. companies. Such research centers are not merely efforts by multinationals to ingratiate themselves with Chinese authorities; they are also becoming useful and cost-effective parts of the global research effort. But for Beijing their main attraction is that they are educating Chinese scientists in some of the world's latest theories and technologies. And given the promiscuity of

ideas, it is beyond doubt that a degree of cross-pollination between the foreign laboratories and their Chinese counterparts will
occur.

Thus, for reasons that have little to do with indigenous research, China is leaping up the technology ladder. As every year
passes, the conventional wisdom that the country will languish
for years in the domain of mid-technology looks more and more
like wishful thinking. And although domestic R & D spending
is limited, some national science programs have been strikingly
successful. The most famous is the space program, following the
astronaut Yang Liwei's successful space orbit in 2004. In the construction of powerful supercomputers to help in complicated scientific research, progress has also been impressive. A decade ago,
China did not have a single supercomputer ranked among the top
five hundred in the world. But by the end of 2003 it had nine, and
its fastest, DeepComp 6800, built by Lenovo, was ranked four-
teenth. Its biotechnology is also world class in some areas. Its scientists are developing a safe "pebble bed" technology for nuclear
power stations and a "clean coal" system that may allow China to
derive energy with vastly reduced carbon emissions. It is, in fact,
difficult to think of an area of technology in which China does not
have credible ambitions to lead the world.

It is said that when Zhou Enlai, Chairman Mao's urbane premier,
who was educated in France, was asked his opinion of whether
the French Revolution had been a success, he answered without
irony that it was too early to tell. Like many sayings attributed
to Chinese leaders, that one may be apocryphal. But its longev-
ity springs from the validity of the insight that it offers: fortune
in China has often waxed and waned according to cycles that are
measured in centuries. One way to identify these cycles was in
charting the accumulation and dissipation of dynastic energy, or
the time it took for heaven to withdraw its imperial mandate. Another way to order the long passage of Chinese history is through
the integrity of trends and ideas. And it is in this regard that 2005
was a very rare year indeed. Although it did not make any of the

world's newspapers or Web sites, it was in 2005 that an idea that has done more than anything else to condition China's fate in the past two hundred years finally came full circle.

To understand this cycle, it is necessary to return to its beginning: the arrival of Lord George Macartney, envoy of King George III, at the court of the Qing dynasty emperor Qianlong in 1793. Macartney was a veteran diplomat who had served British interests in the court of Catherine the Great in Russia, as governor of Grenada in the Caribbean, and as an administrator in Madras, India. He had gone to China with unusual luggage: telescopes, a planetarium, celestial and terrestrial globes, a great lens, barometers, clocks, air guns, fine swords, Derbyshire vases, porcelain figures, and a carriage were just some of the items that made it intact to Beijing after a long voyage over sea and land. His aim was to use these items to impress the court of Qianlong and secure the undertaking of the emperor to open the vast Chinese market to trade. Macartney had also brought with him George Staunton, a twelve-year-old pageboy, who had spent the journey learning the Chinese language with a tutor so that he could make a short speech to the emperor in his own tongue.

Qianlong, who was in his eighties, was impressed with Staunton and plucked an embroidered pouch from his own belt to give him in recognition of his linguistic efforts. But there was no such warmth toward Macartney, who first refused to kowtow in the customary way and then proceeded to make a tiresome list of demands. The emperor instructed his mandarins to send Macartney back to England with a note to inform King George that China had not the "slightest need of your country's manufactures."

That much of the story is commonly cited, but it is less well known what Macartney confided in his diary on a melancholy voyage home. It was "futile," he wrote, for the Chinese to resist British goals of opening up China for trade because that was tantamount to trying to "arrest the progress of human knowledge."

Futile or not, Qianlong and subsequent emperors resisted the trading ambitions of the British and other European powers in almost every way they could. For nearly the next two centuries, the interplay of foreign covetousness and Chinese reluctance was the ordering force behind events. At times this conflict of desires escalated into warfare, and at others it subsided into brooding inaction. The British, having failed to open the door through diplomacy, resorted to the evil gambit of selling opium to an increasingly addicted population.

In 1790, four thousand chests of opium entered China, but by the 1830s there was almost ten times that amount. When the Chinese emperor of the day banned the drug, the British sent a fleet from India to pound the Chinese into submission in the first Opium War. A second Opium War followed a couple of decades later, when Beijing again tried to limit the inflow of narcotics. These periods of partial openness followed by phases of atavistic reclusion set the tone of relations with the outside world until the 1949 Communist revolution, when foreign missionaries were thrown out, treaty ports were closed, and trade with capitalist countries was limited. But Westerners never lost their lust for the China market.

Almost always, then, from the time that Qianlong met Macartney, the West had been clamoring at a door that was sometimes kept ajar but never unreservedly open. In the first few years of the twenty-first century, however, the lingering reservations toward free trade began to fall away. When China joined the World Trade Organization in late 2001, it was for the first time in its history agreeing voluntarily to open its markets according to a set of rules and principles set down by an extraterritorial body. Then, at the first full ministerial meeting of the WTO China attended, it showed free-trade credentials that were in no way inferior to those of the industrialized West. And the pendulum of centuries started to swing. As China's prowess in manufacturing showed itself ever more clearly, so the countries of the developed world found an ever greater number of ways to keep Chinese goods out of their domestic markets. Antidumping clauses were invoked, import-surge safeguards dusted off, and political reasons cited.

By the time of the textile trade dispute, which simultaneously brought the European Union and the United States to loggerheads with Beijing in 2005, it had become clear that when it came to manufactured products, China was for the first time since Macartney's trade mission more open to the world than the world was toward China. Bo Xilai, the Chinese minister of commerce, caught the irony of this tectonic shift in an interview with the BBC in Beijing:[10]

> I think the doctrine of free trade is an outstanding one. The free-trade doctrine has propelled the economies of Europe and the U.S. to a soaring path of development over the past two hundred years. It has also been a doctrine that Europe and America have propagated as a glorious doctrine. They have brandished the banner of free trade and gone around the world doing commerce and making money and becoming developed countries. But now that a developing country that is quite poor and has a GDP per capita of only one-thirtieth of theirs has found a few textile companies that can finally compete with European counterparts, they want to close their doors and engage in protectionism. This, in fact, is a double standard. When they had a comparative advantage, they encouraged the whole world to open its doors, but when they discover that one developing country is becoming more competitive, they say, "OK, enough. Let's close the door now."

One day, as the textile spat raged on, I was writing at home when my phone rang. It was Jane Macartney, a friend who works as the London *Times*'s bureau chief in Beijing and who also happens to be a direct descendant of Lord George Macartney. We chatted for a while about this and that, and then our conversation turned to textiles. Her view was adamant. It was pointless for Europe or the United States to resist Chinese exports if China had the comparative advantage. What was Europe doing still making textiles anyway? she asked.

That view is surely valid from a theoretical perspective, but if past is prologue, theory may prove inadequate in foreshadowing actual events. Qianlong and other Chinese leaders spent roughly two centuries testing the futility of their country's resistance to free trade, and the reason they did so was simple: they knew they could not compete. The superiority of Europe and, later, America in the production of "manufactures" was unassailable. Now, though, the shoe is on the other foot. It is increasingly clear to companies, industries, and governments in the developed world that in manufacturing they cannot match China's might. The big question for the future, therefore, is whether the world's door will remain open.

That question may take years or decades to be answered. Nobody can tell what the final outcome will be, but one thing seems certain. The competitive strain that is visible in the artisan communities of Italy and in the industrial heartlands of America, Germany, and France is spreading. Yet China's impact on these developed world economies is uneven. Not everyone is being adversely affected. Broadly, the powerful, the international, and the wealthy are reaping huge benefits, while those in the middle are suffering in either relative or absolute terms. Middle-class people in medium-size enterprises in industrial heartlands comprise the group most likely to be laid off, downsized, or offered wages that do not keep pace with inflation. In Germany it is the *Mittelstand*, the midsize firms forming the backbone of the industrial base, that is being decimated. In the United States, the Midwest — including such states as Ohio and Illinois — is hardest hit. In France, Italy, Spain, and, to a lesser extent, the United Kingdom (which lost much of its industry in the 1970s and 1980s) it is also companies occupying the center of the spectrum that are — on average — finding life increasingly tough.

This dichotomy of influence springs from globalization's great failing: although goods, services, and capital are mobile across borders, jobs are much less so. Even if workers wanted to move themselves and their families to different countries to work in unfamiliar conditions, the restrictions on such movement are legion. This means that by and large, people cannot move to the companies that need them, so the companies must move to the workers. But pulling up stakes and shifting to a place like China, with its welter of regulations and customs, represents a cost and a risk that most medium-size and family-run businesses are unable or unwilling to absorb. The result is that the beneficiaries of the cheap, diligent, and often skilled labor available in China are overwhelmingly the multinationals. And the benefits they have reaped have been handsome. According to a recent study, about 25 percent of the profits that American multinationals make these days derives from their foreign subsidiaries. Or, to put it another way, 25 percent of the market value of these companies—a whopping $2.7 trillion—is built on profits earned by overseas arms. But ultimately these profits come at the expense of the industries and jobs that sustain Middle America.[11]

On an individual level too, the impact of this type of outsourcing also seems to be hitting employees of the middle and lower echelons of a company disproportionately hard. The managers who make the decisions to outsource their production processes or send them offshore rarely move overseas themselves; they continue to direct operations from the head office. Those who lose their jobs are more likely to be on the factory floor or in engineering or in the lower levels of management. But while it is staff from the middle and lower ranks of a company who will find themselves on the job market—almost always looking for a lower-paid position—the managers who orchestrate the outsourcing often benefit twice over from the initiative they have taken. If their bonuses are linked to profit performance, as they almost always are, then they benefit directly from the cost savings they achieve. They are also likely to see the value of their shareholdings and stock options rise as the company's financial performance improves.

Obviously, life looks very different for those whose jobs were outsourced. As in Rockford and other declining manufacturing areas, people who lose $20-an-hour jobs in high-end manufacturing companies are unlikely to find similar employment. They often end up taking a part-time position in the service sector that pays less than half their former salary. The impact of this, writ large, is that the American middle class is shrinking. The wealthy segment of society is growing, as is the impoverished segment, but the middle-income bracket is starting to hollow out. According to the U.S. Census Bureau, the number of employed Americans who earned between $25,000 and $75,000 fell in 2003, and the number of people earning both more and less than that increased. The number living below the official poverty line climbed by 1.3 million in 2003, to 35.9 million Americans. Overall, real wages — that is, wages minus inflation — have been either stagnant or falling across the U.S. economy, while in some areas of manufacturing the decline has been striking.

So far, the trend to outsource has been concerned mainly with manufacturing industries, but over time the number of service jobs moving to China and India could eclipse those that have moved from manufacturing. The McKinsey Global Institute, in a worldwide study of outsourcing, has calculated that 9.6 million U.S. service jobs could theoretically be sent offshore today.[12] If that was actually to happen, the U.S. unemployment rate would rise to 11.4 percent, from 5 percent in mid-2005. A similar potential exists in the large European economies.

These trends, taken together, foreshadow a political crisis. Although many multinationals are benefiting from trade and investment with China, those companies represent only a narrow, albeit politically powerful, cross-section of opinion in the United States and Europe. They are no match, ultimately, for the middle-class voters who determine the future of Western democracies at the ballot box. If these voters turn against free trade with China in large numbers, there may be little that politicians can do to prevent the West's door to the Middle Kingdom from creaking shut. Of course, such a course would be inimical to the interests of free trade and, quite possibly, inimical to the interests of the middle-class voters themselves. But as Qianlong showed at the end of the eighteenth century, national leaders can and have acted against the economic interests of their people. It may well happen again.

Notwithstanding that scenario, not everything for the United States and Europe is gloom and doom. This is because, in spite of its impressive performance over the past two and a half decades, the graphs that track China's trajectory do not all point upward.

In fact, the country is riven with weaknesses that, to a significant degree but not entirely, are the byproducts of its success, or the alter ego of its competitiveness. China may be a burgeoning economic force, but it cannot rewrite the rules of comparative advantage. What the theory of David Ricardo, the eighteenth-century economist, described is that no country can enjoy a competitive edge over everywhere else in everything that it does and makes.

That insight is fundamental to China's situation today because much of the country's prowess in manufacturing has been caused by a strenuous, state-sponsored skewing of domestic economic inputs. The aim of this orchestration of advantage has been to resolve China's most fundamental problem: the creation of jobs. The government has set out deliberately to ensure that its manufacturing sector will be a world-beater. So it keeps the cost of electricity artificially low, prices water at a fraction of its real value, puts a cap on the price of some categories of coal, subsidizes oil to make it cheaper to industry and transport, ensures that workers cannot form independent unions so they have little power to bargain wages upward, barely implements its own environmental laws so as not to hobble industry with extra costs, promotes savings so its banks are always flush with capital to lend, and provides generous tax rebates to any company that exports its goods.

All this has helped create a manufacturing sector that is undoubtedly earthshaking, but at what price? That, broadly, is the subject of the final four chapters of this book. The sacrifices made in the service of manufacturing have created shortcomings, frailties, and deficits that have to be compensated for somehow. And already, in the quest to make up for its deficiencies, China has started to affect the world in a way that is no less profound than the impact caused by its strengths. In many cases these deficiencies are the source of an appetite, not for jobs, capital, technology, and trade surpluses, but for energy, resources, education, and respect, which the Chinese are obliged to buy from other parts of the planet.

6

Not Enough to Go Around: Natural Resources and Environmental Catastrophe

THE ANYUAN COAL MINE is known throughout China because it was one of the places in which Mao Zedong cut his revolutionary teeth. When he worked there in the 1920s, fomenting disaffection among workers toward their German bosses, the mine was one of the main sources of fuel for the Yangtze River basin and an early industrial base in the poor interior province of Jiangxi. By the time I got there, though, most of the coal reserves, along with the ideological poignancy of the revolution, had been exhausted.

The place had a desiccated feel to it, as if it had been plundered and left with little but memories. A cavernous museum devoted to Mao and the glory of the revolution stood on top of a hill, but the city of Pingxiang, which stretched out beneath it, was anything but resplendent. Its streets were dirty, thronging with unemployed miners, and full of brothels masquerading as hairdressing salons. But that was not the worst of it. Whole neighborhoods had begun to sink into the disused pits and mineshafts that had provided the town with its livelihood for a century. In some areas, the thin slivers of land that had concealed gaping subterranean holes had suddenly given way, causing the buildings they had supported to tumble into them. In other areas, schools, hospitals, and houses were slowly and unevenly subsiding into the earth like ships listing at anchor.

★

I climbed up the muddy hill where the coal mine's first shaft had been sunk, passing through an old arched gateway as I went. On each gatepost, large red characters urged, "Carry forward the revolutionary tradition. Strive for greater glory." At the top of the hill I met an old woman selling "white rabbit" sweets from the front window of her home. While we talked, three or four children came running up the mud path, each clutching enough money to buy a single white rabbit wrapped in rice paper. The woman reached into a plastic jar, took out the sweets one at a time, and handed them to each child with a smile and a few kind words. From where I stood by her jar of white rabbits, I could see the hall where Mao and his comrades had organized unions and worker revolts. In the other direction, on top of another muddy hill, the engines that winched miners up and down the mineshafts were silhouetted against the horizon. One of those shafts, the old woman said, ran right underneath her house, and it had claimed more from her family than the miners had ever taken out of it.

Her eldest son was the first to be swallowed by the hill on which she lived. In 1990, at the age of twenty-seven, he was trapped in the shaft beneath her home after some equipment malfunctioned. He died below ground. A few years later, her husband succumbed to lung cancer brought on by breathing coal dust without respiratory filters. Photographs of her son and husband, both in black and white, hung above an alcove that abutted the house's only room. The alcove seemed to have taken on the roles of shrine and living room simultaneously. It had a clean white tile floor, which contrasted with the muddy concrete of the rest of the house, and a big television in the corner with an embroidered cloth hung over its screen.

The old woman pointed to the alcove and the TV. They had been paid for by her late husband, bought with the compensation award from their first son's death, and they represented something tangible that had emerged from the transience of two lives. But the sense of solidity the old woman saw in them was itself only relative. Long, jagged cracks an inch or two wide had opened in the house's main wall. The place where the woman stood as she sold sweets was sinking perceptibly into the hillside. The wooden front door, on which the character for "prosperity" was stuck, hung in a doorframe that had once been rectangular and upright but was now slipping into the shape of a parallelogram. "The hill beneath these walls is completely hollow. It has all been mined away," she said. "All the houses on top of it will probably end up in the mineshaft one day. But it is OK for now. There is nothing to worry about until the cracks get to about six inches wide."

The era of communism in China, as in the former Soviet Union, has not been kind to the environment. A combination of neglect, overpopulation, careless industrialization, and the inability of a planned economy — in which prices are fixed by state fiat — to put an accurate value on nature's gifts has contributed to a dire environmental crisis. Everywhere there are signs of distress. The deserts of the north are marching toward the towns and cities on their fringe. Waterways that just ten years ago were gushing torrents have slowed to a trickle or disappeared altogether. Food is often contaminated with illegal and alarming levels of animal hormones and agricultural chemicals. New diseases such as severe acute respiratory syndrome (SARS) and avian influenza appear with regularity. Air pollution is so bad that as many as 380,000 people may die prematurely each year by 2010 because of respiratory ailments.[1] Animal and bird species face extinction or loss of habitat as wetlands and forests vanish. Several towns and cities like Pingxiang are sinking into underground holes that have been burrowed by miners or emptied of the groundwater they used to hold.

These problems, or their antecedents, have been around for decades. It is no revelation to assert that the edifice of Chinese statehood rests on frail ecological foundations. But what is new — and world-shaking — is the projection of this environmental exhaustion into the international arena. Extraordinary as it now seems, the famine that followed Mao's Great Leap Forward in the early 1960s took place for the most part without the outside world's knowledge. More than thirty million people died of starvation while China watchers debated whether hunger was, in fact, widespread at all. Now, though, the appetites unleashed by the rise of the world's most populous nation are felt even in the most remote corners of the earth. The forests of Indonesia and Papua New Guinea, the fish of the Pacific Ocean, the iron ore extracted from mines in Australia and Brazil, the soybeans grown in Latin America and the United States, the fresh water that flows into the Mekong River, the oil underground in the Middle East, the gas from Russian Siberia, the cashmere from goats on the Mongolian steppe, and hundreds of other resources and commodities are subject to voracious demand from a burgeoning China.

It may seem obvious that the rise of a great nation will result in great appetites and that those appetites will, in their turn, drive up the international prices of the commodities in demand. But history also provides alternative precedents. The prices of grain and meat in the United States actually fell during the last three decades of the nineteenth century, when waves of immigrants arrived, because the clearing of more and more land for agriculture increased the supply of food. China, however, is not blessed with excess farmland. Around half of its land mass is uninhabited, so one-fifth of humanity is crowded onto just 7 percent of the world's cultivatable land. Not only do domestic producers find it difficult to keep up with the surge in domestic demand, but the ongoing degradation of the environment and the exploitation of natural resources also means that the ability of producers to respond to demand signals is actually regressing with time.

China's growing appetite, along with that of India, is helping to create profound shifts in the global terms of trade. Prices of commodities began to pull out of a twenty-year slump in late 2001, which, not entirely by coincidence, was also exactly the time that China joined the World Trade Organization, cementing the links of 1.3 billion people to the world economy. It was difficult in the year 2000 — the bottom of the twenty-year cycle for most commodities — to imagine the boom in oil, base metal, and many agricultural commodity prices that has since occurred. In the same way, in 1969 and 1970, on the eve of a roughly ten-year commodity boom, it was hard to believe that crude oil prices would rise much from their prevailing level of around $1.70 a barrel. Now, though, the global surge in prices of almost everything humans need to run their factories, feed themselves, and build homes is easier to understand. Hundreds of millions of Chinese have begun to seek a new life, and many of the things they demand — fuel, metals, food, materials, and a certain quality of life — are simply not available in sufficient quantities within the boundaries of their environmentally exhausted nation.

Indeed, China's endowments are deeply lopsided. The profound damage done to its physical environment contrasts with the prodigious strength of its human capital. The disequilibrium that results from this mismatch explains, in a nutshell, both the intensity and the polarity of the influence China exerts on the world. At one extreme, the world has never had to deal with such a large, cheap, and versatile workforce joining the global economy in such a short period of time. At the other, never before has so large a country emerged so quickly from so eviscerated a natural base. These starkly different characteristics explain why China can drive down the average level of working wages and the prices of manufactured products worldwide, while propelling the prices of most sources of energy and commodities through the roof. The cleavage between these areas of influence falls neatly between the things China makes and the things it needs.

At the top of the list of needs is oil. The United States in the twentieth century was able to fuel its development with oil drawn from deposits in Alaska, the Gulf Coast states, Oklahoma, offshore Louisiana, California, and Illinois. But China's geology is less fecund. China made a few large discoveries in the 1960s and 1970s, but in the past two decades its production has fallen far behind domestic demand. Twenty years ago, it was the largest oil exporter in East Asia. Now it is the second-largest oil importer in the world. In 2004 it accounted for 31 percent of the global growth in oil demand, suggesting that the rise in the price of oil to above $60 a barrel in mid-2005 was to a significant degree due to the influence of Chinese demand.[2] China's appetite is growing at a pace that makes a mockery even of expert predictions: in 2005 it consumed almost as much oil as the U.S. Energy Information Administration thought it would need a full five years later. And, as always, from a per capita perspective, the potential was mind-boggling. In 2001 Americans were using more than eleven times more oil per person than the Chinese. Indeed, if the Chinese were ever to consume at the American levels of 2001, they would need to guzzle three times the world's total consumption.

The main catalyst behind China's appetite is the mismatch in the size of its population and its resource base. But that is not the only cause; another is the decades of wasteful exploitation and disrespect for the environment that characterized the Communist era. Mao, who was frank in his hostility toward nature, set the tone for subsequent leaders. In 1940, at the inaugural meeting of the Natural Science Research Society, he articulated his vision. "For the purpose of attaining freedom in the world of nature," Mao said then, "man must use natural science to understand, conquer and change nature and thus attain freedom from nature."[3] Those comments had in them the seeds of the disasters and damage that followed: the 1960s famine, desertification, pollution, erosion, water shortages, and disease. They also acted as a basic mantra for the heroes of the age — men such as Wang Jinxi, the "Iron Man" who discovered oil in Daqing, the country's largest oil field, in the far northeast near Russia.[4]

Iron Man Wang, who died in 1970 but is regarded as an icon of socialist reconstruction to this day, came to Daqing from a small oil rig in the northwestern province of Gansu, a place where, as he put it, "no grass grew and when the wind blew, the pebbles rolled." He had been a child laborer before the revolution and had only a rudimentary education. But he possessed an uncanny facility for saying and doing the right thing at the right time. When he went to Beijing as a "model worker" and had a brief meeting with Mao, he capitalized on the moment by staying up all night to write a panegyric to the Great Helmsman. When he saw that Beijing buses ran on coal gas stored in large, unsightly bladders on their roofs, he announced that this was a national humiliation that could be rectified only by the discovery of more oil. A year later, when his soon-to-be-famous number 1205 drilling team did strike oil in Daqing, he was ready with just the right turn of phrase. China, he said, was about to "take off its oil-poor hat and cast it into the Pacific Ocean" — the inference being that America would have to learn some respect for a new China powered by the vast oil field of Daqing.

Yet these rhetorical triumphs were mere preparations for the Iron Man's defining moment. A few years after finding the first oil, his team was drilling at another rig in the big-sky wilderness next to Siberia, at well number 2589. They had been there for weeks, with no result. Wang's shin had been half crushed in an accident with a piece of machinery, but he refused more than a brief visit to the hospital. Within days he was back at the derrick, barking orders as he hobbled around on crutches. Then, suddenly and unexpectedly, the rig struck oil at a depth of 2,300 feet, sending a gusher 30 feet into the air. The workers rushed to cap the spouting crude by dumping tons of cement mix on top of it. But the pump that was used to mix the cement with sand in a slurry pit near the derrick failed to function. Unless something was done, the oil would all go to waste.

Iron Man leapt into action. He tossed away his crutches, jumped into the slurry pit, and began twisting his body to and fro, using his torso as a surrogate cement mixer. Other workers followed his example, and as they stood there gyrating back and forth, one of the most famous photographs of Mao's era was taken. It was published in newspapers and hung in public places as the whole country was exhorted to learn from the spirit of the Iron Man. The black-and-white photo hangs on the wall in the Iron Man Wang Museum in Daqing. It shows Wang with his posture twisted, the slurry splashing above his waist and his face creased into an exhilarated roar.

If these events seem a little too perfect really to have happened, that is a feature they share with the broad body of China's propaganda mythology. Some might wonder, for instance, how a news photographer happened to be waiting near a lonely drilling rig in the wilderness just at the moment it unexpectedly struck oil. Nevertheless, the story of the Iron Man and the slurry pit has stuck in the national consciousness. An attendant at the Iron Man Museum told me I was a "backward element" after I questioned whether it was possible to mix tons of cement just by twisting your torso. Such skepticism is a minority view. Even the premier, Wen Jiabao, is a fan of the Wang Jinxi legend; he noted a couple of years ago that if you placed all the wells Wang's team had sunk on top of each other, they would reach to the peak of Mount Everest.

What has attracted quiet scrutiny, however, has been the effectiveness of the oil extraction techniques used during the first thirty years of the oil field's life. Statistics on the recovery rates of oil from underground deposits are, like much else about Daqing, still a state secret. But geologists and experts told me that in the first two decades of drilling, as much as 90 percent of the oil was wasted—either left unrecovered underground or spent in gushers that colored the pastures around the wells black. This was partly the result of old, inadequate machinery and drilling techniques and partly because the focus of the teams that followed the Iron Man's shining example was to find as much oil as quickly as possible so as to win propaganda plaudits. Little attention was paid to the technical task of ensuring that deposits were not wasted. Indeed, the use of technology itself was antithetical to the Iron Man spirit, that human will could overcome anything nature could throw at it.

Nobody is yet ready to admit that China's current dependence on imports of foreign oil is due, at least in part, to the wasteful exploitation of an oil field that was in its day a symbol of self-reliance. But Daqing today is a study in how things have changed. The "nodding donkey" rigs that stand by bus stops and in hotel forecourts still rock rhythmically up and down, and the cloying smell of crude still pervades the atmosphere. But production is falling year after year, and the city's mayor speaks at length about the need to diversify into new industries. The most famous resident there these days is another man named Wang, Wang Qiming, an intense, slightly built geologist who talks nonstop in acronyms, jargon, and scientific terms. His job is to find ways of squeezing more oil out of the aging and increasingly complex field. For this he has earned the nickname "Iron Man of a New Era."

We met in a hall belonging to PetroChina, the state oil giant that owns and runs Daqing, and sat in two chairs at the end of the room, looking at each other over a small table furnished with teacups on paper mats. A line of officials and oil company executives sat behind Wang on his side of the room, in the manner usually adopted for formal meetings. But Wang's enthusiasm for his subject meant that any formality was short-lived. Within a few minutes he was on all fours on the soft pile carpet, poring over large, detailed geological maps, pointing out the fissures and strata in cross-sections of rock, which to the trained eye were telltale signs that a river had changed its course at some point in the Jurassic period. He also spent time explaining the method he had pioneered to bring abandoned oil deposits to the surface by first pumping groundwater down their disused well shafts to flood the underground caverns that used to contain oil. When the pressure had built up sufficiently, pumping could resume, he said, and the mixture of oil and water that came to the surface could be turned back into pure crude in a treatment plant.

It all seemed rather convoluted, and as I listened to the flow of his explanations, I began to wonder what Wang felt about the contribution of the man whose nickname he had partially appropriated. The answer was singularly lacking in the type of praise that is customary for a national Communist icon. "Our work is not the same. He was the leader of a well-drilling team. I am responsible for the development of the oil field. I graduated from a university and he came over from Gansu," he said. "He basically relied on brute strength, whereas we rose up through bitter struggle using our brains. In those days we did not have any experience of oil extraction." This roused my curiosity, so I asked another question. But I got my nicknames in a jumble and ended up calling him the "Second-Generation Iron Man." Suddenly the effervescent explanations stopped and he gazed at me steadily over his glasses. "The name is New Era Iron Man," he said. "But if you can't manage that, just call me New Era."

I wondered whether his disinclination to share an identity with the Iron Man of an earlier generation derived from vanity or from the fact that his whole career had been dedicated to cleaning up the mess that Wang Jinxi and his pioneering comrades had caused.

China knows from experience the way in which a lack of available resources can hold back the development of the nation. One of the main reasons why the country fell so far behind Europe in the nineteenth century was that a surging demand for wood from a fast-growing Chinese population pushed prices to levels that inhibited economic activity. The cost of building a seagoing ship in 1820, for example, was seven times that in 1550, so trading vessels were increasingly constructed in Southeast Asian shipyards, where wood was plentiful. The seven-thousand-ton vessel that Zheng He, the famous mariner of the Ming dynasty, used to explore much of the known world would have been prohibitively expensive for most of the three hundred years before the current era — a fact that may help explain why China turned in on itself.

Voracious deforestation continued throughout the nineteenth century, and in some places the wood shortage was so acute that families burned little but dung, roots, and the husks of crops for fuel.[5] In Henan, Shandong, and other provinces where population densities were among the heaviest, forest cover dwindled to between 2 and 6 percent of the total land area, or to between one-twelfth and one-quarter of the prevailing levels in European countries such as France at that time. With fuel so expensive and so scarce during the eighteenth and nineteenth centuries, the chances that an industrial revolution could have taken place in China, as it did in Great Britain, were remote. From 1800 to the 1930s, the population increased by between 150 million and 225 million people, and the general level of forest cover on the central plains was so thin that even trees in protected areas could not be saved from illegal felling by people desperate for firewood.

These precedents have bred a visceral aversion in Beijing to the notion that it might run out of the things it needs to progress. And history is not the only guide. Since Deng Xiaoping's ascent to power in the late 1970s, the Communist Party has defined its legitimacy in terms of delivering economic growth and using its economic power as a lever to attain greater international prominence. It cannot achieve either of these things without oil, but fortunately it can import enough to make up the shortfall. However, this dependence on a foreign commodity for 40 percent of its needs has put Beijing in an acutely uncomfortable position. Its growth and legitimacy depend squarely on the supply of a fuel source controlled in the main by regimes that are unstable, unfriendly, or in the sphere of influence of its strategic competitor, the United States. Driven by this discomfort, Beijing and its large state oil companies have tried with increasing urgency since the country became a net importer of oil in 1992 to shore up supply lines and reduce their vulnerability in virtually any way possible.

The three large state oil companies had invested in nearly thirty overseas oil and gas development projects and had committed more than $5 billion by the end of 2002. But the short history of these deals has been checkered. Obviously in a hurry and clearly in need, the Chinese side almost always paid a significant premium above the market price for the reserves it was able to buy. In some cases, the deals that were arranged politically fell apart later, and in others, foreign oil companies maneuvered deftly to block the overtures of their Chinese competitors.[6] Nevertheless, the China National Petroleum Corporation, the largest state oil company, has managed to purchase assets in Sudan, Iraq, and Kazakhstan. Other companies, such as China National Offshore Oil Corporation (CNOOC), have secured long-term supply contracts from places like Australia. But all told, the volume of oil imports that are either owned or under long-term supply contracts amounts to a small proportion of the country's total requirements. If Beijing was to enjoy anything approaching real security of supply, it needed to do deals of a different magnitude, something that would make its companies real players. But as it tried to do these deals in the outside world, it bumped up against barriers that, though invisible, were nevertheless more stubborn than the most complicated subterranean geology.

One case in point was the attempted acquisition by CNOOC of a large U.S. counterpart, Unocal. It was clear from the beginning that this bid was going to be about a lot more than oil and dollars. The nickname it went by in CNOOC and its team of advisers from Goldman Sachs and J. P. Morgan suggested something of a grand design. They called it Operation Treasure Ship, after the vessel that Zheng He used to "sail the western oceans," and in which, according to the British historian Gavin Menzies, he may well have discovered America long before Columbus.[7] Zheng He was a tall, dashing man who distinguished himself at court through his ability, and the advisory team's use of the treasure ship allusion signified a journey of discovery, a voyage into alien waters with an uncertain outcome. The Unocal bid would be potentially perilous but ultimately rewarding — certainly for the bankers, who stood to earn some $300 million in advisory fees.

The man leading CNOOC's bid, Fu Chengyu, the company's CEO, was as close to a corporate Zheng He as can be imagined. Tall and square-jawed, the fifty-four-year-old had also risen through his ability. Unable to finish his university studies because of the chaos of the Cultural Revolution, he was assigned at the age of twenty to Daqing, in 1972, a time when the oil field was still in thrall to the legend of the Iron Man, who had died only two years earlier. From those nationalistic beginnings, Fu's career took a more cosmopolitan turn. In the early 1980s he was one of the few young people selected by the government to study abroad, and he earned a master's degree at the University of Southern California. Following his return to China, he became a rising star in a strategic industry that was one of the first to open to foreign investment. CNOOC in those days had a monopoly on offshore exploration and so was the only joint-venture partner available for the big foreign oil companies, which poured hundreds of millions of dollars into the dream of striking it rich in the seas off China's south and east coasts. Fu, therefore, had developed his expertise working alongside or for the world's oil majors.

By the time he launched the bid for Unocal, he ranked as one of China's most credible corporate ambassadors. Urbane and sophisticated, he could claim to understand the ways of the West better than virtually any other head of a Chinese state enterprise. If anyone was going to lead China to "go out," as the former president Jiang Zemin was fond of describing outward investment, it was Fu Chengyu. But it was clear from the image that his public relations advisers had started to create for him that Fu also had his qualms. He knew his plan was audacious; it was the largest attempted overseas acquisition by a Chinese company. It was also an attempt to buy a strategic asset at a time when America's national security guard was heightened by the war in Iraq. So in his first few interviews, Fu was at pains to stress his cosmopolitan credentials. He emphasized his background in California and his experience with Western oil firms and even his unusually Western adoration for coffee. "People in China think I am strange because I do not drink tea," he told one interviewer.[8]

But this amounted to little more than a manicure. The problem that Operation Treasure Ship faced was nothing less than a gale-force clash of political economies. First of all, insistent questions were asked about how closely connected CNOOC was to the Communist Party. After all, as commentators pointed out, Fu — in common with all the bosses of large, strategic Chinese state companies — was first and foremost a civil servant. He had been appointed by the Party's personnel department, and if there was any doubt about where his true loyalties lay, then one had only to think of his predecessor, Wei Liucheng. Wei had been running the company one day, and then the next was appointed to the senior post of governor on the southern island of Hainan. Also revealing was that Fu, in addition to his job as head of CNOOC, the listed company, was head of the wholly government-owned state parent, which held 70.6 percent of the listed company's shares. Such an ownership structure put it beyond doubt that CNOOC would,

if push came to shove, place the interests of the Party above anything else.

Indeed, telltale signs of a dual agenda had already surfaced in
the way the bid was conceived. Fu had first met with Charles Wil-
liamson, the CEO of Unocal, on the day after Christmas in 2004
and began canvassing support for a bid among the upper echelons of the Communist Party in February 2005. Having secured
the go-ahead from the government, CNOOC appointed Goldman
Sachs and J. P. Morgan as advisers on the deal and on March 7,
2005, submitted a first bid that valued Unocal at between $16 bil-
lion and $18 billion. All that was fine, but the problem was that
CNOOC's board had not been formally notified of any of these
plans until after the company's financial results were released on
March 30.[9]

The response was predictable. The board's four nonexecutive
directors—a former Shell senior executive, a former Swiss ambassador to China, a Goldman Sachs banker, and an Australian
solicitor—were taken aback. They were told matter-of-factly that
there was an auction going on for a company valued at nearly as
much as CNOOC itself and that their support would be appreciated so that the financing could be locked in. In effect they were
being asked to agree to an $18 billion deal on the back of an enve-
lope. They refused.

One director, Erwin Schurtenberger, the former Swiss ambassador, who had warned of a backlash in U.S. public opinion, resigned.[10] For several weeks after the board dustup, there was a
stalemate. Valuable time was lost to Chevron, a U.S. oil company,
which had already made a bid that had been recommended by
Unocal's board. But CNOOC had not given up, and it later raised
its original offer considerably, valuing Unocal at more than Chevron had. But it was not a knockout blow, allowing Chevron just
enough space to mount a counterattack. The company picked
its straight-talking veteran vice president Peter Robertson, who
pulled no punches. He went straight for CNOOC's most vulnerable characteristic. "We are not competing with this company. We

are competing with the Chinese government," he said. "I think it is wrong."[11]

Robertson's point was not solely political. He was also pointing out that because of its close relationship with the Chinese authorities, CNOOC could call on financing at concessionary terms that were unavailable to Chevron. But as media coverage around the bid swelled — and given time by CNOOC's boardroom conflicts — the focus of attention in America switched more and more to issues of national security. To counter this, CNOOC paid top dollar, hiring the law firm of Akin Gump — and its attorney Daniel Spiegel, a former permanent representative to the United Nations under Bill Clinton — to help it face the political storm. But eventually it was all in vain. A vote in the House of Representatives went against CNOOC's interests, referring the bid to President George W. Bush on the grounds that its implications for national security needed to be reviewed.[12] When Fu heard that, he knew the game was up and withdrew from the competition.

How bruised CNOOC was can be gauged by the reaction of the company's chief financial officer, Yang Hua. He said the use of political prejudice to deny China access to the energy it needed amounted to a violation of human rights. "What are human rights?" he asked at a news conference in Hong Kong. "I'll tell you what it means. It means having guaranteed access to energy. It means having petroleum to run your car."

But whatever the lessons of CNOOC's failure, one thing was clear. The influence of the Party, so critical to the creation of China's manufacturing prowess, had been an unambiguous impediment when it came to the cause of acquiring key American corporate assets. First, Fu had to get the permission of Party elders for the bid, a process that put him in breach of his company's rules on corporate governance and then fomented a crisis of confidence on his own board. Then the subsidized lending that CNOOC had lined up from state banks gave Chevron a legitimate target on which to concentrate its efforts. And last, as media attention around CNOOC's links to the Party intensified, Fu was unable to distance himself from his political bosses — meaning that his arguments never quite addressed what American opinion saw as the main issue.

My student days in China in 1982 were spent at Shandong University in Jinan, the capital of a province that lies midway between Beijing and Shanghai. The officials in charge of my intake took it upon themselves to introduce foreign students to aspects of China's history and culture. They organized trips to the beautiful port city of Qingdao, to the birthplace of Confucius in Qufu, and even to the far northwestern frontier region of Xinjiang, where Turkic Muslims live alongside Han Chinese. The officials were generous and indefatigable hosts, and we students, for the most part, were not as grateful as we should have been.

Of all the trips we went on, the one that sticks most clearly in my memory was also the shortest distance from Jinan. We were put on a bus and driven out to the Yellow River. As we traveled, I was full of imaginings of the raging, gurgling torrents of treacherous water that we would see when we got there. A university official fed these images by standing at the front of the bus and talking excitedly about the river's significance. It was known both as "China's pride" for the fertility it bestowed on the land around it and as "China's sorrow" for the floods that destroyed what it nurtured. The reason why Jinan had not been built along its banks, in the manner of many cities that line the Yangtze and Pearl rivers, he said, was that the Yellow River was simply too tempestuous.

As we approached the river, an empty floodplain opened out on either side of the road. Soon, a newly built suspension bridge came into view. Its thick iron cables looked from a distance like the rigging on a tall ship. We drove halfway across it and stopped. When we got off the bus, I ran to the railing on one side of the bridge and leaned over to get a better view of the mother of Chinese civilization. What I saw was very disappointing. Instead of the angry, churning waterway of my imagination, there was a dark brown, narrow channel resembling nothing so much as a mudslide in flow. My fellow students and I found it hard to believe that this was the fearsome watercourse that over the millennia had probably caused more deaths than any other single geographical feature in the world.

Records of the carnage are so old they marked the start of Chinese history itself. One ancient flood, in 2297 B.C.E., was said to have led to a horrific loss of life; and since 602 B.C.E., when meticulous records began to be kept, the river has burst its banks more than 1,500 times and changed its course 26 times. In recent centuries, the human toll from the regular deluges has risen along with population densities. In 1887 the river tore through its banks at a point in the province of Henan, inundating eleven cities and putting an area of 50,000 square miles under water for two months. Between 900,000 and 2 million people are thought to have died. In 1943 some 3 million peasants in Henan died of starvation after their crops were destroyed.

But the most infamous disaster came on June 9, 1938, during the second Sino-Japanese War, when a retreating Chiang Kaishek, the leader of the Nationalist government, broke the dikes at Huayuankou, in Henan, at a time when the river's floodwaters were close to their peak. The aim of this desperate action was to stall the Japanese advance, but the results were catastrophic: up to 900,000 died as the flood swept over 9,000 square miles of the North China Plain, and another 12 million were made homeless. As a military strategy it was disastrous. The Japanese vanguard did have to wait a few weeks before resuming its southern progress, but as news of the action spread, Chiang's popular standing plummeted.

As my classmates and I looked down on the muddy flow below us, it seemed hardly credible that it had been responsible for so many harrowing pages of history. I think the administrator must have noticed our scoffing, superior reaction. He walked over to us and said, "Do not look down on the Yellow River, because if you do, you are looking down on the Chinese people themselves." I did not know at the time that this was a quotation from Chairman Mao. Its inference was based on the accurate observation that although the Yellow River may not seem impressive for much of the year, its power is deceptive. Its salient feature, the one that gives it its name, is that it is the most silt-laden river in the world. It carries up to sixty times the load of the Mississippi-Missouri river system, which is itself often called "the Big Muddy." As the river's velocity slows along its lower course, the silt in the water is deposited on the riverbed. This deposit builds up until the bed stands above the floodplain around it, and the only things that prevent a flood are the dikes holding the water in. In some parts of Henan, for instance, the river is "suspended" some thirty-five or forty feet above the floodplain. All it takes is a sudden flood crest, caused by heavy rain in the upper reaches, and the pressure can become unbearable.

The challenge over four thousand years and more to control the floods became the story of Chinese history. China was one of the great hydraulic societies, such as those that grew up along the banks of the Sumer, the Nile, and the Indus. The connection in all of these places between civilization and rivers flowing through arid but fertile areas is irrigation. The political structure needed to organize people to dig canals and to allocate fairly the use of water resources also lent itself to other types of construction, to city planning, state religion, education, and to a class with the leisure to pursue mathematics, science, and philosophy. It is not a matter of chance, therefore, that some of the earliest scientists also blossomed in those areas.

Such societies placed a premium on historical records because through these, rulers could study how their ancestors had dealt with floods and consider how they themselves might be able to guard against them. There was, in addition, something deeper than this: the methods used to combat floods have also influenced political philosophies that remain prevalent to this day. One school of thought, that of the Taoists, was relatively laissez-faire. It maintained that it was better not to build huge dikes because, although these would reduce flooding in average years, they were liable to burst when floodwaters were really ferocious, thereby exacerbating the death toll when disasters occurred. This philosophical approach recommended keeping human habitation off the floodplains so that when the river spilled from its bed, the damage would be relatively mild. The other school of thought, the Confucian way, aimed to control nature. It required the construction of strong dikes, the regimentation of society, and strict hierarchies.

Both philosophies have been used, often simultaneously, on different parts of the river. But the Confucian approach has been prevalent, not only on the Yellow River but also on the Yangtze and others. In fact, the ideogram for "political control" in Chinese — zhi — shows three drops of water next to a dike or platform.

There are other examples of the political efficacy of irrigation. The construction of the Zhengguo Canal, the first to be built in China, laid the foundation for the rise to power of the state of Qin. It was completed by the Qin in 246 B.C.E. and irrigated about 200,000 acres in the Wei Valley north of Xian, and it led to such prosperity and population increase that the state of Qin became the first to unify China after a long period of internecine strife. The power of that state — and its ability to organize — can be seen at the tomb of the Qin emperor near the central city of Xian today. It is guarded by a life-size army of terracotta warriors, some eight thousand of them. However, both the canal and the Qin empire were short-lived. The canal silted up and became useless about 150 years after it was built. Furthermore, the Qin population pressure caused farming to expand into the loess plateau.

Thus the link between hydraulic control and political power is ancient. In recent years, though, it has taken on a symbolism that is extremely uncomfortable for Beijing's rulers. The river known as "China's sorrow" for its power and ferocity now elicits pathos for a different reason. It is running dry. In almost every year since 1985 it has failed at times to reach the sea. In 1997 it was dry in Shandong for a full 226 days. The problem is entirely man-made. Since the founding of the People's Republic, the area of irrigated land along the river has grown twentyfold. Well over half the water in the river is taken for industry, agriculture, and residential use, but it is estimated that only about one-third of the water used for agricultural irrigation actually reaches the crops. The rest spills out of irrigation ditches or sinks into the soil beneath the eight large dams and thousands of small ones that have been built to control the river's fury. Farmers are virtually heedless of the need to conserve water, which costs as little as one bottle of mineral water for thirty cubic feet.

Conservation in general appears to be a blind spot. Perhaps it is the case that after thousands of years of political organization to control the consequences of too much water, the machinery of the state has not had enough time to readjust to the reality of too little. This might explain why the officials in charge of the Yellow River Conservancy in Jinan were, as late as 2004, still using the first twenty minutes of their briefings to journalists to explain the measures they were taking to control flooding from a river that was by then little more than a trickle.[13] There may, however, be a more telling explanation for China's ineptitude in conservation: the authoritarian political system that was born on the banks of the Yellow River, grew up through thousands of years of dynastic despotism, and was refined by five decades of communism is simply not configured for the niceties of tending to nature. Behind virtually every environmental disaster lurks a failure of politics or policy. Elizabeth Economy, in *The River Runs Black,* tells the story of how the basin of the Huai River, an area the size of England that covers parts of Henan, Anhui, and Jiangsu provinces, became a toxic hazard for the 150 million people who live there.

The problem started in the 1980s when tens of thousands of small companies, including pulp and paper mills, chemical factories, and dyeing and tanning plants, sprang up along the river and began dumping their toxic waste into it. By the early 1990s there were clear signs of distress. The water in many areas was unfit to drink, cancer rates were twice the national average, and, according to one report, for years none of the boys from certain villages in the Huai River area were healthy enough to pass the physical examination required to enter the armed forces. But when Beijing resolved to address the problem, things merely got worse.

When local authorities were ordered by Beijing to resolve the problem, they released the polluted water that had been building up in their reservoirs and tanks, and in so doing, unleashed a tide of black liquid that killed almost everything it touched as it flowed downstream. Millions of fish died and thousands of people were treated for dysentery, diarrhea, and vomiting. At this point, no less an official than Li Peng, the then premier, got involved, ordering the closure or relocation of thousands of factories, with the aim of halting all waste pollution by 1997 so the river would run clear by 2000. Several hundred factories were indeed closed, but they opened up again almost as quickly. By 1998 and 1999 it was clear that the campaign was going to fail; reports of people dying from being exposed to the noxious gases and chemicals in roadside ditches were regularly reported in the newspapers, and in 1999 the Huai ran dry for the first time in twenty years, ruining crops and killing millions of fish. Nevertheless, Xie Zhenhua, head of the State Environmental Protection Agency, stepped forward to proclaim that the campaign had been successful and the Huai's water was drinkable again.

There was a time when such a barefaced lie would have become a propaganda truth, but by the late 1990s some newspapers were bold enough to report the real situation. It emerged that the waters of the Huai, far from being clean, were so toxic that, by the government's own classification standards, they could not even be used for irrigation.

On the Yellow River, as on the Huai, the root cause of the crisis is the lack of political accountability. Local officials in China's top-down hierarchical system can be supervised only from above, not from below. So the people who live in cities, towns, and villages cannot choose their leaders or criticize them if they do a bad job. The partial exception to this is in the country's 900,000 villages, where, under an experiment with democracy, local people can directly elect their village chief but not the more powerful local Communist Party boss.

The vertical nature of the system has predictable results. Local officials strive to fulfill the criteria on which they are judged by their superiors. These include boosting local industrial output, providing employment, and raising tax revenues. Compared with these considerations, environmental protection is a second-ary concern, an issue that may have to be dealt with at some point but can usually be postponed until the next batch of officials take their posts. In any case, as long as a local official keeps his supe-riors happy, it matters little what the people he governs think of his tenure. Similarly, the pyramidal structure of the system means that, more often than not, neighboring towns, cities, and prov-inces will have a competitive rather than a cooperative relation-ship — an alignment that helps to explain why the Yellow River's upstream provinces routinely use more than their allocation of water and cut down many more trees than they should.

Conservation in any part of the world is most successful in communities where citizens have the responsibility and the right to hold local officials accountable for their promises. But in China, notwithstanding the growing role of some embryonic nongov-ernmental organizations, these conditions do not exist. Problems therefore deteriorate until they are so grave that they can no lon-ger be hidden from central authorities. But by the time these au-thorities are called in, it is often too late for conservational solu-tions and Beijing must resort to sweeping, radical policies. In the case of the Huai, this amounted to the overambitious and ulti-mately unsuccessful decree to halt all industrial waste pollution by closing down thousands of factories. In the case of the Yellow River, it was to commission the largest civil engineering project since the Great Wall: a $60 billion plan to transport a river-load of water from the Yangtze and its tributaries to the Yellow River basin and to parched northern cities such as Beijing and Tian-jin. The project, which was already under way in 2005, envisages digging three canals, more than six hundred miles in length, and pumping the water northward.[14] But even before the scheme had started operating, environmentalists were questioning the effi-cacy of the Herculean efforts required. For one thing, some of the water to be pumped was expected to come from heavily polluted sources, including the Huai. For another, when the price of water is increased — as it must be — the incentive for theft by the com-munities through which the canals pass is set to rise.

The costs of patching up China's wounded nature are only just beginning to be realized. Beijing had until recently tended to act as if it could postpone payment for its environmental deficit by refusing to acknowledge it. But now, as China faces up to reality, it is clear that repairing the devastation it has suffered is a task so onerous that it could slow down, or even derail, the country's stellar economic trajectory. When a researcher at a state think tank in the northern province of Shaanxi, in the coal-producing heartland, calculated a "green GDP" for the province (that is, the economic growth rate minus its cost in resource depletion and environmental degradation), he estimated that Shaanxi had hardly grown at all in the past twenty years.

Regardless of whether such estimates are accurate, they hint at the magnitude of a concealed debt. Streams and rivers are drying up all over the northern half of the country, and water tables are falling precipitously as wells, many of them illegally dug, are sunk ever deeper into dwindling reserves of groundwater. Altogether some 400 out of 668 large Chinese cities are short of water, and the incidence of rationing is growing. Still, the pressures of population, the demands of a burgeoning industrial expansion, and the inability of the political system to inculcate a conservation mentality are taking their toll. China uses between seven and twenty times more water to generate a unit of GDP than the developed countries of the world.

Of course, the crisis extends beyond water and beyond national borders. On the World Bank's list of the twenty most polluted cities on earth, sixteen are in China. Acid rain falls over 30 percent of its territory. Although some large showcase cities such as Shanghai and Beijing are being cleaned up, rural areas are becoming a dumping ground for toxic waste. Chinese environmentalists tend to see the problem as at least partly imported. The factories that multinational companies have set up have turned China into the workshop of the world but have also made it the "rubbish tip of the world,"[15] one senior official once told me. But this view is at variance with how much of Europe, America, and the rest of Asia regards the international impact of China's environmental failure. In a growing number of ways Beijing is catching the censure of overseas nongovernmental organizations, "green" pressure groups, and even governments.

Air pollution, once considered a local affliction, is increasingly being viewed as an intercontinental problem. A study by Daniel Jacob, a Harvard professor of atmospheric chemistry, traced a plume of dirty air to a point over New England, where samples revealed that it had come from China.[16] Concern centers on mercury, a highly toxic pollutant given off by the combustion of coal. The U.S. Environmental Protection Agency recently reported that a third of the nation's lakes and nearly a quarter of its rivers are now so polluted with mercury that children and pregnant women are advised to limit or avoid eating fish caught there. Scientists estimate that around one-third of the mercury settling into the soil and waterways of the United States comes from other countries, China in particular. Josef Pacyna, director of the Center for Ecological Economics at the Norwegian Institute for Air Research, calculates that China spews around six hundred tons of mercury into the air each year, accounting for nearly one-quarter of the world's nonnatural emissions.[17]

The effect on the world's forests of China's rise is still more palpable. In 1998, in response to grievous flooding along the Yangtze that was caused partly by chronic deforestation around the headwaters of the river, Beijing placed tough restrictions on logging. In the meantime, the world's largest furniture and papermaking industries have grown up. The result of these two developments is that China has become by far the fastest-growing market for timber products and paper pulp in the world. From 1997 to 2003 China's timber product imports surged threefold, while imports of paper and pulp more than doubled. The impact of this voracious appetite, which shows no sign of abating, has been increasingly ruinous for the world's primary forests. The rain forests in Indonesia, Myanmar, and central Africa, and the boreal woodlands of Siberia, places known as the "lungs of the planet" for their role in turning carbon dioxide into oxygen, are disappearing at unprecedented rates to satisfy Chinese demand.

In both rain forest and woodland, logging restrictions are circumvented by various underhand and illegal methods. In Russia, licenses to log virgin boreal woodlands are very difficult to obtain, but not if the area in question has been damaged by fire. So the criminals who supply Chinese logging syndicates first set fire to large areas and then obtain permits to fell the timber there. In 2003 some 54 million acres of spruce, fir, Scotch pine, and oak were destroyed or in some way affected by fire.[18] U.S. satellite photographs recorded 157 fires across almost 27 million acres, sending up a plume of smoke that reached Kyoto, Japan, three thousand miles away. The felled trees are a nonrenewable resource that may have taken up to five hundred years to grow in frigid tundra temperatures.

In Indonesia, an area the size of Switzerland is illegally logged each year, and although reserves of teak, ramin, and meranti hardwoods have been virtually exhausted, vast tracts of protected merbau trees in remote provinces such as Papua have become the latest target of illegal logging syndicates. A complicated network involving Malaysian logging companies working with falsified documents, Singaporean warehouses, Hong Kong middlemen, and merchant ships from the Middle East ensures that loads of merbau are delivered to secondary ports, among them Zhangjiagang on the lower Yangtze, every week. Most of the merbau felled is used as flooring for the millions of new middle-class houses being built in Shanghai, Beijing, and other large cities. The size of the illegal trade is considerable: in 2002 China cleared the import of 8.5 million cubic feet more Indonesian timber than Indonesian authorities cleared for export. The International Tropical Timber Organization, a United Nations–backed intergovernmental agency, estimates that five out of every ten tropical logs shipped worldwide are bound for China; and the Worldwide Fund for Nature reckons that 44 percent of the timber imported into China has been illegally felled.[19]

But in terms of potential damage to the global environment, China's demand for soybeans may be having an impact at least as deleterious as its requirement for timber. The shortage of water in northern provinces, where most domestic soybeans have been grown, has led to a decline in output even as demand for beans from an increasingly affluent population has shot up. The inevitable result has been that imports have surged, and in the space of a decade China has gone from being a marginal presence in international markets to its current position as the world's biggest importer by some margin.

Brazilian farmers have moved quickly to satisfy China's hunger, felling swaths of the Amazon rain forest to plant new fields of soy. In 2004 the rate of clearance of the Amazon was the second highest on record. An area of 16,000 square miles—nearly the size of Belgium—was cut down over the course of the year, which is to say that the forest was disappearing at the rate of six soccer fields every minute.[20] Environmentalist groups say that the deforestation is a national shame. The Amazon rain forest, which sprawls over an area the size of the contiguous forty-eight states, is home to 30 percent of the world's animal and plant species. The trees are also a vital source of oxygen for the world, but this supply is being undermined by forest fires, which release hundreds of millions of tons of carbon dioxide and other greenhouse gases into the atmosphere every year.

Greenhouse gases, mainly carbon dioxide, are so called because they accelerate global warming, melting the polar ice caps and possibly triggering all kinds of unforeseen weather phenomena. China is both a culprit and a victim in the planet's warming trend. It is now the second-largest producer of greenhouse gases after the United States, following a 33 percent increase in emissions of carbon dioxide between 1990 and 2002, to 3.4 billion tons.[21] Changes in the domestic climate have been observable. The 1990s was the warmest decade in more than a hundred years, and since 1950 there has been a gradual reduction in precipitation nationwide. This has contributed to the falling volume of water in the six major rivers since the 1960s; and an unpredictable cycle of droughts and flash floods is becoming more pronounced. On the coast, sea levels are rising and inland vegetation is moving to higher altitudes. And the glaciers in the Himalayas and other high mountain ranges are melting at an alarming rate.[22] At the current pace of deterioration, two-thirds of China's high-altitude ice fields, which account for 15 percent of the planet's ice, will have melted by 2050, environmentalists estimate.

In an interconnected world, the environmental stresses of a nation China's size cannot be regarded as distinctly a domestic problem. Yet curbing the waste and appetite that are exacerbating some profound global climate trends is not going to be easy. The country has only just embarked upon a developmental journey that has so far faithfully followed the path blazed by the United States in its ascent to wealth and prestige. An American-style communications infrastructure is being built. Chinese dream of buying a car, a house, a first-class education for their children, and a range of consumer goods conferring status and convenience, just as they do to middle-class families in Europe and America. As disposable incomes rise, people are eating more protein and using more electricity to run their computers, televisions, and household appliances. But in spite of the resemblance China bears to America in an earlier stage of its development, the chances that the Chinese will one day be able to consume at the same rate as Americans do today are close to zero. It is not that they will choose to be more frugal. It is simply that the world does not have the resources to cater to 1.3 billion Chinese behaving like Americans.

Perhaps, in the end, the lack of alternatives will force China to adopt a whole new approach to resources that is based on recycling, conservation, and clean fuels. But the cost of implementing such a strategy would seriously erode the country's industrial competitiveness, so progress is unlikely to be rapid. And in the years that it takes to reach that hazy goal of environmental responsibility, the international tensions released by China's appetite for foreign resources and the abuse of its own environment may escalate sharply.

7

The Collapse of Social Trust

MENCIUS LOOKS STERN and pinched about the mouth in portraits that purport to show his likeness, but his teachings are among the most gentle to have issued from the golden age of Chinese philosophy, which spanned the few centuries before the birth of Christ. In the same way as his contemporary Plato, whose existence he would not have known about, Mencius — or Mengzi, his Chinese name — was concerned with the most crucial and vexing of questions: how men could be good and how society could prosper.

His teachings revolve around *ren*, a word that is often translated as "benevolence" but also has the wider, more general sense of "goodness." The most important property of *ren* was compassion, or not being able to bear that others should suffer. It meant a feeling of responsibility for the suffering of others, such as was felt by the legendary ruler Yu, the subduer of primeval floods: "If anyone were drowned, Yu felt as though it were he himself that had drowned him," Mencius wrote. Another mythical leader, the counselor I Yin, was also said to have possessed *ren*, for if he knew of a single man or woman anywhere who was not enjoying the benefits of wise rule, "it was as though he had pushed them into a ditch with his own hand; so heavy was the responsibility that he put upon himself for everything that happened under Heaven."[1]

Empathetic feelings such as these, the sage said, are the natural birthright of everyone. But just as in modern times, our best intentions at the start of the day can be diverted by the complications of living, so *ren* can be worn away, leaving a mean spirit where

★

there was once a natural magnanimity. Education, however, can temper such regressions and keep people from having their charitable feelings pared to the nub by competition for scarce resources. Mencius described what he meant in the allegory of Bull Mountain:

> The Bull Mountain was once covered with lovely trees. But it is near the capital of a great state. People came with their axes and choppers; they cut the woods down and the mountain lost its beauty. Yet even so, the day air and the night air came to it, rain and dew moistened it till here and there fresh sprouts began to grow. But soon cattle and sheep came along and browsed on them and in the end the mountain became gaunt and bare, as it is now. And seeing it thus gaunt and bare, people imagine that it was woodless from the start. But just as the natural state of the mountain was quite different from what now appears, so too in every man (little though they may be apparent) there assuredly were once feelings of decency and kindness; and if those feelings are no longer there, it is that they have been tampered with, hewn down with axe and bill. As each day dawns, they are assailed anew. What chance then has our nature, any more than that mountain, of keeping its beauty?[2]

The link between man and nature that Mencius made is as valid today as it was more than two thousand years ago. His hometown, a place called Zoucheng, in a corner of Shandong province, wears the strain of population on its sleeve. Large areas of land are sinking into exhausted coal mines underground, just as in the city of Pingxiang far away to the south. The low hills that surround the town have lost most of the trees that in Mencius's day would have covered them. Slag heaps stand next to industrial plants that spew dust and smoke into the air. And if the experience of Qi Yuling, a slight woman in her late twenties with bright eyes and hair pulled tightly into a bun, is anything to go by, the degradations of nature are mirrored in society.[3]

Qi was in her seventeenth year when her life altered course.

One day, her brother came running from her school, swung open the wooden door of their house, and with an expression of sheer joy announced that Qi had passed her exams and was accepted by a technical college in the nearby city of Jining. He had just spoken to her teacher, who said that it was so. Qi then hurried to the school, but as she approached her teacher, she noticed the shadows in his face. He told her that her brother must have been mistaken. There was no notice from the Jining college of her acceptance.

Qi followed her feet back home, reflecting that her education was over. The single-plank bridge that spanned a chasm between those who wore cloth shoes and those who wore leather shoes was no longer there for her to cross. The life that seemed to stretch out before her would be the one that her parents had known: tilling the fields close to their home in a village near Zoucheng. The money that her parents had invested in her schooling had been wasted, and her horizons would be as limited as theirs had been. Mencius's mother was legendary for having moved house three times so that her son could sit at the feet of the best teachers. But Qi had had only one chance, and she had blown it.

Those among her school friends who had passed the entrance exams drifted away, first to college and then to city jobs. When they returned to the village they wore the bright fashions of the city, and some came in black cars that they parked incongruously outside their parents' ramshackle houses so the whole village could take note. They barely acknowledged the friend they used to walk hand in hand with to the school gate and play hopscotch with in the cement yard. To them, Qi had become the embodiment of everything they had striven to leave behind. At first the nonchalance of her former school friends was hard to bear, but as the years passed Qi's exam failure faded in memory and life found familiar rhythms. Only occasionally did something happen that would give her pause for thought.

One of those times was when she applied to leave the village and go to Zoucheng to get a factory job. To do this, she needed to move her *hukou*, or residence permit. But when she went to the authority in charge of keeping everyone's *hukou*, she was told that her permit could not be found. A few days later, it reappeared. A *hukou* is probably the most vital document a Chinese person owns, and so Qi did wonder how the village authorities could have been so bumbling and forgetful.

It was not until eight years after her exam failure that she began to realize that something really was amiss. One day when she was in Zoucheng, there was a knock at her parents' door back in the village. A young woman stood in the doorway clutching bags full of gifts. She said she had come to congratulate Qi on the birth of her new baby. Qi's parents were flummoxed. They had not heard that their daughter was pregnant, and there had been no mention of a baby. In any case, they told the visitor, she did not live in the village these days; she had moved to the city and had not been back for a while. Perhaps the gifts were intended for someone else, maybe another young mother in the village, the parents suggested.

But the well-wisher stood her ground and became a little petulant. She had come to see Qi Yuling from this very village, a colleague of hers at the Bank of China branch in Tengzhou city. People had informed her that this house was where she lived. Well, the parents answered, their daughter was indeed called Qi Yuling, but she did not work in any bank and not in Tengzhou. She was in Zoucheng, and, having been laid off from her job in a ferroalloy plant there, she was doing odd jobs to make ends meet. The visitor took her presents and returned to her car.

When Qi heard of the perplexing visit to her parents' house, she decided to go to the Bank of China branch in Tengzhou to satisfy her curiosity. She asked at the counter if she could speak to Qi Yuling, but the service assistant told her that "Director Qi" was away on maternity leave and would not be back for a few weeks. As Qi turned to leave, she came face to face with a bulletin board with photographs of the bank's key personnel pasted on it. In the bottom right-hand corner she saw a face that was instantly familiar. It was Chen Xiaoqi, a former classmate. The two had not met since Chen had passed the exams for Jining Business College. The photograph showed a slightly changed appearance: her hair was styled with ringlets and waves and her expression had grown quite serious but there was no mistaking her old friend. Beneath the picture, a nameplate read, "Qu Yuling, director of the savings department."

The realization that not only her identity but also her life had been stolen came slowly to Qi. Chen was a rather lazy pupil at school, but nobody doubted that she would do well in life; her father was the Communist Party secretary, the highest-ranking official in their village. He could tap into a power network that threaded from the village to the county and then to the city of Tengzhou itself; there was not much in this small corner of Shandong province that he could not make happen. So when Chen got a place at the college, nobody was surprised. It was not until the evening of the day that she had visited the bank that Qi began to suspect Chen had somehow taken the slot at college that should have been hers. It was a bewildering feeling as she awoke to the understanding not that she was someone else but that someone else was her.

Over the next few weeks, she pieced the details together. Chen's father had intercepted Qi's exam certificate (though not before a teacher had let slip to Qi's brother that Qi had passed). Then Chen's father had bribed or threatened several school officials into silence. He arranged for his daughter to take all of Qi's personal files to the Jining college so the admissions office would not notice anything untoward. Chen had then registered for the accounting course that Qi had wanted to study, and she passed. Of course, Chen's assumed name was on her diploma and was the basis on which she won her job at the Bank of China, the most prestigious of the country's "big four" state banks. The lie had to be sustained. When she wanted to transfer her *hukou* from the village to Tengzhou where she worked, she had to borrow Qi's. When she got married, she again had to use Qi's documents, and when her baby was born, its mother's name was registered as Qi.

So complete was the deception that it was unclear, when the case eventually went to court, whether even her husband had known who Chen really was.

But when Qi first approached Chen's father with the question of why his daughter was using her name, the Party secretary did not attempt to deny it. He said it was nothing that should concern her. Chen was only "borrowing" it for a while. Qi was inclined to take his advice; perhaps it was not such a big deal. But as the investigation continued and she discovered the examination slip showing that she had passed, it became more and more difficult to let the issue rest. Then one day Chen sent a representative to Qi's parents' house with 5,000 renminbi as a "token of respect" that would be theirs if they would agree to drop their concerns about the name.

"He just kept saying that it was only a name. What was the difference? We should just forget about it, take the five thousand and move on," Qi said as we talked in a hotel room in Zoucheng. "The arrogance of it was unbearable. As if five thousand were the value of a stolen life." When Qi and her parents refused to accept the money and declined to drop their investigation, Chen sent some thugs around to beat the family up. That only increased their determination, and after a long legal wrangle a court found in Qi's favor. Chen was ordered to pay 98,000 renminbi in damages.

When we met, it was just before the lunar new year, the Year of the Wooden Cockerel. After our meeting, as I saw her to her moped, I gave her some white sorghum liquor and a two-liter bottle of sunflower oil, which the shop had given away free as an inducement to buy the liquor. She refused them at first, saying that she had not told me her story in order to receive anything in return. But after a while she agreed to accept the gifts, and we spent several minutes, as dusk was falling, shifting the oil this way and that to make it fit in the basket on the front of her motorbike. Eventually she drove away in the direction of the temple to Mencius. I also decided to go that way and walked for an hour or so. When I got to the temple, the moon had risen over the old cedar trees that stood in front of the main hall. It was a scene of haunting beauty. I got out a small booklet of Mencius's quotations that I had bought earlier in the day and read: "If beans and millet were as plentiful as fire and water, such a thing as a bad man would not exist among the people."

The story of Qi Yuling presents a microcosm of the breakdown of trust that bedevils the whole of Chinese society. In saying this, I do not mean to give the impression that everyone is untrustworthy or unreliable. That would be far from the truth. Most people that I have come across have been decent and honest, and some have shown kindness and hospitality that would be rare in the West. Neither would it be true to say that Chinese culture fails to value integrity.

China's history is replete with reverence for people who were upright, loyal, and altruistic. The great philosophers Confucius, Mencius, Zhuang Zi, Lao Zi, and Mo Zi, to name but a few, were all concerned with virtue in its crucial manifestations. Nevertheless, trust is a commodity constantly under siege. Poverty and the competition for scarce resources impinge upon it. The ideological vacuum that replaced communism undermines it. The daily diet of propaganda disorients it. The venality of officials devalues it. The ascendance of a value system dominated by money hollows it out. What is left is a society in which describing someone as honest can just as easily be a gentle criticism as a compliment. Even official newspapers have highlighted the problem, rating a "crisis of trust" as one of the top ten ills of the country.

The vast industry for counterfeit products and the violation of intellectual property rights, described in earlier chapters, is part of the general crisis. But the problem goes much deeper than that. The influence of artifice is almost omnipresent, and identity is an item to be bought and sold. In Beijing and other cities, the cell phone numbers scrawled with spray paint on walls and under overpasses have been put there by scam artists advertising fake papers—residence permits, work permits, university degrees, identity cards, you name it. A whole identity makeover with a Ph.D. in rocket science can be bought for less than $100. People use these to assume new identities, launder a dubious past, and secure city jobs.

But they are by no means the only people masquerading as someone else. The media regularly reports cases of criminals who have gone around the country pretending to be some senior official and enjoying the pampering of sycophants before finally being exposed. In a nation where a uniform bestows unquestioning respect, the number of people impersonating police and military officers is astonishing. Beijing authorities said that in the five years up to 2002, they had apprehended more than 10,000 phony police officers in the capital, along with 320,000 fake uniforms, badges, and weapons.[4]

A practice called *you chang xin wen* ("news with bonus") has become a staple of the newspaper business. Many, if not most, Chinese journalists these days expect to find several hundred renminbi tucked in an envelope along with their press release when they attend a news conference on a corporate announcement. Similarly, many will not agree to write an article on a company unless they get paid in advance. The practice is so blatant that the PR companies that organize news conferences inform their corporate clients airily that "everybody does it" and advise them on how much money to put in the envelopes.[5] The few news organizations that have a strict no-bonus policy, such as *Caijing* magazine, are regarded as heroic trailblazers for an impartial media, and indeed the quality of the reporting in the no-bonus newspapers and magazines is on a different level from the rest. But the "news with bonus" mentality has spread to many fields, including soccer. Referees have often accepted bribes to swing matches with a few deft dubious decisions. Such people are called "black whistles," and every time a black whistle is uncovered, the media is up in arms.

One of the most intriguing identity subterfuges involves the number plates on officials' cars. It has long been the habit of the Beijing traffic police (the real ones, that is) to avoid apprehending cars with an official number plate, because the risk of incurring the wrath of the powerful person within is too great. Consequently, official number plates confer a license to drive in as cavalier a fashion as you like. That makes them valuable on the black market. But, as with everything else, there is a hierarchy. It is much better, for instance, to be in a car identified as belonging to the Beijing government than one from an outlying province. Better than any local-government car would be a black Mercedes with central-government plates. But best of all is the protection accorded by riding under the cover of a single, red character, *jia*, meaning "armor." Placed just in front of the license number, a *jia* denotes the Central Military Commission, the most powerful body in the land after the politburo. *Jia* plates are not easy to get hold of, but for people with connections, they too can be bought. The investment is soon recouped by the freedom from parking fines, speeding tickets, and other inconveniences.

All of these activities contribute to a large and growing underground economy that is not captured in the official figures and is therefore ignored except in special studies. Neither the World Bank nor the International Monetary Fund nor the brokerage houses that analyze the ups and downs of China's growing global influence make allowances for the size of the underground economy. This is clearly a significant oversight. In some provinces, such as Zhejiang on the east coast, the underground economy is almost institutionalized. Scores of underground banks provide financing for private companies that still find the traditional state-owned lenders reluctant to cooperate. In Guangdong, especially around the cities of Shenzhen and Guangzhou, hundreds of thousands of unlicensed factories operate in the twilight of symbiotic relationships with local officials. Tax evasion is endemic all over the country, as is shown by the regularity of scandals involving fake value-added-tax receipts. The size of the underground economy is by its nature difficult to estimate, but one Chinese scholar who has spent years studying it, Yao Jianfu, says it could amount to about one-third the size of the official economy.[6]

In other words, the gray area in economics may be huge. And in personal relationships too. The incidence of extramarital affairs, paternity tests, prenuptial agreements, and divorce rates is surging in the cities along the east coast. Private detectives, a job description that did not exist just over a decade ago, now number in the hundreds of thousands and are increasingly employed by one lover to trail another, or by a wife to check up on her husband. In the southwestern city of Chengdu, a chambermaid walking into a hotel room was intrigued to find the following note on the bed, written in a feminine hand:

Dear Mr. Song:
Please excuse my deception. It was due to my job. I'm a love detective and I was hired by your lover to test your love. I have now got your ID card and underwear as proof. You have loved each other for three years and are now preparing to wed. Please go back to your lover's side.

At the end of the letter was written the name of the detective agency, Hunting Fox, its address, and the signature of the writer, Xiao Qing — the assumed name of the young female detective who had lured Song to the edge of seduction and then left with his underpants when he was in the shower.

Xiao Qing was the epitome of Chinese beauty. She was twenty-seven years old, five feet six inches tall, slim, with curves and white skin. Her face was an oval that drew to a gentle point at her chin, and her almond eyes were dark and shining. When she smiled, a shallow dimple formed in one cheek. Although she looked innocent — she applied just enough makeup to suggest the glow of good health — she understood male psychology. Her client for this assignment was Ms. Yun, a plain-looking twenty-five-year-old who worked as an accountant in a foreign company and earned 6,000 renminbi a month. The cost of hiring Xiao Qing to lure her fiancé was just 1,000 renminbi. Not much more, observed Yun, than the price of a Burberry shirt. It was nearly Christmas, and there was barely three weeks to go before she was to marry Song, who worked for a private trading company. He was wealthy and in many ways a good catch, but Yun was fretting that he had grown cold of late and their relationship was getting stale. She had to fathom the depth of his love.

Xiao Qing waited by the elevator in the building where Song worked. As he entered, she asked him to hold it for her and then thanked him with a charming smile as she took her place close to him. Song walked to the coffee shop across the street and she followed. As he passed her in the shop, she nudged her bag onto the floor. He picked it up and Xiao Qing said, "You work in that building. I work there too. I came here only a week ago by myself. I don't have any friends here." They exchanged name cards and began to meet from time to time.

On Christmas Eve, Yun called Song to ask if he was free to go out that night. They were not Christian, but Christmas Eve is nevertheless an occasion, a time when friends and lovers get together to eat. But Song had already agreed to see Xiao Qing, so he told Yun he was very busy at work. That night they danced and drank, and Xiao Qing pretended to lose her bag. Inside were the keys to her house and her cash, so when Song offered to take her to a hotel, it seemed as if fate had had a hand in the decision. In the hotel room, she suggested he take a shower first. But when he emerged from the bathroom, he found her gone and the letter lying on the bed.

Yun felt the money had been well spent, and even though Song apologized several times, she decided to take time out of the relationship to reconsider their future.

In the end, no more than feelings were hurt. But at other times the breakdown in morality has descended into pure evil. Two of the most shocking cases in recent years have involved commercial activities: the sale of fake baby milk powder to unknowing parents and the transfusion of HIV-contaminated blood to villagers in the northern province of Henan. In both cases, local governments were implicated in crimes that caused death.

The milk powder tragedy began when some forty companies in several provinces hit on the idea of selling powder that looked like the real thing but was in fact a cheaper, less nutritious substance, inserted into packages bearing counterfeit brands. It contained just enough protein to keep a baby alive for six to eight months but not enough to promote growth and development. Instead of dried fortified milk, the powder contained a mixture of sugar, flour, and gluten. The companies that sold it reasoned that the more sickly and malnourished the babies began to look, the more fake powder their parents would feed them. That would be good for sales.

In the event, it turned out almost as the companies had hoped, though with one variation that also worked to the companies' advantage. The powder made the babies' heads swell up and their cheeks grow chubby, even though their bones remained small and brittle and their internal organs underdeveloped. The big heads convinced many parents that all was well, and so they delayed taking their babies to the hospital. About a dozen are known to have died of malnutrition in and around the city of Fuyang, in Anhui province, where the scam was most prevalent.[7] Many hundreds more are thought to be in poor physical and mental health and will probably be affected for the rest of their lives. When the case was cracked in 2004, several Fuyang officials were fired or put in prison for complicity with the milk powder companies. But this has had little effect. Within months of the sentences' being handed down, new fake milk powders were on the market in Fuyang and elsewhere.

Children were also among the victims of the HIV scandal, which has been unfolding in villages in Henan since the mid-1990s. Back then, there was a shortage of blood in local hospitals and a society that was not accustomed to donating it. Local officials set up blood collection centers and offered to pay around five dollars for a donation, a significant sum for a peasant in one of China's poorest areas. Indeed, the main limitation to what became a roaring trade was anemia, which set in when a person had given too much blood. So the collectors switched to taking just plasma — that way, they could extract the blood, pool it with that of other donors with the same blood type, skim off all the plasma at once, and then return the remaining blood to the donors.

The arrangement seemed to suit everyone, though it was also a sure way to spread diseases throughout the donor community. Nobody is quite sure how or when HIV-tainted blood entered the blood supply, but it spread rapidly. AIDS, the disease that is brought on by the HIV virus, is estimated by health workers to have spread to a million Henan peasants. Around 100,000 children have become orphans. Local governments, which profited from the blood collection centers in the first place, have tried to cover up the scandal, arresting AIDS activists, closing down orphanages, and conducting a strenuous campaign to keep the issue out of the national media. It seems unlikely, however, that they will be successful in the long run. Pierre Haski, the China correspondent of *Libération,* the French newspaper, has obtained official documents showing that branches of the Henan government knew that HIV was being spread through the contaminated blood long before they did anything to stop the blood trade.[8]

The horrific nature of such cases provides a bleak commentary on contemporary society. It also detracts from the national image. To some people, that may seem a mere inconvenience. But the reputation of a country, like that of an individual, is of inestimable value. China has much going for it in this regard: an ancient culture, sparkling traditions in literature and the arts, the accumulated wisdom of thinkers over thousands of years, the size of its potential power, the taste of its cuisine, kung fu and other martial arts, the diligence and intelligence of its people, the gleaming skyscrapers in cool new cities such as Shanghai, and of course the cuddly giant panda. But against these positive associations are a raft of less alluring images: shabby products, counterfeit goods, ripoffs of intellectual property, exploited labor, human rights abuses, the 1989 Tiananmen massacre, official nepotism and corruption, the persecution of religion and other forms of spirituality, a sick environment, outbursts of angry nationalism, and opposition to the exiled Dalai Lama. All or any of these impressions, plus others too numerous to mention, can coalesce to shape the attitudes of people in the West when they read the label "Made in China" on products. The resulting image, or brand, is often far from positive, and Chinese companies pay handsomely every year for the poor perceptions held in the West.

The cost incurred flows mainly from the way in which global

capitalism is configured. When a consumer item is sold in a shop, most of the money paid goes to the owner of the brand, the distributor, the advertiser, and the retailer. The manufacturer, which in more and more cases is a separate company contracted by the brand owner, gets a relative pittance for its work. China, as is obvious from even a brief trip around the Pearl River Delta, is firmly at the manufacturing end of this value hierarchy. The girls and young women laboring away at their tables making shoes in one of the world's largest shoe factories, the Taiwanese-owned Pou Chen in the city of Zhuhai, near Hong Kong, get around 1 or 2 percent of the price paid by customers in the United States and Europe for the brand-name shoes that they make.[9] The same is true at Galanz, the factory that single-handedly makes about 40 percent of the world's microwave ovens on contract for foreign brand owners. And it is the same story for almost every manufactured product that Chinese companies make. Seventy percent of the world's photocopiers, 70 percent of its computer motherboards, 55 percent of its DVD players, 30 percent of its personal computers, 25 percent of its TV sets, and 20 percent of its car stereos — to name but a handful — are made in largely brandless factories by workers who get no more than a few percentage points of the final sale price. In fact, all of the work done in China — the sourcing, manufacturing, transporting, and exporting — rarely qualifies for a return of more than 10 or 15 percent of a product's sales revenue.

This may seem unfair. Certainly, the effort expended by a typical migrant worker who is far from her village, working fifteen-hour days without benefits or union protection under a management regime that may use fines as a motivational strategy, is not inconsiderable. But it is the advertising, marketing, and sales executives in Europe and the United States, as well as the shareholders of the brand-owning company, that take the lion's share of the value from the product that the migrant workers create. No doubt the brand holders sometimes feel uneasy about this arrangement; the most common plea I have heard during scores of visits to contract manufacturers has been, "You can write anything you like,

but please don't report the names of the brands that we manufacture for." It may be that brand holders wish to shield their customers from the discomfort of knowing the working conditions
under which their products were made. Or it may be that they
feel that any association with China could undermine the image
they are trying to project. Whatever the reason, the underlying reality is that world trade is arranged in this way. The customer is
the ultimate arbiter, and if customers in the United States and Europe think that the greatest portion of a product's value derives
from its logo, then most of the commercial rewards will continue
to accrue to those who build and sustain the brand.

Chinese companies that try to build their own brands, meanwhile, bump up against a series of barriers, not least of which are
the associations that go along with their national identity. It is not
easy to create an aura of quality, consistency, or "cool" among
overseas consumers if the news coverage from your country centers on repression, corruption scandals, worker exploitation, and,
for many people, a vague and menacing presence called communism. Thus Chinese firms are condemned to surrender much of
the value that comes from making and selling things to foreign
companies.

This disadvantage has not escaped the notice of Beijing's leadership. Wen Jiabao, the premier, speaks regularly about the need
for companies to concentrate on creating and building their
brands, and events such as the Olympic Games, to be held in Beijing in 2008, are being viewed as a rare opportunity to launder the
country's reputation in the eyes of the world. But until that reputation is overhauled — and it will take more than the Olympics to
do it — Chinese corporations are likely to find other ways to build
their brands. Near the top of the list of preferred strategies is the
acquisition of foreign brands.

The outward investment of Chinese companies has become an
identifiable trend. Lenovo, the Chinese computer company, paid
$1.75 billion for the personal computer unit of IBM, an American
icon. TCL, an electronics company, bought Thomson, the French
TV maker, and its German counterpart, Schneider, and took a ma-

jority stake in a cell-phone-handset joint venture with France's Alcatel. BOE Technology bought the liquid-crystal-display unit of South Korea's Hynix Semiconductor for $380 million. Haier, the consumer electronics maker, launched an aggressive but ultimately unsuccessful bid for Maytag, another American household name. Such sorties have prompted comparisons with the outward extension of Japanese corporate might at the end of the 1980s, when Mitsubishi bought Rockefeller Center in New York and Honda, Toyota, and Sony made investments in other arenas.

But there are important differences between the internationalization of Japan Inc. and the first faltering foreign steps of Chinese companies. The main difference is that Chinese manufacturers (the energy and resource companies are in a separate category) are being pushed overseas through weakness rather than strength. In the case of Lenovo, for instance, the acquisition of IBM was motivated not by a desire to encroach on the U.S. computer market but to defend itself at home, where it is being squeezed by competition from giants such as Dell and Hewlett-Packard.

Another difference is that many of the Japanese acquisitions followed inroads that their formidable brands had already opened up. They had real corporate clout. By the end of the 1980s, Japan had been an emerging Asian powerhouse for nearly four decades, and Sony, Hitachi, Sharp, Sanyo, Nissan, Toyota, Honda, and many other brands were already household names. But Chinese brands, perhaps because of the speed of China's rise, have been given very little time to establish themselves. So when TCL bought Schneider and Thomson, it decided to keep selling the European brands rather than substitute them with its own. This was not the only expression of relative weakness. TCL's chief executive, Li Dongsheng, also acknowledged that his company was being *driven* overseas by the paucity of profits at home.[10] The problem of oversupply was endemic in China, he said, and profit margins were therefore perennially thin. The only answer was to build a bulwark in offshore markets, where decent margins could be collected to reinforce the home front. This amounts to a reversal of usual business logic, but it is surprising how many Chinese bosses employ it.

The big exceptions to this tendency are those Chinese companies that enjoy monopoly or near-monopoly conditions at home. These firms — the oil giants PetroChina, Sinopec, and CNOOC; the telecom operators China Telecom, China Mobile, and China Unicom; and some of the financial institutions — are flush with cash and intent on snapping up opportunities overseas for rather different reasons. Nevertheless, the magnitude of the task facing Chinese manufacturers in building their brands abroad and in acquiring foreign counterparts is sizable — though that is unlikely to stop many from trying. Indeed, the world could be on the brink of a deluge of outward-bound Chinese investment. As the trend continues, heroes, villains, and legends seem certain to be created.

Legend, in fact, was the English name of Lenovo before the company found out that others abroad were already using it, and had to change. That is unfortunate, because no word describes the ascent of Liu Chuanzhi — the man who started his career as an IBM sales representative in a borrowed suit and twenty years later bought the company — more accurately than the one he gave to his corporation. His experience could not have been more different from those of Bill Gates, Larry Ellison, Steve Jobs, and other luminaries in the U.S. information-technology industry, and in some respects his curriculum vitae appears a little lacking. Liu can hardly speak a sentence of English, has almost no experience operating in markets beyond China, and is by no means a technological visionary. Yet, like several other Chinese entrepreneurs over the age of fifty-five, he graduated summa cum laude from the school of hard knocks.

Liu was born in 1944 into a family without a single revolutionary credential to its name. On his father's side there were bankers, which is to say capitalists. His mother's father had been the finance minister of a famous warlord, which is to say both capitalist and of suspect loyalties. As a boy, Liu dreamed of being a pilot, but his background barred him from even applying. A gifted scholar at his university, he wanted to join the Communist Party but was prevented from doing so because of a perceived lack of feeling toward workers and peasants. With these disadvantages, he had to turn himself into a "needle wrapped in cotton" — someone who could do things that he disliked and yet appear cheerful. One of his first moves was to volunteer to collect excrement from the public toilets on one street to prove he was not aloof from the masses. He shoveled out the nightsoil, put it in a cart, and hauled it away to be used as agricultural manure.[11]

Such efforts paid off. By the time he had graduated in radar technology, he had found favor with his teachers and fellow students. He was also known as a good public debater, a skill much in demand in the early years of the Cultural Revolution. In 1968 he was assigned to a good job in a research institute in Chengdu, a city in the southwestern province of Sichuan. But only a few months after he got there, Mao had come up with a new idea: all young intellectuals should be sent to the countryside to learn from peasants. Liu went first to till paddy fields on a farm near Macao and then to another farm in Hunan that used to be a labor camp for criminals. In 1970, however, his luck changed and he was transferred to Beijing to work as an engineer in the prestigious Academy of Sciences' Institute of Computing Technology. Even though the Cultural Revolution was still in full swing and most "intellectual" institutions had been disbanded, the institute was allowed to continue with its work because it was designated as a military unit, "Army BJ 116."

By the early eighties, China had stood down from its war footing and military budgets were being cut. The Institute of Computing Technology had more than a thousand scientists and five hundred workers on its payroll when its funding was slashed. For Liu, as it turned out, that was to be the luckiest break of all. The institute could no longer afford to keep so many intellectuals in its suffocating embrace and encouraged several young scientists to find an income by themselves. A group of them set up the cumbersomely named New Technology Development Company of the Institute of Computing Technology of the Chinese Academy of Sciences in December 1984. Its headquarters was a sixty-five-square-foot cinderblock bungalow that served as the institute's gatehouse. It had a cement floor, no sofa, no armchairs, and no computers; just two benches and two desks with three drawers each. From the outside, it was about as unprepossessing as could be imagined. But that was where Lenovo got its start, and the timing could not have been more auspicious. In the same month as the scientists moved into their spartan gatehouse, the government of Deng Xiaoping approved a document that stated, famously, that some people would be allowed to get rich first.

"Rich" would not have described Liu then. Like the forty other scientists' families at the institute, he lived in a one-room, forty-square-foot brick structure that he built with his own hands in the institute's bicycle parking lot. He and his colleague Li Qin, who was later to become a vice president of Legend, used to go together to fetch sand from a nearby construction site to make the mortar between the bricks. The two of them built the kitchen together, and Liu plastered newspapers on the walls and put a reed mat on the ceiling. He, his wife, and their newly born son lived in these cramped quarters. One day, when Liu's wife was washing a lot of clothes, a sock dropped unnoticed into a cooking pot and nearly became soup. Liu's salary was just over $13 a month, a wage on which a family had to save patiently for months just to buy a pair of cotton long johns.

But things were changing. The institute gave him 200,000 renminbi in seed money to get his company started, along with the authority to spend the money how he wished, to employ whom he liked, and to decide business strategy by himself. Unlike other entrepreneurs at this time who branched off on their own, Liu saw the value in maintaining strong links with the institute. He gained the respect that the institute's name offered and the close relationship with the government that it signified, and he had access to the institute's research and expertise.

In spite of this, however, his first business ventures ended in failure. He and his colleagues lost their bearings and started to trade all manner of products, looking for quick profits. They bought and sold electronic watches, sneakers, track suits, and refrigerators, and managed to lose two-thirds of the seed capital to a swindler in Jiangxi who had promised to sell them TVs. That could have been the end of Liu's business career had it not been for the decision of the Academy of Sciences to buy five hundred IBM computers. Liu and his team landed the contract to maintain those computers and earned back their losses. As he got to know the computer business better, he could not help noticing the markup that retailers were making by selling imported products such as those from IBM. The import price for IBM's PC 286 was 20,000 renminbi, but retailers sold them for 40,000. Liu had an idea of what he was going to do next.

Later, he remembered his first meeting as an IBM sales rep. "I was sitting in the last row in my father's old suit for the whole day and didn't get a chance to talk," said Liu, a powerfully built man with a broad face and prominent canine teeth. "It was all new and startling. Even in my dreams I never imagined that one day we could buy the IBM PC business. It was unthinkable. Impossible."

Those early days after he jumped into the sea of business were difficult and unpredictable. Liu had to swallow his pride on many occasions, drawing on the resilience that he had built up during his turbulent student days. Once, when Liu was angling to secure a license, a man in his twenties cursed him to his face, but he still invited the young man out to dinner and flattered him enough to achieve his aim. On another occasion, Liu and his associates spent 25,570 renminbi to buy ten TV sets, two refrigerators, and ten bottles of Maotai wine as "gifts" for officials who needed to be kept sweet. Yet another time, he waited all night by the door of a defaulter with a brick in his hand, and when the unsuspecting man returned home, he got such a shock that he paid up. But although Liu could be tough on outsiders, he lavished attention on those who worked for him. In 1989 food was hard to come by in Beijing and inflation was galloping ahead at a fierce pace. So Liu went to

Shandong and lent peasants there 100,000 renminbi, telling them that they did not need to repay with money, only with vegetables and pork.

That is what doing business in the 1980s was like. But as his employees ate the pork and vegetables that had come by train from Shandong, they worked on a project of global significance — their first computer. As soon as the prototype was cobbled together out of smuggled parts intended for the computers of other companies, Liu began to harbor dreams for the future. The company's name was changed to Legend, and a strict — not to say militaristic — corporate culture that Liu fondly called the "Spartacus matrix" was adopted. All employees had to go for a morning run, then sing the Legend song, and then study. If managers were late for a meeting, they had to stand in a corner as the meeting progressed.

It was around this time too that the company developed its breakthrough product, a circuit board that would allow IBM PCs to process Chinese characters. The Chinese language system helped them sell imported PCs, which gave them distribution experience and an understanding of consumer needs. In 1990 they started to assemble PCs under their own brand name as well as sell printers for Hewlett-Packard and computers for AST, a now defunct U.S. manufacturer. Following that, business took off, and in 1994 Legend was listed on the Hong Kong stock market. The company copied Hewlett-Packard's sales management system and applied it to the network it was increasingly using to sell its own branded products in China, and it also copied HP's employee ID card. Liu acknowledged once that Legend was the rising brand, but HP was Legend's teacher.

In the late 1990s and in the first two years of this century, things seemed to go swimmingly. Legend computers became the market leader and then extended their lead over IBM, HP, Compaq, and others. At its zenith, the market share of Legend computers hit 30 percent. But after China's accession to the World Trade Organization, which dispensed with many of the restrictions hobbling the foreign competitors, Legend's rivals began to make up lost territory. Liu described the dynamic like this: "In the past, Chinese enterprises competed with foreign counterparts rather as in a race between a turtle and a rabbit in a swamp. The foreigners, the rabbits, complained that the race was unfair, but after China's WTO accession, we are now competing on a racetrack."

Things began to go awry. The company, by now called Lenovo, saw its share of the domestic computer market slip to around 27 percent in late 2004 and early 2005. Hundreds of young Chinese companies sprang up, copying exactly what Liu had begun twenty years earlier, assembling cheap, serviceable computers from a grab bag of parts and selling them at discount prices. Various attempts to diversify into other businesses failed. A fervent hope that making cell phone handsets would deliver much-needed profits proved misguided after the industry was savaged by the old afflictions of oversupply and price wars. A highly touted initiative to set up an Internet portal, FM365, with AOL Time Warner and a planned investment of $200 million foundered over a lack of chemistry between the two companies. And the rabbits — especially one called Dell — were starting to move so quickly into the China market that the turtle, for the first time in eight years, feared that it might surrender its position as market leader. All these problems in the domestic market led Liu to look for a dramatic solution. He found it in IBM.

After buying the American icon, he explained his reasoning. "What we did was to let the turtle ride on top of the rabbit and let the rabbit run. IBM is the rabbit, and Lenovo is the turtle on the rabbit's back. Let it take us forward."

There could be no doubt after that comment that Lenovo saw the IBM acquisition as part of the answer to its domestic troubles. But Liu, who was due to retire from his day-to-day involvement with the company after the deal was done, also saw IBM as a route into unfamiliar foreign markets. "What do we want from this deal?" Liu asked. "We want brand. Can we build up our own brand? It is tough. We want teams of internationalized talents. IBM already has such teams. We want market, distribution, and sales networks. IBM has them. We want technology. IBM has it."

Acquisitions such as the ones by Lenovo and TCL are attempts to enrich China's impoverished repertoire of corporate brands. On a human level, the same impulse for respect and invisible capital motivates a demand for overseas education. Although Beijing's record in improving the availability and quality of the education it provides for its people has been impressive, there is an insatiable thirst for more. And the "branding" that comes with a degree from a respected foreign university such as Harvard and MIT or Oxford and Cambridge is valued at least as much by Chinese society as the knowledge that may have been acquired from studying at a "name" institution.

It is difficult to overstate the potential demand in this area. In the past, for instance, the flow of qualified Chinese applicants to such universities was circumscribed by a lack of financial resources, substandard teaching in many Chinese schools, and an imperfect mastery of the English required for qualifying examinations. But now that China's middle class has swelled to include between 150 million and 200 million people, and education loans secured against property are available from state banks, the potential increase in applications is enormous. English is becoming less of a barrier now that an estimated 200 million Chinese are studying it. Teaching standards are shooting up, and hundreds of thousands of gifted children who just a decade ago would have been denied anything but a rudimentary education are now thriving under competent instruction. What this portends for the world can be seen in the number of participants in the 2004 International Science and Engineering Fair, run by Intel, the American semiconductor company. In the United States, 65,000 students competed in local fairs; in China, 6 million did.

It did not take long before the number of Chinese applicants to schools and universities abroad bumped up against limits imposed by physical capacity and the availability of visas. These constraints, in turn, have fostered a second phenomenon: China has embarked on an intensive program to build new, world-class colleges and universities. By around 2015 it plans to have funneled an additional $550 billion into education, investing in centers of excellence that will train scientists able to lead the world in their fields. Given the extraordinary success of the government's efforts so far (increasing the proportion of the college-age population in higher education to roughly 20 percent from just 1.4 percent in 1978), such goals do not appear to be overambitious. Already in engineering, the focus of the nation's education efforts, China is training some 442,000 new undergraduates a year, along with 48,000 graduate students and 8,000 Ph.D.s. These figures could more than double over the next decade if the government can fulfill its plans. By comparison, the United States — which during the modern era has given the world the telephone, the lightbulb, the airplane, the automobile, the refrigerator, the television, the personal computer, the global positioning system, and thousands of other inventions — is training only around 70,000 new engineering undergraduates each year.

Faced with such prospects, a mini gold rush is under way among American and European universities seeking opportunities to establish full campuses in China or at least to offer courses in existing Chinese universities. Such joint ventures did not exist before 1995, but now there are more than seven hundred foreign academic programs being taught in China. Leading the way are American institutions, ranging from large public colleges like the University of Maryland to smaller private entities such as Lakeland College in Sheboygan, Wisconsin. Educational establishments from the United Kingdom, Australia, Canada, Japan, and Singapore are also either building campuses or pursuing cooperative ventures. The foreign schools are sometimes motivated by the lure of untapped income from the world's fastest-emerging market for education, but they are finding that the low tuition fees they can charge often fail to offset the cost of employing professors from overseas. In the event, some foreign professors schedule trips to China for short bursts of lectures before returning home to teach the rest of the syllabus over the Internet.

Notwithstanding the problems encountered in delivering an education of a Western standard to Chinese students in China, the trend is expected to continue, mainly for economic reasons.

The cost of building a campus is a fraction of what it would be in the United States or Europe, foreign textbooks are sold by official decree at a deep discount to their prices overseas, and swapping foreign lecturers for their mainland counterparts has helped to keep payrolls in check. All of this has meant that the cost of teaching students until graduation in China is significantly lower than in the West, even if they are attending a foreign campus that has been transplanted to a Chinese city. That has stark implications for the future of education worldwide. The current outflow of Chinese students to universities in Europe and the United States may in the not-too-distant future start to be matched by an inflow of foreign students looking for an economical education, at a foreign campus in China or even at a Chinese university.

8

Communism vs. Democracy

ANY OF THE WEAKNESSES and deficiencies described in the previous two chapters can be traced back to one overarching contradiction: China tries to run an increasingly sophisticated capitalist economy with a political system that was designed to issue crisp commands from a single source of authority, and to be obeyed. This observation is not controversial, nor is it insightful; political scientists have been pointing out as much throughout the era of reform since 1978. Indeed, it is widely accepted that China's crisis of trust, environmental malaise, rampant piracy, and official corruption derive at least in part from systemic inadequacies thrown up by the country's transition. For much of the past two and a half decades, these problems have mainly been the concern of the Chinese themselves and a limited circle of Sinologists abroad. The intricacies that surrounded the dichotomy between communism and capitalism were primarily the preserve of academic political scientists. But since China has become an inescapable global force, the glaring mismatch between its political and economic polities has become an issue not just for Beijing but also for Washington, Tokyo, Brussels, London, and other national capitals.

That is because the influences that China has on the world are all external expressions of internal affairs. Just as the decisions of the White House invite international scrutiny from the governments and people affected by them, so China's trade partners increasingly feel the need to address the systemic sources of the issues they are confronting. Signs of this trend are already in evi-

★

dence. The reasons that the bid by CNOOC, the Chinese oil company, for its U.S. counterpart, Unocal, foundered all had to do with American misgivings over China's political economy. Similarly, protectionist sentiment welling up in Congress, industry associations, and trade unions derives much of its impetus from arguments that the Chinese *system* puts U.S. competitors at an unfair disadvantage.

As a result, the spotlight is falling ever more unsparingly on a number of sensitive issues: Beijing's insistence on keeping the renminbi's value fixed at what American critics think is an unjustifiably low rate; the government's ban on independent unions for migrant workers so they have little power to campaign for more pay; the domestic prices of water, electricity, and oil, which are kept low by administrative fiat or state subsidies; the heavy restrictions on capital flows, which act as a mechanism to support Chinese banks; the many industries in which foreign investment is limited; the incapacity of the state to bring counterfeit pirates to book; the export of pollution to neighbors because of ineffective environmental safeguards; and the illegal felling of rain forests overseas by China-based syndicates.

Thus China's vulnerability to international censure — and therefore to the protectionism and obstructionism that threaten to frustrate its economic ascent — flows in almost every case from the unevenness of its political and economic transition. But if so much is at stake, why is it that Beijing does not accelerate its political reforms and adopt the type of law-based, multiparty democratic system that has proven itself as an effective regulator of capitalist economies all over the world? That's the 64-million-renminbi question, and one on which there may be no consensus or answer for a long time to come. One way to elucidate the issues in play, however, is to consider the life and career of Cao Siyuan, one of China's most brilliant and dogged advocates of reform.

Cao is a short, rotund man with thick spectacles and unruly hair. His face, with its gentle folds and bunched-up cheeks, looks as if it has been molded by laughter. And, as you get to know him, this impression is reinforced. He laughs frequently, often at his own jokes, and with various seismic intensities. The lowest gradation is a good-natured chuckle, which either peters out into conversation or rises to a more generous eruption that can escalate to the highest pitch of hilarity: a wheezing, body-reverberating guffaw. In conversation he can be lyrical or blunt, but he is rarely bashful about letting his audience know of the part he has played in some of China's pivotal moments. He dramatizes his speech by slipping from time to time into the third person. Devices such as "And what do you think Cao Siyuan did next?" or "When Cao Siyuan heard that, he . . ." are deployed as he gets closer to the point he wants to make. Yet he can also be self-effacing. Even though he spent six years working in Zhongnanhai, the exclusive compound that houses the ruling elite in central Beijing, he says his own role there never amounted to more than that of a "seventh-grade, sesame-seed-size official." He also enjoys poking gentle fun at his roly-poly physical appearance. After making an observation along the lines of "In those days I was a mere slip of a thing, no more than a bag of skin and bones," he will pause mischievously to watch for his listeners' reaction. If he senses a flicker of incredulity, the reverberating laugh may follow.

In China he is not well known by his real name, but if you mention Cao Pochan — "Bankruptcy Cao" — to someone, you may get a nod of recognition. The foreign media, to which he sometimes makes himself available, often call him, on second reference, simply "Mr. Bankruptcy." His nickname comes from the fact that he was the architect of China's first bankruptcy law. That may not sound like much. But in the late 1980s bankruptcy was at the cutting edge of the ideological transition from communism to capitalism. It was the Rubicon that, once crossed, rendered hollow any lingering pretense that Beijing was trying to build an economy along Communist lines. Communism was all about production, not profit and loss. But bankruptcy not only recognized financial performance, it also made it the key criterion for corporate survival. Once bankruptcy had insinuated itself into the code of commerce, other expressions of capitalism were sure to follow.

Companies would have to cut costs, improve productivity, and put a value on their assets. The "iron rice bowl" notion that factories existed to provide lifetime employment for the proletariat and production for the masses was doomed to dereliction.

On one of the first occasions that I met Cao, we had dinner in the St. Regis Hotel with the editor of the *Financial Times* and other colleagues from London. The St. Regis is a self-styled "six-star hotel," and the restaurant we had chosen offered some of the most upscale Chinese cuisine in Beijing. As we arrived, we were shown past a painted lacquer screen to a table in a discreet corner, where Cao, settling into his chair, called over the waitress and made an impromptu order. A few minutes later it arrived on a bed of ice in a boat made of woven rattan, beneath a mainsail carved out of a white radish and placed artfully around a carrot mast. Over the boat's prow sat the sculpted head of a dragon, hewn from a sizable block of pink turnip. We all stared as the waitress lowered the boat and placed it diagonally across the center of our table. We peered in to see what she had brought. It was *long xia*, "dragon prawn," more commonly known as lobster. The dinner passed convivially, with Cao, in an ebullient mood, charming us with his wit and insights. At the end, after we bade him a fond farewell, the editor called over the waitress and took the check. As he looked at it, I could not tell whether the expression that formed on his face was a grin or a grimace. "No wonder they call him Mr. Bankruptcy," he said. The lobster we had consumed turned out to be of the Australian-reared, air-freighted, $300-a-pop variety.

During the dinner, though, Cao said something that to me, at least, was well worth the price of the lobster. I was to keep his words with me throughout my seven-year reporting assignment. I came to see them as a basic formula for understanding the twists and turns and ups and downs of China's political economy. *Gaige tai kuai, jiu luan. Gaige tai man, jiu si*, or "When reform is too fast there is chaos. When reform is too slow there is stagnation." Put another way, it meant that without the liberalization of controls on the economy, growth would slow and eventually stop. But if the pace of liberalization was too fast, the rapid growth that resulted could spill over into disorder. On the face of it, this was straightforward enough, but there was an added, paradoxical twist: the legitimacy of the Communist Party sprang from both growth *and* control. Yet in order to get more of one, it had to sacrifice part of the other.

Without fast growth, Beijing has no chance of meeting its job creation targets, and too few jobs could mean social instability. But surrendering administrative control to the invisible hand of the market saps the essential power that sustains a single-party state. So the Party is a reluctant reformer, and in areas where control is critical to maintaining its rule, the Party has tended to resist liberalizations that go beyond the superficial. The reluctance also means that when things are going well and the economy is riding high, reform generally decelerates, only to pick up again when the tide of growth ebbs. The waves of activity created by this interplay of government fear and covetousness define the economy's momentum.

Some call this the "business cycle," but that does not quite capture it. It is, like a lot of things in China these days, a sort of amalgam, a yin and yang, of business and politics. And Cao, by the nature of his work as a leading advocate of reform, has found himself bound up with its undulations. Typically he would be busiest during the cycle's troughs, when the government was receptive to ideas of how it might generate growth. During the booms, however, his services were less in official demand.

His ebullience during the St. Regis dinner was partly due to the fact that in 1999 China was weathering the aftermath of the Asian crisis and the government was receptive to ideas. But his mood that night was in strong contrast with the torment he had been through. His troubles had begun in 1989, the year that a boom created by the first decade of reforms overheated, kindling the grievances that fueled antigovernment demonstrations in Tiananmen Square. When those protests were eventually crushed by the tanks and troops of the People's Liberation Army, Cao and many others were rounded up and thrown in jail. He had not been a leader of the disturbances or one of a number of "black hands" whom the government accused of inciting students to protest the nepotism, corruption, and despotism of the Communist Party and, later, to demand an all-out shift to Western-style democracy.

Nevertheless, he had been involved in the drama in a different way, one that reveals a tantalizing missed opportunity for political reform. In addition to being the author of the bankruptcy law, Cao at that time was also a policy adviser to Zhao Ziyang, the head of the Communist Party. Zhao was not exactly a democratizer, but he was part of a minority of Chinese leaders who seemed to believe that economic and political reform were two sides of the same coin. He had suggested a number of mainly technical ways to make the bureaucracy more accountable to the people it ruled, but before any of them could be implemented, he became embroiled in a series of events that would be his and Cao's undoing. He argued against using military force to quell the protests in Tiananmen Square, fielding fierce opposition from his hard-line colleagues. When they prevailed and imposed martial law about two weeks before the troops were called in, Zhao was put under house arrest and remained there until his death in early 2005. Cao, though, made a desperate attempt to save his boss and prevent the army crackdown.

Audaciously, Cao treated the institutions of the state as if they were part of a democracy. The plan was to turn the National People's Congress (NPC), the toothless legislature that is used to rubber-stamp Party directives, into a political tiger. Working with Li Shuguang, another Beijing academic, he cited Article 29 of the nation's constitution — the statutes of which are often neglected — to argue that the imposition of martial law against a peaceful people's demonstration was in violation of the principle that the People's Liberation Army "belongs to the people." It was clear, Cao and Li went on, that the only way forward was for the NPC to impeach Li Peng, the premier, for imposing martial law in the first place. Given that an impeachment of this type had never before been attempted and that the NPC had never been used to check Party power, it was surprising that Cao's initiative made any headway at all. Yet he and Li managed to collect fifty-seven signatures, all from people on the NPC's top committee, in support of impeachment. In the end, of course, Premier Li crushed the attempt to unseat him and ordered the military crackdown that began on the evening of June 3, when Cao was also arrested. Nevertheless, if his attempt to use the NPC to impeach a premier had succeeded, China's future might have been radically different.

Cao was released from jail just under one year after his arrest at a vegetable market near his office. He was freed along with another 210 people who were, according to the official Xinhua News Agency, being given "lenient treatment" but who would be severely punished if they failed to repent of their "criminal activities" and began doing "evil" all over again.[1] In common with almost all of those arrested following the massacre, Cao was not charged with any crime or offered an apology when he was released. As far as he was concerned, he had acted entirely in accordance with the rights afforded him by the constitution. In any event, he kept a low profile for most of the rest of the 1990s, declining media interviews and concentrating on a new career as an adviser for his own company, the Siyuan Bankruptcy and Merger Consultancy.

So it was with some relish that, with the economy faltering in 1998 and 1999, Cao returned to his role as an activist. He was forthright in his opinions and sometimes mischievous in his turn of phrase. When I asked him what was meant by the term "the collective leadership," the way that newspapers then described the pinnacle of Party power, he replied, "Collective leadership means never knowing which bottom should be spanked." Later, he had the following to say about being critical of the government:

> Often when I am making speeches, people ask me, "Cao Siyuan, will the central government be able to accept your points of view?" I say: "Why do you always ask whether the central government will be willing to accept them or not?" What is the central government? They are servants. They are the servants of the people. You cannot use acceptance as a standard to judge

servants. For example, if at home I hire a maid to do the cooking, I do not try to do everything the maid wants. The maid should ask me what I like to eat. The relationship between citizens and public servants should not be transposed.

But in spite of his daring, he was not a dissident, and if you asked him to describe his role in life, he would say:

I think that on the dramatic stage there should be different types of actor. There should be those with red faces, those with white faces, clowns, beauties, sages. In the same way, on the stage of history there should also be different roles. If you said that red faces are good, then I ask, is it good to have a whole stage full of red faces? Nobody is able to be everything, so what should Cao Siyuan be? The result of my research is that I should be a student of the people. As a student of the people, how do I define my job? I define it by making suggestions. I am a "suggestive student of the people." I suggested making a bankruptcy law. I suggested having people in to listen to the National People's Congress. I suggested privatization, etc. I specialize in suggestions and I don't complain. Is it that there are no complaints at the pit of my stomach? No! My whole belly is full of complaints. The problem is that complaining does not solve problems. In my articles I never criticize people, never complain, I only write prescriptions. If someone is ill, I never say "They should die, they should have died long ago." I say "They still can be saved" and the prescription is as follows.

As 1999 wore on, with urban unemployment surging and outbreaks of social unrest proliferating nationwide, the prescription Cao had in mind was privatization. He could see that private companies were far more dynamic than their state-run cousins and that they could provide the jobs the country badly needed. He could also see that the central government was reluctant to give free rein to private enterprises because, by their nature, they represented a dilution of state control. Although the NPC had passed an amendment to the constitution in 1998 saying that private enterprise should be regarded as a "component part" of the economy, it left no doubt that state enterprises should remain dominant. Another indication that Beijing was ambivalent about the rise of the private sector: Jiang Zemin, the president, was traveling around the country making speeches pledging that the government would never promote the privatization of state enterprises. Cao, meanwhile, was also traveling the country, urging the exact opposite. It was highly unlikely that their paths would cross; it is easier, as the Chinese say, to climb a tree to catch a fish than it is for an ordinary citizen to gain an audience with the general secretary of the Communist Party.

But then, out of the blue, an opportunity presented itself. Cao was invited to speak at a forum organized by *Fortune* magazine in Shanghai. When he looked at the program, he saw that he would be onstage in the auditorium just a few hours before Jiang himself. Prior to leaving Beijing, he called me excitedly. He told me I should be ready for some news. I asked what sort of news, but he would say only that he was going to drop a bombshell. Later, in a speech he made to overseas Chinese in New York, Cao described what happened at the Shanghai forum:

Where do you think Cao Siyuan was when Jiang was giving his speech? Sitting about thirty meters away! When he finished and returned to his seat, I put books in both of my hands and waltzed over to him. Some people say the head of state is closely protected by guards, so how can you get near him? When I gave a speech at Columbia University, someone asked me if I could have been shot walking over to him. So how was it that I was able to march up to Jiang Zemin while keeping life and limb intact? Well, because when I worked in Zhongnanhai for six years, I was able to ingest deeply the code of the secret service. That code, however, I regret I am unable to share with you today.

Anyway, Jiang was just sitting there with his gaze directed forward when this fattypuff lumbers into his field of vision from the right. He turns to look and suddenly our lines of sight cross. He is staring at me and I am staring at him. I meet his gaze and walk over to face him. I discover that Jiang Ze-min's eyes are glistening. Maybe he is thinking, Who is this guy? I don't do the normal thing and say who I am, I just put one of my books into his hand. He sees the book title, *The Wind and Clouds of Bankruptcy,* and at the bottom it says, "Author, Cao Siyuan."

He says, "So you are Cao Siyuan," and I say, "At your service." Then I give him thirty seconds to remember how our paths once crossed by saying: "Thank you, Chairman Jiang, for your generous support when you were mayor of Shanghai and I came to do an investigation on matters related to the bank-ruptcy law. I have written about your support in this book, on page 111."

When he heard this, he was, of course, happy. A smile spread across his face, and it was during his delight that I offered him the second book. The second book was *Society's Righteous Path Toward Privatization.* He has just been on the podium saying, "We are absolutely not doing privatization," and here I am not only doing it, but doing it right under his nose. If Jiang had thrown a wobbly and slapped the table and said "Take him away!" I would have been finished. But I calculated that there would be another outcome. Maybe he would not only keep his temper, but he might also think, "Why is Cao Siyuan so auda-cious? Why is he calling it *Society's Righteous Path Toward Priva-tization?* Maybe I should find out for myself by reading the book."

But there was no way I was going to leave it at that, just giv-ing him the books and leaving. So I pulled out a name card and gave it to him, saying, "If you need anything, call me."[2]

Jiang did not call, and it is not known whether Cao's bomb-shell had any impact on the course of privatization. What is true, though, is that at the Sixteenth Congress of the Communist Party, in late 2002, the constitution was amended to put private business on an equal footing with state corporations. In addition, private entrepreneurs were allowed to join the Party, and a small handful were even given invitations to attend the congress itself, in the Great Hall of the People.

Then, unfortunately for the cause of privatization and for Cao's well-being, the economy began to take off again. Growth in 2003 surged, and the pressure on the government to create jobs abated. The Communist Party had had to surrender considerable control to deliver the growth it needed: since 1998 it had privatized almost all of the country's urban housing stock, laid off more than twenty-five million workers from state companies, allowed hundreds of thousands of state companies to free themselves from the burden of providing medical care for employees and schooling for their children, and promulgated new freedoms, allowing tens of millions of people to travel from the countryside to cities in search of work.

But since the growth spurt that followed those liberalizations kicked in, Beijing has taken the opportunity to consolidate its power. It has conspicuously failed to follow through on the Sixteenth Party Congress's promise to put private enterprises on an equal footing with state corporations. Private companies are still restricted from "strategic sectors" such as retail banking, investment banking, basic telecom services, newspapers, television, publishing, oil and gas extraction, power generation, railways, ports, and petrochemicals. In addition, private companies still find it difficult to get permission to be listed on the stock market, and only 40 out of the 1,600 listed companies are private. They also run into obstacles when trying to secure financing from an overwhelmingly state-run banking system, receiving as little as 10 percent of the total bank loans annually. As Yasheng Huang of the Harvard Business School notes, private companies, far from being accorded equal status with their state brethren, are actually treated worse than foreign companies.[3] The latest example of this was in the sale of several multibillion-dollar equity stakes in state banks in 2005. Foreign financial institutions have shelled out more than $20 billion to buy the various minority stakes on offer, but participation by private Chinese companies has been barred.

In fact, the first two years of the tenure of Hu Jintao, who took over from Jiang Zemin as Party chief in late 2002, have been marked by a distinct emphasis on the primacy of large, efficient state-owned companies. Corporations such as the oil giants Petro-China, Sinopec, and CNOOC, all of which are rising in the rankings of the world's largest companies, are considered models of state capitalism. But as Hu and his administration promote the interests of large state firms, the nonstate reform agenda has slipped and Cao's situation has also taken a turn for the worse. Following a conference he organized in the eastern port city of Qingdao in mid-2003, during which he called for a major overhaul of the constitution, his phone has been tapped, he has been followed, and he was banned from making or attending public speeches. His clients have been warned away from him.

These days Cao is back to living the low-profile life that he remembers from the previous boom, in the mid-1990s. He maintains contact with his circle of friends, finds work here and there, and continues to write essays and books. But there is at least one difference between now and then: technology has allowed him a wider audience for the short poems that he writes in a classical meter and sends out from his cell phone. Those that I have received have been elegantly written and melancholy. Many allude to unappreciated service, a theme that is almost as old as China itself. One poem recalled Qu Yuan, a brilliant and upright adviser to an emperor in ancient times who hanged himself when he could no longer be loyal to his monarch and to the interests of his country at the same time. Another poem, received at the time of the midautumn festival, when the Chinese admire the moon and think existential thoughts, went like this:

> Year after year, when the autumn wind picks up,
> We say goodbye to summer and welcome the frost.
> If you plant melon, melons grow. Beans yield beans.
> Sweet or bitter, who can dictate which?
> Eating melon, gazing at the moon,
> The world is multipolar yet singular, love is universal
>   yet in one heart.

The last line, read another way, can also mean "The world is mul-
tipolar yet singular, charity resides with the central government."

The main problem with China's political system is that it does not
permit the checks and balances necessary to supervise and regulate a capitalist economy in an efficient manner. In a democracy,
this is achieved by configuring the system so that each organ of
government and each economic entity is regulated or overseen by
another external and independent body. The whole edifice is then
supervised by the will of the voting public. But a Communist political system is engineered to venerate and sustain a single source
of authority. Thus the Chinese Communist Party is officially held
to reside above everything, including the law. There are no direct,
public elections for Party posts (some experimental village-level
elections that have been permitted are for the non-Party post of
village chief), so there is no mechanism to allow political renewal
through a popular mandate. Each level of the bureaucracy reports
to and takes orders from officials on the next rung up, creating
a giant pyramidal structure in which the chain of command is
mostly vertical. No organization engaged in governance is permitted to exist independently of the Party. Even nongovernmental organizations, of which there are an increasing number, are
supposed to maintain an affiliation with a Party body and to support its work. Religions, too, are free to practice as long as they
accept — at least nominally — that the Party, which is atheist, is a
higher authority than their own spiritual leader.

Such a system does not lend itself to supervision by external
forces because it recognizes no authority greater than its own.
That does not matter in a centrally planned economy, in which
the Party is master of all it surveys. But it is far from adequate in
a capitalist system animated by the antagonism of competition.
It has become clear in recent years that the Party is fully aware
of this mismatch and has poured enormous energy into attempt-
ing to create the impossible: a system of self-regulation in politics,
law, and the economy under which all parties are equal but the
Party is more equal than the others.

The waste generated by this grand project of political engineering is evident in many places, but nowhere is it more pronounced than in the most democratic of all capitalist institutions, the stock market. In the West, stock markets function by allowing the investing public to supervise the actions of corporate decision makers. If investors do not like the strategy of a CEO, they can "vote" against it by selling their shares. But in China the system has been turned on its head, so the bosses of publicly traded companies do not have to suffer the indignity of listening to the opinions of minority shareholders. In fact, every aspect of the system has been designed to extract a maximum of public money while surrendering a minimum of accountability. Companies typically float less than one-third of their share capital, so even if minority shareholders banded together, they would still be unable to influence the decisions of the board of directors. Lax disclosure rules mean that listed companies are required to divulge a bare minimum of financial information, and even that, it has transpired, is often false. The decision as to which companies may be listed is made not on the basis of financial health but by Party officials, with the predictable result that only a small number of listed companies are private and the rest are the corporate offspring of the Party and the state.

With so many of the state's interests at stake, the market regulator, the China Securities and Regulatory Commission (CSRC), does not even pretend to be independent. Shang Fulin, the CSRC boss, takes his orders from a "leading group" of Party officials who dictate what should happen in the financial sector. He regularly makes public statements about how he is taking steps to boost share prices and drive the index upward. And when prices edge down, other Party branches can be called upon to join a chorus of bulls. The starkest example of this was in 1999 when, in the aftermath of the Asian financial typhoon, the *People's Daily*, the official mouthpiece of the Party, tried to lift a soggy market by declaring on its front page that securities markets were facing "uncommon opportunities for development" and that the Party had "firm confidence" on behalf of investors.[4]

But as the years have passed, the costs to China from its regulatory laxity have been expressed in a legion of corporate corruption scandals. One of these involved a department store and distribution company based in Zhengzhou, the provincial capital of Henan, China's largest province. The company, Zhengzhou Baiwen,[5] was run by Li Fuqian, a former soldier who had started in the shop as a counter assistant in the mid-1970s, after leaving the army. In those days that was a dream job, because people who worked in shops had access to rationed commodities before anyone else. Baiwen was owned by the Zhengzhou branch of the Communist Party, so it was naturally one of the first chosen for a stock exchange listing, even though it did not meet a prerequisite that it had to be profitable. A small lie was required, but Li and his associates decided to tell a big one: they claimed that the company's profits had increased thirty-six-fold in the ten years before its flotation in 1996. When those numbers were announced, the investing public took note, and Baiwen's share price soared.

In 1997 the company was named a "red flag," a rare official distinction that denoted it was a model from which others should learn. Li was also selected as a "model worker" at a Party ceremony in Beijing, and when he got home, he maneuvered himself into the posts of chairman and Party secretary of Baiwen in addition to the position of president, which he already held.

From then on, he made all decisions single-handedly. A few months after that, he issued the order that the company should attain "double 8" — reaching 8 billion renminbi in sales and 80 million renminbi in profits, even though he knew these figures bore no relation to the company's actual performance. They were in fact double the numbers the company was then publicly announcing, and those were already wild exaggerations. In reality, Baiwen was losing millions. But on the strength of the falsified figures, it managed to raise another large dollop from the stock market, which Li poured into a dizzying array of schemes, run by people to whom he owed political debts.

When the company toppled, Li was fined and thrown in jail. But the most extraordinary passage in the story was yet to come.

The CSRC, or the shadowy Party officials from whom it takes its orders, decided that even though Baiwen was insolvent several times over, it should not be declared bankrupt or have its stock market listing revoked. The government, which still owned most of Baiwen's shares, ordered the state to arrange a bailout, and after some restructuring, the company just carried on trading.

The malignancy that Baiwen represented has spread, and the stock market has been rocked by one scandal after another. In 2001 the CSRC found forty instances of companies faking their results, including one called Yinguangxia, which fabricated almost $100 million in profits.[6] Around the same time, several stock price manipulation scandals were also making headlines. The worst involved Yorkpoint, a science and technology company based in the southern boomtown of Shenzhen, which managed to enlist the help of around 120 financial institutions, mostly securities companies, in twenty provinces and municipalities to spend more than $500 million dollars to push up the company's share price before taking profits and letting it crash.[7]

In 2004 one of China's most respected companies, the car-parts-to-ketchup conglomerate D'Long, was also caught in fraudulent dealings worth an estimated $3.6 billion.[8] Later in the same year, Huayin Trust and Dalian Securities were dragged down after it came to light that the chairman of both companies had engaged in a $3.1 billion fraud.[9] Southern Securities, an industry pioneer with impeccable connections to the Communist Party, also succumbed in a $2.4 billion scandal that mainly involved executive theft.[10] In 2005 the chairman and the chief financial officer at Yili, a dairy company of nationwide renown, were arrested on suspicion of embezzling $50 million.

Similar problems and others afflict the banking sector, and there, too, the lack of regulatory independence is a root cause. The "big four" banks, which control more than half of the country's deposits and loans, are all owned by the state. Their presidents dress like bankers and talk like bankers, but they are, in fact, high-ranking Party officials who are appointed to their posts by the Party's personnel department. After having served their term, the executives are rotated back to positions at the top of the People's Bank of China, the central bank. While in their jobs at the "big four," the presidents all insist that their banks are "commercial." What they mean is that the decision a bank makes in regard to lending money to a company is based solely on the judgment of whether that company will be able to repay its debt plus interest. Following several years of reform, this claim may be more true than it used to be, but the reality is still that if an important state company needs a loan, or a big state project needs funding, the "big four" can be counted on to oblige, regardless of commercial considerations. In return, these banks can feel secure in the knowledge that they will never be allowed to fail, no matter how many bad debts pile up on their balance sheets. The central bank, which regulates the banking industry alongside the recently established China Banking Regulatory Commission, has a track record of bailing out the "big four" every time they need it.

The cost to China of this system shows up in the money that the central bank has spent on bailing out the "big four" and other financial institutions. If the various cash infusions and bad-debt relief for the state banks over the past five years are added together, it transpires that China has allocated nearly $250 billion to bolster its banking system. And the task is far from over. Standard and Poor's, the rating agency, estimates that it may cost the government another $190 billion to clean up the balance sheets of the two worst-performing members of the "big four," the Industrial and Commercial Bank of China and the Agricultural Bank.[11] Additional money will be needed to rehabilitate the tens of thousands of rural credit cooperatives, which are thought to be mostly insolvent, and scores of city commercial banks, another weak pillar in the financial architecture. It is quite possible, then, that the total bill for returning the financial system to health could come to more than $500 billion — or, to put it another way, enough money to build twenty Three Gorges dams across the Yangtze River. Even after that money is spent, the governance deficiencies that contributed to the bad-debt problem in the first place may remain. The probability is that until state banks are divorced from government influence and subjected to the discipline of knowing they may fail, the incidence of reckless, corrupt, and state-guided lending will continue.

In the natural environment, too, similar shortcomings are evident. According to Pan Yue, the outspoken deputy head of the State Environmental Protection Agency (SEPA), the degradation of the environment is exacerbated by the absence of an independent system of supervision. All too often, local authorities own the companies that they regulate and are therefore often unwilling to make them abide by costly environmental safeguards. Meanwhile, the local branches of SEPA are dependent on funding from local authorities, so they have little power to enforce any measure that is unpopular with their mayor's office or, for that matter, with state-run companies that may have strong links to the mayor's office.

The legal system is also beset by such conflicts of interest. Local governments fund local law courts and appoint judges and other legal officials, so a mayor's office can be confident that any ruling it deems important will not go against its interests. Some courts are more compliant than others; a few in Beijing, Shanghai, and other large cities have highly trained legal staffs and are relatively independent, but most provincial and municipal systems lack legally trained staff. When asked, many local officials will claim that their courts are independent and impartial, but sometimes this façade slips. The vice mayor of Wuhu, the second city in Anhui province — famous for the car company Chery, which is owned by the mayor's office — once told me that if Volkswagen was worried that Chery might have violated its intellectual property rights, then it was welcome to come to Wuhu to settle the issue in court. "Let's see who wins," said the vice mayor. Volkswagen decided, in the end, that it would not pursue the issue through the courts.

In other places, such as the northeastern city of Shenyang, the legal system has at times suffered a near-total breakdown. In 2001 the Shenyang procurator's office, a key legal agency, was in thrall to a local mafia boss called Liu Yong, who swaggered about town shooting rival gang leaders with his pistol, ordering the city's police force to torture people who disobeyed him, and engaging in corrupt commercial schemes with the mayor, the taxation bureau, and several other parts of the Shenyang government. Liu even used his connections to get himself a post in the local branch of the National People's Congress before he, the mayor, and several others were arrested and thrown in jail.[12]

It is difficult to put a figure on how much corruption has cost China over the years. But there is no doubt that the bending of rules and massaging of accounts that helped boost economic activity in the early stages of the reform era no longer describe the problem. The abuse of power has now become a debilitating, multibillion-dollar-a-year scam that is eroding the efficiency of almost every organ of the Party and state. The Organization for Economic Cooperation and Development, a group of wealthy nations, estimated in a report that in 2004 corruption in China accounted for between 3 and 5 percent of that year's gross domestic product — between $50 billion and $84 billion.

Such estimates are necessarily based on imperfect data and may well be conservative. Indeed, an examination of government accounts by Li Jinhua, the auditor general, in 2004 suggested that corruption is uniformly present throughout the government — all of the thirty-eight central government ministries and organizations that he investigated were discovered to be cooking their books or using their influence to extract illegal fees.[13] Another audit, in the southern province of Guangdong, one of the country's most economically advanced areas, showed a similarly high incidence of malfeasance. It found that no fewer than four hundred officials were corrupt. Jiang Zemin, the former president and Party boss, said toward the end of his term in office that official corruption had become so injurious that it was jeopardizing "the very existence of the Party and the state."

If that is the case, then why does the Party decline to launch the political reforms necessary to save itself? And why does it continue to preside over a system of governance that is inadequate in serving its burgeoning, increasingly sophisticated economy? There is unlikely to be a single answer. One explanation may be that the economic reforms of the past twenty-eight years have generated so much wealth that Beijing feels able to bank-roll its systemic inefficiencies. Another may be that, contrary to the aura of confidence it strives to project, the Party is so neurotic about the erosion of its executive power that it is in no mood for political liberalization. But in my view the most powerful inhibitor of political reform is corruption itself. Local governments in many parts of the country have been hijacked by special interest syndicates that typically consist of government officials and the most influential local business leaders. These secret syndicates exist to enrich their members, often at the expense of the public, and so they are implacably opposed to any reform that could unravel the web of relationships that boost their bank balances.

No one knows how prevalent these syndicates may be, but a surge in the number of public protests directed at local governments suggests a sharply deteriorating situation. The number of "mass incidents"—the Ministry of Public Security's catchall term for sit-ins, strikes, group petitions, rallies, demonstrations, marches, traffic-blocking, building seizures, and other forms of unrest—reached 74,000 in 2004, an all-time high, and involved 3.7 million individuals. In 1994, by comparison, there were about 10,000 such incidents, with just 730,000 participants.[14]

In 2005 the numbers continued to rise. Although no "mass incidents" have escalated into coordinated, nationwide movements, the dramatic increase in local protests shows that material enrichment alone does not guarantee greater public contentment. In fact, the outbreaks have grown in recent years at roughly the same rate as the economy—that is to say, around 9 percent. In the overwhelming majority of cases, the flare-ups have been sparked by the arbitrary behavior of local government officials who seize land and other assets from ordinary citizens but offer little or no compensation.

There are any number of case studies that demonstrate how officials abuse their administrative powers to enrich themselves and their cronies. In 2003 I began to follow a saga that was played out in the wilds of the northern province of Shaanxi, in towns and villages on the dusty loess plateau, but nevertheless held relevance for the outside world. That is because if incidents such as this come to define the modus operandi of local Chinese governments, then the chances of Beijing being able to bring its political economy into line with international norms may be slim.

The first time I met Feng Bingxian was on one of those rare summer days in Beijing when the hills beyond the western suburbs were visible from Tiananmen Square beneath a fathomless blue sky. I found Feng sitting in the coffee lounge of the VIP section of the Beijing Hotel, next to the banquet hall where Mao had once hosted Nikita Khrushchev, the former Soviet leader. Feng was a thin, wiry man with a cheerful, animated face, and he sat, dressed all in black, behind a glass of kiwi juice. Next to the juice was a Nokia cell phone and the key to a suite costing more than $100 a night.

He had phoned me to say that he was petitioning the government to take action against the wrongs that he had suffered. Foreign journalists regularly received such calls and were frequently reluctant to follow them up because they usually led to hurried, furtive encounters with desperate people in back alleys near the premises of the State Petitions Office, a holdover from imperial times when people of conscience wrote memorials to a supposedly benevolent emperor. It was not the inconvenience of such assignments that made them unpopular, but their hopelessness. Only about two out of a thousand petitions actually led to a resolution, and in most cases petitioners would be kept waiting for years for any news of how their complaint was being processed. But Feng, with his VIP suite and his cell phone, was clearly a different sort of activist.

He was the representative of ten thousand or so private investors in about six thousand small oil wells that had been confiscated without compensation by the authorities in fifteen counties in Shaanxi. The investors were a varied bunch. Some were wealthy entrepreneurs, but the majority were peasant farmers who coaxed a living out of the inhospitable Yellow Earth Plateau, an eroded buffer that protects the central plains from the advancing sands of the Gobi Desert. Many of the farmer-investors had sold their land and furniture to raise money for prospecting. After losing their wells, their income had dried up, and some had turned to loan sharks to fund their children's schooling. The aim of their collective petition was to implore the central government to intervene on their behalf and see that their wells were returned.

Disputes between individuals and local mandarins are common throughout the country, but in some ways this one was different. It was almost certainly the biggest concerted challenge by private-sector interests of their local authorities since private enterprise was first permitted in the early 1980s. To me, that made it an important story. It was a test of the tidy theory that sooner or later single-party politics would bump up against an increasingly free-market economy, and when that happened, the Party would have to yield. Thus the Shaanxi oil well dispute seemed a manifestation of a crucial stage in the country's political evolution.

Feng was blunt about where I fitted into his plans. He had considered appealing to the law courts in Shaanxi but dropped the idea because, as everyone knew, the judges were appointed and paid by the very officials whom the oil well investors wanted to sue. He had tried the State Petitions Office, but not yet to any avail. The local media had found his story too risky to run. So, he said with a worn smile, that left us, the foreign press. There was a chance that our articles, translated into Mandarin, would make it into the "Big Reference," a confidential digest of foreign reports that is circulated only to top cadres. If they saw it, they might be sympathetic, he said.

I said that to write the story I needed to quote him by name and to get the Shaanxi government's version of events. After some persuasion, he agreed to let me use his name. A few days after my article was printed, he received an unexpected, late-evening knock at his hotel room door. Three men, all in black, told him that they were there to take him to a senior official who was interested in hearing his case. The elevator that they took to the lobby was made of glass and ran down one side of the hotel's cavernous atrium. One of the men stood by the door, the other two close to Feng, who could see the lobby-level coffee lounge coming to meet him. Waitresses were wiping down the tables, and along the far wall a fountain made of alabaster animal statues had fallen silent, turned off for the night.

The elevator did not stop at the lobby. It went on to the basement garage, where Feng was bundled into the back of an official car and driven for more than twenty hours to Yulin City, in northern Shaanxi. Without being charged with a crime, he was put in jail. At first his interrogators quizzed him about his contacts with a *Financial Times* journalist, and then they switched to investigating the tax returns from his oil well business. Shortly after his detention, his son called me and, scrupulously polite, asked if there was anything I could do to help. Sheepishly, I said there was not.

Almost a year later, Feng and I met again in Beijing, and far from blaming me for the consequences of our first encounter, he punctuated his account of the abduction, detention, and interrogation with bursts of laughter. He had been released after a month or so in jail on the condition that he would cease his activism. Since then he had lived an itinerant life, sleeping in the apartments of friends or on the office sofas of colleagues, fearful that the police would find him. But there was no question of him giving up. "This used to be about oil wells. Now it is about our rights," he told me. "This used to be a problem. Now it is a cause."

Feng's new strategy was to lobby. He and a growing group of associates had decided to try to win the support of the central government in Beijing by moral suasion and behind-the-scenes activism. Achieving their aim would require turning Beijing against the local authorities in northern Shaanxi, an ambitious scheme that, in essence, amounted to asking the Communist Party to endorse the interests of private entrepreneurs over the actions of the state, or at least one branch of it. But some of the activists felt they had a chance. One of them, Li Zhiying, put it this way: "They say that the arm is unable to twist the leg. That is true. But I ask you, who is the arm and who is the leg?"

Indeed, not all the odds were stacked against the investors. The facts of the case seemed to favor them: in 1994 the oil ministry and the China National Petroleum Corporation (CNPC), the state-owned oil giant, agreed to turn over the prospecting and development rights for a swath of territory in northern Shaanxi to the local authorities. This was an unusual step, because oil was an asset over which the state had monopoly ownership. Nevertheless, the agreement was official and public, and in any case the CNPC had searched for oil in northern Shaanxi and found nothing tempting there.

With little delay, local authorities put the prospecting rights up for sale at around $10,000 for each square-kilometer block. Initially investors were hesitant, but after the first gushers spouted, the trickle of farmers trailing across the loess plateau to buy drilling licenses became a flow. "Nodding donkey" derricks appeared on barren hillsides, their rhythmic pumping exerting a hypnotic pull on would-be wildcatters. Some lost everything. But around ten thousand struck lucky and more than a thousand small oil companies were founded to operate about six thousand wells. Soon, one of the poorest places in all of China began to get rich. Some investors built new houses. Others sent their children off to the best local boarding schools. A few bought cars, and Feng, who until then had worked a series of dead-end jobs in state companies, developed the habit of staying in hotel suites.

But by 1999 their luck was turning. An order from the State Economic and Trade Commission, a ministry-level body in Beijing, instructed local authorities to renationalize the private wells, placing them under the control of the Shaanxi Yanchang Oil Industry Group, a new company to be run and owned by Shaanxi provincial officials. The key provision of this order, however, was that the transfer from private to state ownership should take place by "acquisition, merger, or share purchases," according to the document. It was here that the local authorities of Yulin and

Yan'an in northern Shaanxi departed from their instructions. In the first place, they did not act on the order for four years, for reasons that remain unclear. Then, when they did act, in early 2003, they simply seized the wells by force.

A few years earlier they might have got away with it. But China in 2003 looked as if it might be changing. In March the national legislature passed a landmark amendment to the constitution that gave private property a legal status equal to that which had long been accorded to state property. In other words, private entrepreneurs for the first time enjoyed rights of ownership and legal action that were, on paper at least, not inferior to their cosseted cousins in state-owned enterprises.

Also around this time, Hu Jintao, newly installed as the general secretary of the Communist Party, had upgraded the long-neglected constitution by ordering that the politburo — the pinnacle of Chinese power — should study it and govern according to its principles. The *People's Daily* reflected the emerging zeitgeist by running front-page editorials proclaiming the inviolability of the country's basic law.

This provided Feng and his associates with an opportunity. They formulated a plan to turn the Shaanxi oil issue into a case study, a litmus test of the Party's fealty to its own principles. To do this, he tapped into what is perhaps the most economically liberal official body in China, the All-China Federation of Industry and Commerce, a Party organization with considerable clout. At the federation, Feng found Bao Yujun, a former deputy editor of the *People's Daily* who had also founded the All-China Society of Private Economy Research in 1993. Bao, one of the first officials to call for constitutional protection for private property, saw the Shaanxi case as a natural extension of his work. "This is a classic case of illegal administration and the misuse of administrative power," he said.

Bao first aired the issue for public debate at a conference he chaired a short time later in Taizhou, an eastern seaboard city famous as a crucible of private enterprise back in the 1980s. This attracted so much interest that Bao agreed to chair another meeting, entirely devoted to the Shaanxi case, in the Great Hall of the People in Beijing.

The academics who attended that meeting in the summer of 2004 were a virtual Who's Who of the country's top legal and economic thinkers. On a screen by the podium where Bao sat, the audience watched video footage from the Shaanxi county of Ansai showing evicted oil well investors being brutally treated at an open-air "public arrest meeting." Their transgression, according to the local officials who appear on the smuggled video, was to resist the seizure of their wells. When the video ended, the floor was opened to debate. One academic after another castigated the Shaanxi authorities. "You are the people's government. Your power is given to you by the people," said Li Chengxun, a researcher at the Chinese Academy of Social Sciences, a top state think tank. "The local governments of northern Shaanxi have trampled on the law. The [oil production] contracts they themselves granted to the peasants, they themselves have torn up." Li Yiping, a professor at the People's University in Beijing, saw a broader significance. "China's democracy, future civilization, and future rule of law rely completely on us to rise up and struggle with law-breaking governments, including at this meeting today," he said. "Democracy and the rule of law is a process. It is not something that the government bestows."

For Feng, the meeting in the Great Hall of the People was a watershed event. It imparted moral legitimacy to his cause and cast the problem of the confiscated wells in the wider context of constitutional loyalty. Securing the backing of prominent academics was a considerable achievement—many of them were from state-run think tanks, and some were even policy advisers to the central government.

But there was another windfall. The meeting's proceedings were filmed and edited into a documentary, narrated by a professional who had worked for China Central Television. This was copied onto DVDs and sent to government officials in Beijing and to all levels of the Shaanxi provincial administration. "When they got the DVDs, the pressure on the Shaanxi officials was mounting," said Li Zhiying, the activist.

My attempts to get the Shaanxi government's side of the story had been almost fruitless. Telephone calls to various offices in Xian, the provincial capital, had been met with blanket denials that any dispute existed. Eventually, a director of the Shaanxi provincial news office, Zhang Lin, agreed to answer my questions. He said the wells had been recovered after state television broadcast negative news about the private oil investors. What kind of negative news? "Various. I have forgotten," he said. Asked if it was true that local officials were running the newly established oil companies in northern Shaanxi and benefiting materially from them, Zhang made a clear denial. "It is impossible that officials are directly involved in business. There is a government policy to separate politics from business," he said.

I decided to travel to the area in October 2004 to check his assertions, as well as those of Feng and his associates. The route to northern Shaanxi from Beijing goes via Yan'an, the revolutionary base of Mao and his comrades during the most grueling years of the Communists' guerrilla war against Chiang Kai-shek's Nationalists and the invading Japanese. That era is bathed in nostalgia for many Chinese, and the hillside caves that Mao and his generals once used have become tourist attractions.

Shops near the caves sold packets of coarse grain and other manifestations of the "Yan'an spirit" that in Mao's time had elevated "eating bitterness and enduring labor" into a lofty ideal. The few customers in the shops that Saturday in October were people from Beijing and Shanghai, and deprivation for them was a distant memory. One middle-aged man swayed gently to "Nanniwan," a famous Yan'an song that played on a shop's stereo: "There are crops everywhere, everywhere cattle and sheep. The Nanniwan of the past was all barren hills, with no wisp of humanity. But today's Nanniwan is just not the same as the past."

Six hours north of Yan'an by car is Jingbian, the county in which Feng's disputed oil wells are located. As my taxi climbed through the hills, passing pumping oil derricks to the left and right, I read the slogans on walls and signposts by the side of the road. "Having One Child Is Good," said one. "Everybody Takes Care of Underground Cables," read another. My driver said that, to be understood, their meaning had to be inverted. People here wanted several children because that meant more labor, he said, and telecom cables were often dug up and sold. In Ansai county, the scene of violent confrontations between the local government and oil well investors, there was a large sign reading "Put People First" — the Hu Jintao formulation for a kinder, gentler government.

In Jingbian I went to the office of Gao Zhongcheng, concurrently the deputy mayor and general manager of the Jingbian Oil Drilling Company. Metal plaques on the gate identified the company as both a government and a Communist Party concern. When I entered his office, Gao was not pleased to see me. "What the hell are you up to?" he shouted, breaking up a meeting. I identified myself as a journalist and he said he was calling the police. I told him that I had come to get the Jingbian government's side of the story, but his irritation seemed to deepen. "These are illegal reporting activities. The police will settle this," he said. I was escorted down the corridor to wait in a separate room, and left alone. To my amazement, open on a desk in front of me were stacks of accounting documents detailing production from the confiscated wells. The revenue of Gao's company, according to my hurried calculations, ran to millions of renminbi a day.

I was not sure what the police, when they turned up, would do with me, and I tried to listen through the door to a conversation in the corridor for clues. After a while, one of Gao's assistants appeared with a cup of hot water. When the police arrived after another half-hour, the water was replaced by tea. "Jasmine," said the assistant as he put the cup down next to me. An hour of questions later, I was ordered to return to Yan'an by car.

At the time of writing, some three years after Feng and his fellow petitioners had started their campaign, the case had still not been resolved. There had been no court hearing and no ruling by Beijing on whether the constitutional protection extended to private property applied in this instance or not. Instead, the battle of attrition between the activists and the Shaanxi authorities dragged on and on. But fortune appeared to be on the side of the authorities. For even as they arrested Feng, his lawyer Zhu Jiuhu, and others, only to release them without charges and then arrest them again, they were earning millions of dollars every month from the output of the wells they had seized. Meanwhile, the savings that Feng and the others had put aside from their now distant days as local oil barons were dwindling fast. When they ran out of money, their quest to hold the government accountable for its crimes would become a freedom they could not afford.

9

Can We Be Friends?

A BEAT-UP RED TAXI took me home one afternoon as spring was turning to summer. The driver's accent, which tagged a lazy *er* sound onto the ends of most words, identified him as *lao Beijing*, or "old Beijing" — a singular description. In English we differentiate between London and Londoners, between New York and New Yorkers. But the Chinese language makes no distinction between the alleyways and courtyard houses that make up the old quarters of the national capital and the people whose families have lived in them for generations. Both are called "old Beijing," as if long association somehow fused one with the other.

The alleys in which old Beijing have traditionally lived are called *hutong*, and their layout has helped to mold the city's soul. They are long, narrow, and sometimes lined with ginkgo or other broadleaf trees. In summer, when the heat of the day is subsiding, inhabitants of the courtyard houses take out low stools, place them in the shade of the trees, and sit down to chat. Their conversations can be long and rambling, a Beijing specialty called *kan da shan*, or "chatting a big mountain," in which robust views, cursing-for-the-fun-of-it, and cutting-through-the-bullshit are intermingled with local gossip, old stories, and political satire. Humor is never far from the surface.

Most of the alleyways in Beijing's old quarters have been bulldozed over the past decade, sweeping away more than seven hundred years of history. The graceful eaves of the houses, the pomegranate trees in their carefully tended beds, and the carved stones

★

from which inhabitants in other times mounted their horses have all fallen to a modernizing zeal. A city with an antique charm that rivaled Venice is preserved only in photographs. With the disappearance of its physical contours, the old town's soul now resides mainly in its human manifestation. The people of old Beijing can still be seen walking to the imperial parks — dedicated to the sun, earth, moon, and sky — to fly their kites on the light breezes that arrive in spring and autumn. They also wander, with songbirds in rattan cages or Pekingese dogs tucked under their arms, to their other old haunts, places that once had some local significance but are now road intersections or the forecourts of soaring new office towers. Once in these modern surroundings, they appear a little bereft, as though they have been drawn by the topography of their memories — the knowledge that the stretch of anonymous concrete beneath their feet used to be "dragon's whisker ditch" or "tributary rice-store *hutong*" or the old mosque on Bull Street.

In the years that I have lived in Beijing, one of the things I have enjoyed most has been the company of such people. So whenever I get into a taxi and hear that the driver is *lao Beijing*, I feel a small swell of pleasure. More often than not it means I am in for a fun and interesting conversation. And so it was on this day in late spring. My ride started with the usual mixture of cursing at other motorists, swearing at the Beijing government for letting traffic get out of control, and expressions of dismay at the general state of the world. But amid this banter were the things that made such taxi drivers special: snatches of poetry, four-character idioms, fragments of ancient lore, and wise old saws. Listening to the driver talk, it occurred to me that I was being treated to the linguistic equivalent of an archaeological dig. Layer after layer, the inherited wisdom of an unbroken culture was being peeled back to reveal its artifacts. In one sentence there lay buried a saying from Confucius, followed a few minutes (and 2,500 years) later by a nugget from Chairman Mao, and then, a bit later, there were a couple of things I could not place or date. It was not that the driver was being deliberately obscure, only that the Chinese language is a heavy loam.

When I happened upon a particularly shiny linguistic relic, I would take out my notebook and store it away. On this day, I wrote down "throwing a meat dumpling to hit a dog," which is how the driver spoke of the futility of protesting against the government. Then there was *ou duan si lian*, or "lotus broken skeins join," which described the way small viscous strands, almost invisible to the eye, join two halves of a lotus root after it has been broken in two. It evokes the emotional tug that exists between estranged lovers. That one took a while for the driver to explain, and I had not finished writing it down when I heard the radio being turned up. It was a *xiangsheng*, a rapid-fire comic dialogue that is also part of *lao Beijing* lore. The driver fell silent and I craned forward from the back seat to hear the performance more clearly.

Although I missed some of it, I could comprehend that one comedian was asking the other to name his favorite animal. After some banter back and forth, the other comic answered that his favorites were monkeys, or *hou* in Chinese. He explained that he liked monkeys because they were hairy and loud and boisterous. In fact, he liked them so much that one day, unaccountably, he found that he was missing them. So he went to the zoo to see if he could find any. But when he got there, there was not a monkey in sight. So he called out, "*Hou! Hou! Hou!*" Still nothing came, so he raised his voice: "*Hou! Hou-er! Hou-er-o! Houero! Horro! Hello!*" The laughter from the audience started as a murmur. But when the comic shouted "*Hello!*" again, the laughter grew louder, as everybody evidently understood the implied comparison between Westerners and monkeys.

The end of my taxi ride coincided almost exactly with the punch line. The taxi driver smiled a little bashfully as he took my money and we said goodbye. I was not in the least offended; in fact, I too had laughed. I had long since left behind the hurt I used to feel when my foreignness was mocked. There had been times in my student days, and occasionally later, when I had felt humiliated. Once, in 1982, a few weeks after I arrived at Shandong University, campus administrators had taken my group of foreign students to the theater. I did not understand much of the play we saw, but I do recall that the stock joke of the evening was that foreigners had big noses. I also remember my university track coach, a kind and dedicated man, taking me aside one day after practice to explain that blacks and Caucasians tended to be better sprinters than the Chinese because it had been scientifically proven that they shared more genes with apes. As the years passed, I accepted that some Chinese harbor prejudices as some of us foreigners hold foolishly to ours. That was just the way things were.

The monkey *xiangsheng* on the radio put me in a pensive mood, perhaps because at the time of my taxi ride anti-Japanese demonstrations had been raging day after day in Beijing and other mainland cities. Marches against the Japanese, which were among the few public protests that the authorities sanctioned, had been a periodic feature of the political scene for decades. But these were uglier than others I had witnessed. The vitriol of the taunts, the fact that many of the protesters were in their twenties, and the twisted expressions of hatred and fury on their faces had unsettled me in a way that took me by surprise. No matter how much I tried to rationalize what I had seen, I was beset for weeks by questions that were as insistent as they were banal: Do the Chinese like us? Are we friends? *Can* we be friends with them?

Friendship. It means different things to different people. One kind describes the diplomatic relations between states. Another deals with the feelings between individuals. The first kind of friendship is hard work; it must be structured and scripted down to the smallest detail. The second is spontaneous, haphazard, and voluntary. But in China the boundaries between the two have been blurred by dint of a strenuous, state-sponsored drive to nurture "friendship" between Chinese and foreign individuals as an important instrument of foreign policy. Such efforts are called *waishi*, or "foreign affairs," the goal of which is to try to manage the way China is seen by the outside world, not only by foreign governments but also by the public. The head of the *waishi* system in government is China's top leader, and virtually every government agency, municipal authority, and state enterprise has an office designated to deal with foreign affairs. Friendship is not something the Communist Party is willing to leave to chance.

In some ways this is not unusual. The Soviet Union had a similar system for dealing with foreign guests. But what is perhaps revealing about the Chinese effort is the way that foreigners are described in the training manuals given to *waishi* operatives. These books are designated as "internal," or secret from the foreigners they are intended to help influence. However, several of them have been obtained by Anne-Marie Brady, the author of *Making the Foreign Serve China*, an impressively researched recent book.[1] The rules of engagement contained in the training manuals are intricate and all-pervasive. They stress that intimacy is forbidden and that making friends with foreigners is "work." One phrase that keeps cropping up is *nei wai you bie*, "foreigners and Chinese are different." There are also quoted injunctions from Zhou Enlai, Mao's urbane premier, to the effect that making "friends" with foreign journalists required thorough research and investigation, because *waishi* workers needed to "know your enemy and know yourself." Adding to the sense that *waishi* workers were somehow crossing an elemental divide was the illustration on the cover of one manual from the mid-1990s: a handshake. One hand was smooth and the other covered in thick black hair.

In the same book, a *waishi* aficionado, Zhao Pitao, summed up the mission of foreign affairs workers: "To make friends with foreigners is the effective way to strive for international sympathy and support. It is an important task of foreign affairs work."[2]

One way to cultivate "friendship," the handbooks say, is to create feelings. This can be done in a number of ways, one of which is to find things in common. This does not have to involve politics. It can be children, gardening, sports, almost any subject. But whatever form it takes, eliciting some sense of commonality is essential to the creation of favorable feelings. "Feelings are the response of people to objective events. They are an important motivation for human activity. In order to work on people, we first of all need to establish feelings," says one passage in a *waishi* book called *Zhou Enlai's Diplomatic Art.*

Other ways to nurture feelings included convincing foreigners that they are special. At times, this resulted in a form of theater. In the late 1970s and early 1980s a frequently used device was a kind of charade that involved some small item — a discarded sock, a used razor, or a pack of postcards — that a foreigner had left behind in a hotel room. Shortly after the foreigner had checked out, someone (usually a local *waishi* official) would jump into a car and rush after the foreigner's taxi or bus, flag it down, and hand over the item to the embarrassed but thankful visitor.

In the late 1980s foreigners who exhibited friendship would be given privileges. This often involved the deployment of China's most powerful chimera: its population. The foreigner would be either charmed by the adulation of crowds or seduced by the exclusivity of a one-in-a-billion reception. Examples of the former variant in this genre included the "spontaneous" crowd of tens of thousands that hailed Craig Barrett, the then CEO of Intel, in the southwestern city of Chengdu. They surrounded him in the streets chanting *"Ying-te-er, Ying-te-er"* ("Intel, Intel"), until Barrett, by his own admission, began to feel like Elvis Presley.[3] Later, Intel approved the chip-packaging-plant investment that Chengdu had been angling for. Edgar Bronfman, who was then chairman of Seagram, had a similar experience in a remote village by the Yangtze River in 1998. His beverage company had promised to invest in a $55 million orange orchard that would help transform the local economy.[4] After he debarked from a cruise ship that had taken him downriver, he saw thousands of peasant farmers thronging the hillsides, clogging the streets, and waving from rooftops. The feelings engendered in Bronfman were so strong that when Seagram was later bought by Vivendi, a media company, he insisted that the orange orchard be kept as a special unit, even though it was about as far from the core business as can be imagined.

Sometimes it is exclusivity rather than popular adulation that is employed. The foreigner can see the multitudes about him as he is ferried around town in a limo with a police escort but is kept separate from the hoi polloi, in the manner of a mandarin in a sedan chair. More rarefied gradations of exclusivity are reserved for people like Rupert Murdoch, the magnate who controls News Corporation. During the years he has been trying to crack the China market, he has gained access to the inner sanctums of Communist power. He has had dinner with the most powerful men in the country inside Zhongnanhai, which is guarded just as fiercely as the old, imperial Forbidden City ever was. He has also enjoyed the virtually unique privilege of addressing a lecture hall full of future leaders in the Central Party School. The theme of his speech — the efficacy of an open media — contrasted neatly with the fact that the school is strictly off-limits to both Chinese and foreigners unless they have secured prior approval.

Yet the privileges granted, the warmth, the closeness, and the respect are all calculated to achieve utilitarian aims. That these friendships are nothing more than temporary arrangements for mutual benefit is evident in example after example. Yet no case is clearer than that of Edgar Snow, an American journalist and author who became acquainted with Mao when the future chairman was the leader of a guerrilla force based in Shaanxi. The following passage, recorded in Snow's unpublished diaries, shows just how powerful the *waishi* principle of "creating feelings" by making foreigners feel special can be. It describes the arrival after an arduous journey of Snow and George Hatem, a Lebanese doctor who was also to become a firm "friend of China," at the Communists' revolutionary base.

> The bands and troops fell behind us and marched up the main street to the accompaniment of slogans shouting, "Welcome American comrades! Hurrah for the Chinese comrades! Hurrah for the world revolution!" etc and posters and banners of welcome decorated the walls of the town, some written in English, some in Latin-hua and many in Chinese. It was the first time I had been greeted by the entire cabinet of a government, the first time a whole city had been turned out to welcome me. The effect pronounced on me was highly emotional. Had I been called up to make any kind of speech I would have been unable to do so.[5]

Snow was to become China's most famous postrevolutionary friend. His book *Red Star Over China* was to become a bestseller in the United States, and Mao, who called him "friend Snow," had Snow stand beside him on top of Tiananmen Gate on National Day. But it was inevitable that the time for payback would come. When it did, Beijing took its payment in the most valuable currency that a journalist has to offer: his credibility. Unlike many other "friends of China," Snow lived in the United States. He was given a special invitation to come back in 1960, when China was in the midst of the famine caused by Mao's industrialization policies. Beijing hoped that the man who had done more than anyone else to further the image of the Communists in the eyes of foreigners would return to write another book supporting the regime. Mao wanted him to reinforce the claims that there was no trace of famine in China and that the rumors of mass starvation reported in the media were rubbish.

Snow was escorted around the country by George Hatem, who had stayed on in Beijing after the revolution as part of a coterie of professional "friends of China." When Snow's book *The Other Side of the River: Red China Today* came out, it contained the whitewash the Chinese were looking for. Snow declared that he saw no starving people in China, though "isolated instances" of starvation might exist and there was undoubtedly considerable malnutrition. "Mass starvation? No," he said. In fact, an estimated thirty million were dying of hunger.

The *waishi* phenomenon is interesting on different levels. It can be looked upon as an aspect of public diplomacy or as an exercise in social psychology. But I find it absorbing for what it suggests about the Chinese government's attitude toward the outside world. Why did the state feel the need to stage-manage personal friendships, and why did Beijing wish to discourage real friendships based on genuine feelings? Perhaps it had something to do with the "patriotic education" that Chinese schoolchildren are taught and the antiforeign propaganda that sometimes surfaces in state newspapers. In both cases, the foreigners portrayed were not people who were friendly to China. Rather, it was as Chairman

Mao said on top of Tiananmen Gate as he declared the founding of the People's Republic on October 1, 1949: "The Chinese have always been a great, courageous and industrious nation; it is only in modern times that they have fallen behind. And that was due entirely to oppression and exploitation by foreign imperialism and domestic reactionary governments . . . Ours will no longer be a nation subject to insult and humiliation. We have stood up."

Over the past decade or more, Beijing has allowed the Chinese much greater freedom to make real friendships with foreigners, and of course the personal bonds formed have been as intimate, trusting, and loyal as anywhere else on earth. Yet the state continues to try to use its people to contrive an image of China in foreign minds. The most recent example of this is a new set of handbooks published by the state to teach people how to make a good impression on foreigners when the Olympic Games are hosted in Beijing in 2008. The books urge scrupulous politeness, high standards of personal hygiene, and the creation of "warmth" toward visitors.

To some extent, however, this is all artifice. The state's real view of foreigners has not changed. Schoolchildren are still taught that the 109 years before the 1949 revolution were characterized by the treachery of a cabal of Western and Western-oriented countries — Russia, Great Britain, France, Germany, Japan, and the United States — that attacked the old Chinese empire and seized hundreds of square miles of territory.[6] They forced the Beijing government to sign unequal treaties, resorted to gunboat diplomacy, fought two opium wars with the aim of peddling drugs, burned imperial palaces, looted priceless treasures, and humiliated the Chinese people.

All of this, in fact, is true. But what is lacking in the textbooks, or in the stream of newspaper articles and television programs on the same issue, is any sustained attempt to distinguish between historical crimes and current realities. Every schoolchild has to memorize passages of history in which Japanese are described as "devils" and portrayed as evil. Elementary school students learn that the first among ten "must-know" historical facts is that Communist China was founded on "one hundred years of Chinese people opposing foreign aggression."[7]

There is little official attempt to foster a spirit of reconciliation or forgiveness. As demonstrators outside the Japanese embassy in the late spring screamed "devils," "Japanese dwarfs," "dogs," and other epithets, the authorities made no move to calm them down or to educate them about all the aid and investments the Japanese government and Japanese companies have provided to China over the past two and a half decades. No one in Beijing suggested that the Japanese people of today were in any way different from the soldiers of the imperial army that swept through China before and during World War Two. At times it appears that the government has nurtured nationalism into so potent a force that it is in danger of losing control of it. A senior official once told me that Beijing had no option but to allow days of violence by rock-throwing mobs outside the U.S. and British embassies in 1999 after the Chinese embassy in Belgrade was bombed by NATO forces. When I asked him why, he said, "Because we did not want to be called Li Hongzhang," naming the arch-traitor of the Qing dynasty who is universally reviled for signing unequal treaties with foreign powers.

Issues of friendship and nationalism are difficult to pin down and describe. You may even feel foolish for posing unanswerable questions such as "Do they like us?" Yet in some way such inquiries are the most important of all. History shows that the rise of great powers creates tensions, dislocations, and antagonisms among the preexisting hierarchy of nations. The causes of World War One had a lot to do with the rise of an assertive Germany, and the nationalism of a resurgent Japan did much to precipitate the Pacific theater of World War Two. It is true that fostering warmth between peoples may not ultimately be sufficient to prevent outbreaks of violence between states, but it can inhibit the escalation of peacetime competition into outright hostility. And that could be crucial for China and the West, because the competition that is roiling commercial and diplomatic relations is already a powerful force and is set to intensify.

But before getting into that, some balance is required. It must be said that from a global perspective China's emergence is of enormous economic benefit. The value created by the release of 400 million people from poverty, the migration of more than 120 million from farms where they perhaps raised chickens to factories where they churn out electronics, the quantum leap in educational standards for tens of millions of children, the construction of a First World infrastructure, the growth of forty cities with populations of over one million, the commercialization of housing, and the vaulting progress up the technology ladder have helped unleash one of the greatest surges in prosperity in history. The prime beneficiary of this has been China itself, but the mobilization of wealth on such a scale is necessarily, in aggregate terms, lifting the fortunes of the planet.

Some specific advantages are already evident. Beijing's towering pile of foreign currency reserves, which in late 2005 stood at more than $710 billion, has been used to a large extent to buy U.S. Treasury bonds. Not only has this helped the American government to finance public spending and pay for the war in Iraq, but it has also assisted in keeping interest rates low. The depressed level of U.S. interest rates has, in its turn, set a standard for the world and led to a property boom in most developed countries. At the same time, the manufacture of ever cheaper products, such as those on sale in Yiwu, has meant that people's purchasing power has strengthened.

Regionally, however, the benefits are unevenly spread. Overall, the countries that have gained most are those that are rich in energy and other resources but do little in the way of manufacturing. Africa has seen particular advantages. Trade between China and countries in Africa tripled in the past three years and helped power a boom that was expected to carry African growth in 2005 to its highest level in thirty years.[8] In Asia, too, the picture is generally positive. Trade with the ten member nations of the Association of Southeast Asian Nations was expected to exceed $130 billion in 2005,[9] up by about a third over one year earlier. In northern Asia, things have been equally vibrant, with South Korea and Japan now both counting China as their largest trade partner. Australia has been a clear winner, exporting iron ore, alumina, natural gas, and a host of other resources and commodities. In Latin America the picture is more mixed, with a surge in commodity and resources trade offset somewhat by the impact of bruising competition with the manufacturing industries of Mexico and Brazil.

But Europe and the United States, as we have seen, have had a much more turbulent time. And because of the way global power is distributed, it is here that a key challenge to China's future may reside. With trade amounting to more than two-thirds of the size of China's economy (compared with around a quarter for other large economies), Beijing is clearly vulnerable to the protectionism that might follow a withdrawal of the West's goodwill. Many of the achievements of the past twenty-eight years might not have been possible without the infusions of overseas capital, expertise, and technology and the access to foreign markets. But America and Europe, in large part due to homegrown deficiencies, are finding it increasingly tough to identify a net advantage from their engagement with China. So a key question for the future is not so much how China's rise will affect the world, but to what extent the world will *allow* China to continue its ascent. While a general shutdown in trade would have a catastrophic impact on the global economy and is therefore unlikely, even a partial pruning of commercial links or a gradual upsurge in Western protectionism toward China would have profound effects on the world's well-being and create tensions that could spill over into other areas.

From an economic perspective, such an outcome would be irrational, because a curtailment of trade hurts the protected as much as those they are seeking protection against. But such decisions rarely come down to dispassionate economic analysis; they turn instead on the perceptions of electorates — people such as those in

Rockford, Illinois, or Prato in Tuscany, or a thousand other places reeling from China's manufacturing might. And therein lies the rub.

My (admittedly unscientific) impression is that Americans, and to a lesser extent Europeans, do not often credit the Chinese for the improvements they have brought to their lives. As a small test of this theory, I stood outside the Wal-Mart in Rockford asking shoppers if they felt like saying "thank you" to Chinese workers for reducing the prices of what they bought. I got plenty of double takes, a few strange looks, and one man turned on his heel and walked away. Only one or two people had any words of gratitude. I suspect that if I had gone to a mortgage lender and asked home buyers if they felt good about China buying U.S. Treasuries, thereby helping to keep interest rates low, the reaction might have been even more muted.

The point, without being flippant, is that a lot of the "good" that China does for the economies of the United States and the European Union is less visible than the blame it attracts for its deleterious impact on jobs. Thus if a politician runs for office promising to prevent the outsourcing of jobs under "unfair" trade conditions to a Communist behemoth that fails to uphold intellectual property rights, fixes its currency's exchange rate, and exploits its own workers, he can be virtually assured of tapping into a ready-made populist agenda. By contrast, a case built on the accurate but more nebulous argument that free trade benefits those who engage in it may not achieve the same pulling power.

China is peculiarly vulnerable here. The shortcomings of its system of governance mean that China finds it tough to respond to such criticisms. It cannot stamp out piracy, for example, because many of the abuses take place with the connivance of disobedient local governments. It cannot allow independent trade unions to be formed because they might pose an intolerable challenge to the Party's authority. Neither does it have much leeway to allow free fluctuation of the currency, because even a modest appreciation could wipe out the profit margins of manufacturers who have yet to build up their brands. And as for being a Communist behemoth, well, that is difficult for Beijing to address because although it is no longer Communist, it is still ruled by the Communist Party. All of this points to an uncomfortable paradox: China owes its emergence in large part to the free-trade system created by America since World War Two, but in many ways it is still not a creature of that system. In several respects its economy, political system, culture, military posture, and values are different from most of the other nations that have reached maturity under the Pax Americana.

In the past, this may not have mattered much. China's differences with the West have not caused the West to turn away from China during the past two and a half decades (with the exception of a brief period after the Tiananmen massacre in 1989), so why should those differences have any greater impact now? The answer to that question is linked to early 2004, when manhole covers were disappearing from streets all over the world to feed the churning hunger of Asia's rising giant for scrap steel. At that time, a Rubicon was crossed. China's future was destined to be different from its past. Even though the central government did not control the nation's appetite, it had no alternative but to do everything in its power to satisfy it. Failing to do so could have precipitated panic or a sudden economic collapse of the sort that could shake the timbers of Party authority. Whatever else happened, China had to be fed.

A new era in international relations dawned, one defined by the geopolitics of scarcity.[10] Greater and greater competition, both commercial and political, began to set one country against another in pursuit of finite resources and energy. As recently as five years ago, Beijing's leaders hardly had to worry about where and how their companies would secure supplies of oil, gas, and a host of traded commodities and resources. In those days, the nation's demand, though significant, was relatively easily accommodated on world markets. But now China is the second-largest importer of oil in the world after the United States. Its imports of aluminum, nickel, copper, and iron ore have risen from an average 7 percent of world demand in 1990 to a predicted 40 percent by 2010.[11] As a result, Beijing has become anxious in case supplies of crucial resources run out or are diverted to other countries, threatening the growth that produces the twenty-four million new jobs it must create every year. Thus scarcity, or finding ways to alleviate it, has in a few short years leapfrogged up Beijing's agenda to become the key motivator of foreign and domestic policies.

The imperative to tend to its cravings has brought China more and more into strategic and diplomatic conflict with the United States. Because it has no slack in the decisions of where to sate itself, Beijing has had to strike deals for access to resources as they have become available, wherever they have been.[12] Many have been with countries that are rivals of the United States or designated as pariahs by Washington. Because of this, America is watching with rising angst to see if Beijing enters agreements that impinge upon vital interests or threaten its own established energy supply lines. So far, the situation has not revived the dynamics of the Cold War, when great powers jockeyed for influence in Third World countries, but the conditions exist for it to become so.

Take, for example, the Latin American nation of Venezuela, the world's fifth-largest oil producer. It is run by Hugo Chavez, a socialist ally of Cuba's Fidel Castro who has accused Washington of plotting a coup to kill him and seize his country's oil resources. He has used the forum of the United Nations to brand America a "terrorist state" and has pledged at home to reorient his economy away from its dependence on the United States. In spite of this, Venezuela is an important source of oil for America, supplying some three million barrels a day to the world's superpower.

But recently Chavez has started trying to find alternative clients for the oil exports, and China is on the top of his list. He was invited to Beijing in 2004 and got a warm welcome. While there, he signed agreements that could bring Chinese investments in Venezuela's oil sector to $3 billion, double the existing amount. In 2005 the new affinity continued, with Zeng Qinghong, the vice president, receiving a friendly welcome from Chavez in Caracas. The Venezuelan president told Zeng his country had an "extreme interest in becoming a safe supplier of oil and oil derivatives to the People's Republic of China." The not-so-safe subtext, though, was that if long-term supply contracts with China are eventually signed, they may be honored at the expense of the U.S. supplies, and Washington is already on tenterhooks. As Condoleezza Rice, the secretary of state, has said, the United States "welcomes the rise of confident, peaceful and prosperous China" but hopes it will be "able and willing to match its growing capabilities to its international responsibilities."[13] In other words, the United States does not want to see Beijing befriending Washington's rivals in order to divert the oil supplies that sustain American growth.

Elsewhere, the issue is not that China may impinge on U.S. supply lines, but that in its alacrity to shore up supplies, it is forging ties with countries that Washington has made a policy of isolating. Sudan is a case in point. In 1997, when the predominantly Muslim government in Khartoum was engaged in a gruesome war against Christian rebels in the south, Washington banned American companies from doing business in the East African country. This gave the Chinese a clear run at tapping into Sudanese oil reserves. In the years since, Sudan has become China's largest overseas oil project, and China has turned into Sudan's biggest supplier of arms. Chinese-made tanks, fighter planes, bombers, helicopters, machine guns, and rocket-propelled grenades have added new impetus to the civil war between the north and south of the country which has already lasted for two decades.[14] The money to buy those weapons, meanwhile, has come from oil revenues generated largely by the activities of the state-run China National Petroleum Corporation.

China National Petroleum owns 40 percent, the largest stake, of the Greater Nile Petroleum Operating Company, a consortium that dominates Sudan's oil fields. Another Chinese firm, Sinopec, is erecting a pipeline over hundreds of miles to Port Sudan, on the Red Sea, where China's Petroleum Engineering Construction Group is building a tanker terminal. The total investment runs into billions of dollars, and as production has increased, Sudan has come to furnish China with 10 percent of its total oil imports.

But the benefits derived from this have to be weighed against the cost to Beijing's reputation. Not only has China become the chief supporter of a government that has perpetrated repeated instances of genocide, but according to human rights groups and locals quoted by Peter Goodman, a reporter for the *Washington Post*, the construction of Chinese oil rigs has also led directly to the slaughter of Sudanese people.[15]

The U.S.-funded Civilian Protection Monitoring Team, a nongovernmental organization, has asserted that Sudanese government troops have sought to create a *cordon sanitaire* around oil installations by removing the mostly ethnic Nuer and Dinka tribes who lived there. On February 26, 2002, the Nuer town of Nhialdiu was wiped out during one such operation, to make way for a Chinese well that is now pumping in the nearby town of Leal. Mortar shells landed at dawn, followed by helicopter gunships directing fire at the huts where people lived. Antonov planes dropped bombs and roughly seven thousand government troops with progovernment militias then swept through the area with rifles and more than twenty tanks, according to Goodman's report, which was based on numerous local sources. "The Chinese want to drill for oil, that is why we were pushed out," Goodman quoted one man, Rusthal Yackok, as saying. Yackok added that his wife and six children were killed in the operation. The chief of Leal, Tanguar Kuiyguong, who lost three of his ten children on that day, told Goodman that around three thousand of the town's ten thousand inhabitants died and every house was burned to the ground.[16]

There is no evidence, however, that the Chinese government or its largest oil company had any advance notice of the Sudanese government's scorched-earth strategy at Leal. Beijing also brushes off any suggestion that it is complicit in Sudan's genocide. As Zhou Wenzhong, a deputy foreign minister, said in 2004: "Business is business. We try to separate politics from business. I think the internal situation in Sudan is an internal affair, and we are not in a position to impose upon them." A few months later, though, Chinese diplomats successfully diluted the impact of a

United Nations resolution condemning Khartoum, thereby un-
dermining Washington's efforts to threaten sanctions against Sudan's oil industry in protest of other waves of genocide in the
Darfur region of Sudan. Having watered down the resolution,
however, Wang Guangya, the ambassador to the United Nations,
denied that his actions had anything to do with a desire to protect
Chinese state oil interests in the country.[17]

Sudan is by no means the only nation in which Beijing has
pursued energy and resources at the expense of its international
reputation. When the president of Uzbekistan, Islam Karimov,
visited Beijing in 2005, the government rolled out the red carpet
for him in spite of the fact that just twelve days earlier the Uzbek
army had killed hundreds of civilian protesters in a town square
in the east of that central Asian nation. The feting that Karimov
enjoyed in the Chinese capital contrasted with an outcry elsewhere in the world, and with the calls for an international inquiry
from the United States and its North Atlantic Treaty Organization allies, which at that time maintained military bases on Uzbek
soil. In Beijing Karimov got a twenty-one-gun salute in Tiananmen Square, and there was never a public mention of the events
in Andijan, the city in the Fergana Valley where the atrocity had
taken place. It was not long, however, before clues emerged as to
the real motivation behind China's courting of a "reliable friend,"
as the state media referred to Karimov. The Uzbek president had
brought with him a $600 million deal that allowed China National
Petroleum access to twenty-three Uzbek oil fields.[18]

A couple of months after Karimov's visit, it was the turn of
Zimbabwean dictator Robert Mugabe to accept a twenty-one-gun
salute, a small loan, and some encouraging words from Hu Jintao.
Much more substantive than these ties with either Uzbekistan or
Zimbabwe, though, has been China's warming relationship with
Iran, another country high on Washington's list of pariah states.
Iran supplies 11 percent of China's oil imports, so it is already a
crucial resource partner. But the level of reciprocal interest is set to
surge, as Sinopec, the second-largest state oil firm, implements an
oil and natural gas agreement with Tehran that is said to be worth

as much as $70 billion—the biggest energy deal yet by any member of OPEC, the cartel of oil-producing companies.[19] Under this agreement, Beijing is committed to develop the giant Yadavaran oil field and buy 275 million tons of liquefied natural gas over the next thirty years. Tehran has also agreed to export to China some 150,000 barrels of oil per day at market prices for twenty-five years.

The ballast that this deal has given to bilateral ties has made Beijing a loyal friend of Tehran in the U.N. Security Council, where China is one of only five countries with the power to veto any resolution that is proposed. It has put that power, or the aura of it, to work over the past couple of years in deflecting successive attempts by the United States to impose sanctions through the United Nations on Iran's energy sector. Washington suspects that Iran may be developing nuclear weapons technology and had hoped to use the threat of sanctions to force Tehran to demonstrate to the U.N.'s nuclear watchdog that it has not broken the Nuclear Non-Proliferation Treaty, an international agreement that seeks to stem the spread of nuclear weapons and weapons technology. But this avenue now appears effectively blocked by China's maneuvering in the Security Council. The anxiety this causes in the White House is hard to overestimate: preventing Iran from developing the bomb has long been a cornerstone objective in the State Department's global view.

China's willingness to elevate the agendas of resource-rich pariah states to the Security Council is a major departure in the way it conducts itself. Tensions continue to rise, but so far Washington's warnings have gone unheeded. In June 2005 Chris Hill, the assistant secretary of state for East Asian and Pacific affairs, told a subcommittee of the House of Representatives that an important task for the United States and its Asian allies was "to ensure that in its search for resources and commodities to gird its economic machinery, China does not underwrite the continuation of regimes that pursue policies seeking to undermine rather than sustain the security and stability of the international community."[20] A few months later, with no observable change in China's behavior, Robert Zoellick, the deputy secretary of state, was more blunt: "China's involvement with troublesome states indicates at best a blindness to consequences and at worst something more ominous." He added that if Beijing tried to use its influence to "push the U.S. out, they would get a counter-reaction."[21]

The first ripples of that "counter-reaction" may already be evident. The failure of the bid by CNOOC, the oil firm, for its U.S. counterpart Unocal in the summer of 2005 was an indication of how sensitive American public opinion has become toward a rising and potentially threatening China. That is because by objective reckoning, the approach of China's third-largest oil company to the mid-tier American producer in no way represented a threat to U.S. national security. The total output from Unocal's American oil wells, after all, satisfied just 1 percent of U.S. consumption. But in a democracy, it is emotion rather than objectivity that counts. With China courting American rivals in several parts of the world, issuing statements calling on the United States to get out of its military bases in central Asia, and absorbing outsourced American jobs, members of Congress, understandably, did not find themselves in the mood to assist China's oil companies. Neither was CNOOC's cause enhanced by the comments of a Chinese general just days before Congress was due to vote for or against the CNOOC bid's proceeding. In prepared remarks to foreign journalists, the general, Zhu Chenghu, warned that if "the Americans draw their missiles and position-guided ammunition onto the target zone on China's territory, I think we will have to respond with nuclear weapons. We Chinese will prepare ourselves for the destruction of all the cities east of Xian [in central China]. Of course, the Americans will have to be prepared that hundreds of cities will be destroyed by the Chinese." After that, it was no surprise that the House of Representatives voted, 398 to 15, to refer CNOOC's bid for review by President George W. Bush on national security grounds.

Statements such as General Zhu's make a strong impression, regardless of how representative they may be of Beijing's real intentions. The CNOOC failure, though important, was just

one deal. But it illuminates the much larger and very real danger that one day Congress and the American electorate will come
to see China unequivocally as an adversary. If that perception be-
gins to gel, then it may start to condition Washington's thinking
on a panoply of strategic and commercial issues and lead to the
step-by-step reversal of the policy of engagement that has under-
pinned China's rise over the past twenty-eight years. If the sense
of China as an enemy permeates deeply enough into the American political psyche, then a whole range of familiar anti-Beijing arguments—that China is an unfair trader, a manipulator of its currency's value, a pirate of intellectual property, an exploiter of its
own workers, a beneficiary of subsidized financing from its state
banks and others—may grow in potency. But Beijing, goaded
by its insatiable appetite, may have no room to cede ground to
American public opinion, creating an impasse that could trigger
progressively stronger counter-reactions from the White House.

To some, this scenario will seem far-fetched. But there is ample
justification for the view that strategic and military competition
between China and the United States is intensifying. Two inter-
related issues underlie this competition. The first is an established
but incendiary rivalry over Taiwan, and the second is a much
newer expression of Beijing's growing assertiveness: the desire
to guarantee the safe passage back home of the oil and other resources it acquires in foreign climes.

On Taiwan, the situation is noticeably regressing. The background is ostensibly straightforward: China claims that Taiwan is
part of its territory and threatens to invade if the island's leaders
ever declare formal independence. The United States accepts that
Taiwan geographically belongs to China but wants reunification
to happen peacefully and is obliged under an American law, the
Taiwan Relations Act, to come to Taipei's assistance if the mainland ever decides to attack.

Beyond these outlined dimensions, however, things get more
nuanced and emotional. Taiwan's position astride the sea lanes
that skirt through the South China Sea and head toward Japan
makes the island of crucial strategic importance for trade and the

projection of military power in the region. Its attraction to Washington is further enhanced by its democratic government and the assiduous courting of members of Congress by its senior officials. For China, the issue is also highly emotional and nationalistic. Beijing sees the island as a lingering slight on its prestige, a reminder that the humiliations it suffered at the hands of foreign powers in the 109 years before 1949 have yet to be reversed. The cause of reclaiming Taiwan, which it lost in 1895 after a war with Japan, has become a shibboleth of Communist rule.

With the two powers so implacably opposed, any shift in the military balance across the Taiwan Strait is a cause for concern throughout the Asia-Pacific region. That shift has now unambiguously taken place. David Shambaugh, an American expert on the Chinese military, says that following the aggressive upgrading of the People's Liberation Army's capabilities, the balance of military power has tilted decidedly in China's favor.[22] According to recent estimates by the Pentagon, China has more than seven hundred missiles near its southeast coast, facing Taiwan, and is accelerating the buildup by adding seventy to seventy-five missiles a year, up from its previous annual increase of around fifty.[23] Such a deployment, some U.S. and Taiwanese analysts say, could be consistent with intentions to launch a lightning "decapitation" strike against Taiwan, using accurate guided weapons to disable the government, disrupt communications, and force Taiwan to the negotiating table within hours — before the U.S. Navy has had time to sail to Taipei's rescue.

In spite of the standoff over Taiwan, though, the United States and China have managed, since they established diplomatic ties in 1979, to avoid painting each other as future enemies. But this, too, may be subtly changing. On a visit to Singapore in 2005, Secretary of Defense Donald Rumsfeld asked an open forum why it was that China was expanding its missile forces so that it could reach targets in many parts of the world, not just the Pacific region: "Since no nation threatens China, one must wonder: Why this growing investment?" A senior Foreign Ministry official in the audience countered him, also with a question: "Do you truly believe that China is under no threat whatsoever from any part of the world?" Later in the year, on a visit to Beijing, Rumsfeld returned once more to the theme, asking his senior army inter- locutors why China was spending, by the Pentagon's estimate, as much as $90 billion a year on strengthening its military. His host told him that the Pentagon had got its figures wrong, that the Chinese military budget for 2005 was actually only $29 billion, a mere fraction of what the United States spends every year.[24] Nev- ertheless, these exchanges serve to underline America's growing anxiety.

Anxiety levels are set to rise further as Beijing seeks to deepen its military footprint in the Asia-Pacific region, where the United States has been the undisputed arbiter of security since World War Two. China is not trying to incite Washington, but it has no option but to seek to shore up its oil supply lines from the Middle East in the Strait of Malacca, the sea channel between Indonesia and Ma- laysia through which almost all of Asia's imported oil passes. The potential for a conflict with the United States over Taiwan means that Beijing cannot rely on American ships to police the strait for it. China needs to set down its own naval support network in the region, and it has gone about this task with speed and determi- nation.

China has started to implement a strategy to strengthen dip- lomatic and military ties with countries dotted like a "string of pearls" along the route that its oil tankers take on their journey from the Middle East, according to a report prepared for the Pen- tagon by Booz Allen Hamilton, the defense contractor.[25] Each pearl denotes a military facility or listening post that the Chinese may use or are in the process of building. One pearl is Gwadar, a Pakistani naval base that Beijing is helping to construct. When it is finished, diplomats assume, the Chinese navy will enjoy regu- lar access to dock its vessels. In nearby Bangladesh, a container terminal is under construction with Chinese help in Chittagong, another strategic port along the vital sea artery from the Middle East. In Myanmar, whose government receives generous military assistance from Beijing every year, electronic listening posts have been installed on islands in the Bay of Bengal so the Chinese can monitor the activities of the Indian and U.S. navies in the areas around the Strait of Malacca.

Of course, none of this means that a conflict between China and the United States is imminent or even likely. But it does represent a significant heightening of tensions and mutual suspicions. If these spill over into the realm of commerce, as they clearly did during the CNOOC bid for Unocal, then slowly but surely the free-market assumptions of the West that have facilitated China's remarkable ascent since 1978 could start to be undermined. If this happens, the biggest economic event of the second half of the twentieth century could be thrown off course in the first half of the twenty-first, causing dislocations that would convulse not only China but also much of the rest of the world. That prospect, so damaging for so many hundreds of millions of people, is made possible by globalization's most fundamental limitation: although trade increases the mutual economic dependence of the countries that engage in it, trade does not make the peoples of those nations any fonder of each other. Thus, when relations deteriorate because of issues that have nothing to do with commerce, each side starts to resent its dependence on the other, and goodwill can rapidly unravel.

The most worrying recent example of this is the relationship between Japan and China. The two countries are engaged in an economic convergence unprecedented in its rapidity and depth. Some 16,000 Japanese firms do business on the Chinese mainland, and sharply increased trade with China has lifted Japan's economy out of a decade of feeble growth and recurring recessions, while imports from China have lowered costs for Japanese consumers. More than 150,000 Chinese students attend Japanese universities, and a million Chinese work in Japanese companies. In Shanghai, where their business presence is growing sharply, there may be as many as 100,000 Japanese residents. In spite of all this, the two Asian giants are no better reconciled diplomatically or emotionally than they were in 1978, when Japanese business involvement in China was virtually zero.

In fact, politically, the neighbors are diverging as fast as they are coalescing commercially. Popular nationalism in both countries is driving politicians to pander to their constituencies, exacerbating the existing ill will. In Japan, Junichiro Koizumi, the prime minister, makes regular visits to the Yasukuni Shrine in Tokyo, which is dedicated to Japanese soldiers who died for the emperor, thus insulting the Chinese, who know all too well that several of the war criminals who committed atrocities during the second Sino-Japanese War are commemorated there. In China, senior officials who normally prevent street demonstrations from taking place grant regular permission for screaming crowds of anti-Japanese protesters to gather outside Tokyo's embassy. It stands to reason that at some stage deteriorating political and diplomatic ties will spill over into commerce, and the Chinese people may launch sporadic boycotts of Japanese goods, just as they did in the 1930s and 1940s when the war was being fought. Someday one of these boycotts may flare into something bigger, more long term, and more damaging.

But maybe the scenario I have painted is too pessimistic, too black. Indeed, whenever I think of all the issues described above, of how the acrimony, ill will, and strategic competition could one day rupture China's trading relationship with the West, a particular memory recurs, suggesting that these concerns may be overblown.

The memory in question is set in the embassy quarter of Beijing in the aftermath of NATO's bombing of the Chinese embassy in Belgrade. With smoke still rising from the rubble of the Chinese embassy complex, Washington issued a statement saying that the bombing had been a tragic mistake, a case of a pilot under pressure using an outdated map. But Beijing scorned this notion: a politburo meeting was held during which it was decided that the Pentagon had deliberately targeted the embassy, killing some of the staff inside. When this was announced to the people, genuine fury engulfed not only Beijing but most of the country. Indignant crowds of students and ordinary citizens gathered outside the American and British embassies within hours of the news' release, and as the first day of protests wore on, the frenzy mounted. The Chinese military and police guards who are stationed all year round to protect foreign embassies stood by as the demonstrators hurled rocks, paint, and bottles. When someone with good aim managed to hurl a projectile over the wall and smash a window, triumphant cries welled up from the crowd. At times even the guards would join the jubilation.

Meanwhile, foreign residents of Beijing found themselves subject to closer than usual scrutiny from Chinese citizens, who would ask which country they came from. If the answer was Britain, the United States, or another NATO country, the reaction was never favorable. Suddenly the number of self-professed Britons and Americans in Beijing dropped precipitously, while those calling themselves Australians, South Africans, and Canadians surged. One senior British diplomat I knew, when accosted by an angry mob not far from his embassy's front gates, said that he was Albanian. Others, in their desire for bland anonymity, adopted an Icelandic identity.

As dusk fell on the evening of the first day of protests, I was busy covering the event and did not realize how identities were migrating all over town. I felt no animosity toward the Chinese and, naively, could not really see why they would feel it toward me — after all, whether the bombing in Belgrade was a mistake or not was an issue for my government. I had nothing to do with it. I was standing taking notes in the middle of a crowd of several hundred rock-throwing people outside the British embassy when somebody asked me where I was from. I answered "Britain." There was a sudden silence from those around me, and the mob began to back away. Then someone said "English pig." Somebody else added "English dog." A third said "English running dog." The chant began to ripple through the crowd: "English pig, English dog, English running dog." With each refrain, it built in intensity and menace. I could see that something was going to happen, so I pushed my way outward, and the crowd let me pass with only a few kicks, shoves, and punches. When I broke free I ran as fast as a running dog could go. Rocks brushed my legs and hit my left shoulder as I went, and the crowd roared triumphantly at my departure.

By the next morning I had become South African. I was outside the American embassy watching rocks sail through the windows of the ambassador's study. I knew the ambassador was in the building because the British military attaché, using skills he had picked up in Northern Ireland, had managed to evade the crowds, slip down a side alley, and clamber over a high-security fence with sleeping bags for the besieged embassy staff. Then, just as I was interviewing the protesters, I bumped into someone I knew.

She was an influential official in the Chinese Ministry of Foreign Trade and Economic Cooperation and a leading light in the ongoing negotiations to win China access to the World Trade Organization. I counted her as a friend and was happy to see her there. We normally met over coffee in Häagen-Dazs, and in between mulling trade issues, we would chuckle over whether we felt brave enough to eat one of the fattening ice creams on the menu. But as I walked toward her, her face became a mask of fury. When we got to within two feet of each other, she started to rant. I do not have the exact words in my notebook because I just stood there gaping. I do remember that the opium wars came up several times, the century and a half of shame and humiliation, how we foreigners should realize that the Chinese would one day get their revenge, and then we would know what it was like to suffer. I asked her, when she had finished, whether the negotiations to enter the WTO would be derailed because of this. "Of course! How can you talk about trade when the other side is bombing your embassy?" she shouted.

But the episode did not end there. A month or so later we were back in Häagen-Dazs, and she informed me that the deliberations on joining the WTO were proceeding. When I asked her when and how they had resumed, she replied that they had never stopped. "We are prepared to make concessions to benefit ourselves in the long run," she said.

It is this flexibility and pragmatism, visible in China's transformation over and over again, that supplies the counterargument to future scenarios full of doom and gloom. China is perhaps too much wedded to the world, too deeply insinuated into its organizations and treaties, and too dependent on others to bite the hands that feed it.

NOTES

BIBLIOGRAPHY

INDEX

Notes

★

1: RAGS TO RICHES

1. "Shagang Group Purchases German Plant from Thyssen Krupp Stahl," China Business Information Network, December 31, 2002.
2. Shown on the photographic Web site "26 Things in One Abandoned Steel Mill," www.hebig.org/photos/26things/index.php.
3. These figures come from a meeting with Shen and other announcements by Shagang. Other details of the Shen Wenrong and Shagang story are from Yang Shilin, Chen Liming, and Yang Zhiqiang, *Kua Shiji De Chaoyue, Shen Wenrong Yu Shagang De Qiji* (Beijing: Beijing Metallurgical Industry Press, 2000), unpaginated.
4. Joe Studwell, *The China Dream* (London: Profile Books, 2002), 31, 32, 33.
5. Matthew Forney, "It Takes a Village: A Band of Hungry Farmers in Anhui Launched China's Economic Revolution," *Time International*, August 15, 2005, and Jim Mann, "China Denies Return to Collectives," *Los Angeles Times*, May 9, 1986.
6. Forney, "It Takes a Village."
7. This phenomenon has been observed by several researchers, including Yang Dali, of the University of Chicago, and David Zweig, director of the Center on China's Transnational Relations, Hong Kong University of Science and Technology.
8. James Kynge, "Chinese Eye SE Asia Buys," *Financial Times*, February 25, 1998, and interview with the author. Also Benjamin Kang Lim, "China Tycoon Hails Legal Changes," Reuters, February 3, 1999.
9. John Pomfret, " 'Reform Hero' Gets Life Term for Fraud," *Washington Post*, May 31, 2000, and Andrew Higgins, "Enemies Close In on China's Whiz-Kid," *Guardian*, September 17, 1996.
10. Ling Zhijun. Lian Xiang Feng Yun. 2005.
11. James Kynge, "Hope Holds Out for Triumph over Adversary," *Financial Times*, April 29, 1998, and "China's Public Show of Capitalism," *Financial*

★

Times, December 18, 2000. See also Russell Flannery, "Not Just Chicken Feed," *Forbes*, November 14, 2005.

12. Peter Wonacott, "Shopping for China: A Scourge of the Rust Belt Offers Some Hope There, Too," *Wall Street Journal*, November 26, 2004.

13. Elaine Kurtenbach, "China's Tiny Automakers Set Their Sights on the Whole World," Associated Press, July 24, 2005.

14. "Chinese Business: Li Makes Some Costly Calls," *The Edge Singapore*, September 20, 2004.

15. "China at 50: Nation Builders. Zong Qinghou. A Toast to Daring Ventures," *Asiaweek*, September 24, 1999.

16. Author interview with a former classmate of Shen Wenrong's in Jinfeng. He declined to be identified by name.

17. Yang et al., *Kua Shiji De Chaoyue, Shen Wenrong Yu Shagang De Qiji*.

2: THE FUTURE IS THE PAST (EXCEPT WHEN IT ISN'T)

1. Theodore H. White and Annalee Jacoby, *Thunder Out of China* (London: Victor Gollancz, 1947), 13.

2. Quoted in Donald L. Miller, *City of the Century* (New York: Simon & Schuster, 2003), 188.

3. Ibid.

4. Niu Wenyuan et al., *Zhongguo Ke Chixu Fazhan Zhanlue Baogao* [*China Sustainable Development Strategy Report*] (Beijing: Beijing Science Press, 2004), 227, 228.

5. Ibid., 236.

6. Doug Peacock, *Cotton Times*, www.cottontimes.co.uk/workers1.htm.

7. William Cronon, *Nature's Metropolis* (New York: W. W. Norton, 1991), 164.

8. Quoted in Deirdre Chetham, *Before the Deluge* (New York: Palgrave Macmillan, 2002), 117.

9. Marc Faber, *Tomorrow's Gold* (Hong Kong: CLSA Books, 2002), 52.

10. The story of porcelain is discussed at length in Christopher Cullen, *The Dragon's Ascent* (Hong Kong: Pacific Century Publishers, 2001), 127.

11. Joe Studwell, *The China Dream* (London: Profile Books, 2002), 4.

12. Angus Maddison, *Dynamic Forces in Capitalist Development: A Long-Run Comparative View* (Oxford: Oxford University Press, 1991), 10.

13. Adam Smith, *The Wealth of Nations*, book 1, chap. 9, para. 15.

14. Jeffrey Sachs, *The End of Poverty* (New York: Penguin Books, 2005), 150.

15. For several details in this account, I am indebted to research conducted by Zhang Lijia in White Horse village in 2004.

16. Elizabeth Rosenthal, "Study Links Rural Suicides in China to Stress and Ready Poisons," *New York Times*, November 29, 2002.

3: THE POPULATION PARADOX: INNOVATION, PIRACY,
AND THE GRAIL OF MARKET SHARE

1. Joe Studwell, *The China Dream* (London: Profile Books, 2002), 19.
2. Ibid.
3. Graham Hutchings, *Modern China* (New York: Penguin Books, 2000), 340.
4. Author interview and taped transcript, 1999.
5. The $60 billion figure is taken from remarks made by William Lash, assistant secretary of commerce, at a news conference in Beijing on April 12, 2005, the transcript of which was published by the U.S. embassy in Beijing. As an estimate of the damage caused by piracy, it is at the conservative end of the spectrum. Such estimates are very rough, and the true losses resulting from piracy of various sorts may be much higher.
6. Don Lee, "Ripping Off Good Reads in China," *Los Angeles Times,* April 24, 2005, C-1.
7. Anne Stevenson-Yang and Ken DeWoskin, "China Destroys the IP Paradigm," *Far Eastern Economic Review,* March 2005.
8. Author interview, 1999.
9. A good account of the deflationary conditions in the latter part of the nineteenth century can be found in Chris Farrell, *Deflation* (New York: Harper Business, 2004).
10. Quoted in testimony of South Carolina senator Ernest F. Hollings before the US-China Economic and Security Review Commission, "Hearing on China's Impact on the U.S. Manufacturing Base," January 30, 2004, 17.

4: THE TIES THAT BIND: CHINA GOES TO EUROPE

1. There are various estimates of the size of the Chinese immigrant population in Prato, and all are complicated by the fact that many illegal immigrants do not register with the local authorities. The estimate of 20,000 is based on official publications and may well be on the conservative side. Prato has the second-largest Chinese population of any city in Italy, after Milan.
2. Bruce Stokes, "Italian Textile Town Braces for the Worst," *National Journal,* October 2, 2004.
3. I am indebted here to Antonella Ceccagno of the University of Bologna, author of "The Economic Crisis and the Ban on Imports: The Chinese in Italy at a Crossroads," a paper that gives an in-depth account of Chinese immigrants working in Italy. www.nias.ku.dk/issco5/documents/ Ceccagno%20abs.doc.
4. Details such as these come from interviews with Francesco Delfino, gen-

eral manager of the province of Prato, and his staff, and from local government pamphlets.

5. For more about these and other dynamics, see Suzy Menkes, "China: Catastrophe for Creativity or Luxury Opportunity?," *International Herald Tribune,* September 27, 2005.

6. This passage describing and quoting Moritz Mantero and aspects of the Como silk industry draws extensively from Peter S. Goodman, "China's Silk Noose Tightens," *Washington Post,* December 18, 2003.

7. Wei Jingsheng, "Chirac Is Making a Fool of Himself," Agence France-Presse, October 24, 1999.

8. "Chirac Calls for Closer Ties," *Shanghai Daily,* October 12, 2004.

9. James Kynge and Martin Arnold, "Chirac Hails Beijing as Trade Deals Are Set Up," *Financial Times,* October 11, 2004, and "French Firms Sign Big Deals with China," *Business Daily,* October 11, 2004.

10. "Chinese President's Visit Throws Chirac into Hot Water," Agence France-Presse, October 22, 1999.

11. Wei Jingsheng, "Chirac Is Making a Fool of Himself."

12. "Chirac Says EU Measures on Chinese Textiles Not Enough," AFX Asia, May 19, 2005.

13. "Europe's New Protectionism—Charlemagne," *The Economist,* July 2, 2005, and, among many others who reported this speech, Nicholas Watt, "Wake Up and Change, Blair Tells EU," *Guardian Weekly,* July 1, 2005.

14. "March Champion: French Socialist Works to Keep Voters in 'No' on EU Constitution," *Wall Street Journal Europe,* May 27, 2005.

15. Jack Ewing and Dexter Roberts, "The Chinese Are Coming . . . to Germany," *Business Week,* February 21, 2005.

16. Interview with the author, Beijing, November 2004.

17. James Kynge, "Zhu Warns Rural Poverty Poses Threat to Future," *Financial Times,* March 5, 2003.

18. Total government expenditure has been around 21 percent of China's gross domestic product in recent years. See "China Risk: Macroeconomic Risk," *Economist Intelligence Unit,* November 15, 2005.

19. Stefan Theil, "Capitalism? Nein! Schröder and his Social Democrats Rediscover Karl Marx," *Newsweek International,* May 9, 2005.

5: AMERICA BOUGHT AND SOLD: ACQUIRING TECHNOLOGY FOR A GREAT LEAP FORWARD

1. Testimony of Bruce A. Cain, hearing before the U.S.-China Economic and Security Review Commission, Akron, Ohio, September 23, 2004.

2. "Magnum Integrated Technologies Becomes Lead Bidder for Ingersoll," *Metalworking Insiders Report*, July 17, 2003.

3. Al Frink said in this speech and in remarks to the media before the dinner that laws and regulations plus red tape added 22 percent to the cost of doing business in the United States. This and other remarks made to the author before, during, and after the Rockford dinner are on tape.

4. Testimony of Peter Cowhey, dean of the Graduate School of International Relations and Pacific Studies at the University of California, before the U.S.-China Economic and Security Review Commission, February 12–13, 2004.

5. "China Industry: Chery's Big Expansion Plans," *Economist Intelligence Unit*, February 7, 2005, and Mark O'Neill, "Chery Gears Up for U.S. Roll-Out," *South China Morning Post*, April 26, 2005.

6. Brian Bremner and Kathleen Kerwin, "Here Come Chinese Cars," *Business Week Online*, March 26, 2005. See also Alysha Webb, "Chery: Big Ambition or a Pipedream?," *Automotive News Europe*, April 18, 2005.

7. Michael S. Chase, Kevin L. Pollpeter, and James C. Mulvenon, *Shanghaied?* (Santa Monica, Cal.: RAND Corp., 2004).

8. Author interview.

9. Kathryn Kranhold, "China Sets a High Price to Gain Market Entry," *Wall Street Journal*, February 27, 2004.

10. I am indebted to Rupert Wingfield-Hayes, the BBC bureau chief in China, for letting me listen to the tape of his interview with Bo Xilai in May 2005.

11. Diana Farrell, "Trends," *Milken Institute Review*, Second Quarter, 2005.

12. McKinsey Global Institute surveys and reports can be found at www.mckinsey.com/mgi.

6: NOT ENOUGH TO GO AROUND: NATURAL RESOURCES AND ENVIRONMENTAL CATASTROPHE

1. James Kynge, "China Is the Workshop of the World, but It Is Becoming the Rubbish Tip Too," *Financial Times*, July 27, 2004. This article quotes a research paper from the Chinese Academy of Environmental Planning that says the cost to human health from air pollution in the early twenty-first century accounted for 2 to 3 percent of annual gross domestic product and will reach 13 percent of GDP by 2020 if China fails to curb a worsening trend. In the country's eleven largest cities some 50,000 people die prematurely and 400,000 people suffer chronic bronchitis each year because of soot and other tiny airborne particles. If things do not change, the 380,000

figure I give for 2010 will rise to 550,000 by 2020, the research paper suggests.

2. "From T-shirts to T-bonds: China and the World Economy," *Economist*, July 30, 2005, and David Zweig and Bi Jianhai, "China's Global Hunt for Energy," *Foreign Affairs*, September–October 2005, 25.

3. Elizabeth Economy, *The River Runs Black* (Ithaca, N.Y.: Cornell University Press, 2004), 48.

4. Most of the details of Wang Jinxi's life are gleaned from photographs, pamphlets, booklets, recordings, and photocopies on display at the Iron Man Wang Museum in Daqing.

5. Kenneth Pomeranz, *The Great Divergence: China, Europe, and the Making of the Modern World Economy* (Princeton, N.J.: Princeton University Press, 2000), 226.

6. "Kashagan Sale Completed," *International Petroleum Finance*, April 11, 2005. This article describes how the Western oil companies that owned stakes in the Kashagan oil field used their preemption rights to prevent China National Offshore Oil Corporation (CNOOC) and Sinopec from buying into the field.

7. Gavin Menzies, *1421: The Year China Discovered America* (New York: Harper Perennial, 2004), passim.

8. Francesco Guerrera et al., "The Maverick Oil Mandarin," *Financial Times*, June 25, 2005.

9. Francesco Guerrera et al., "Twists and Turns in Log of Treasure Ship's Transglobal Journey," *Financial Times*, July 14, 2005.

10. Ibid.

11. "Chevron Confident about Bid for Unocal," AFX Asia, June 24, 2005.

12. Enid Tsui, "CNOOC Executive Speaks Out about Failed Bid," *Financial Times*, September 16, 2005.

13. Andrew Gowers, editor of the *Financial Times*, and Mure Dickie, its Beijing correspondent, had this experience in October 2003. I experienced a similar explanation in June 1999.

14. Richard McGregor, "Hope for Parched Cities Springs from Canal Project," *Financial Times*, June 9, 2005.

15. This comment was made off the record, so I cannot disclose which official said this to me.

16. Matthew Pottinger, Steve Stecklow, and John F. Fialka, "Invisible Export: A Hidden Cost of China's Growth: Mercury Migration," *Wall Street Journal*, December 17, 2004.

17. Ibid.

18. Tim Radford, "Huge Rise in Siberian Forest Fires Puts Planet at Risk, Scientists Warn," *Guardian*, May 31, 2005.

19. Venessa Leevenessa, "Giant Strides and a Colossal Fallout: China's Miracle Economy May Be Planet's Greatest Threat," Newstoday.com.sg, October 22, 2005. See also Michael Richardson, "Illegal Logging: Calls to Give It the Chop," *Straits Times*, May 14, 2005, and "China's Need for Wood Imperils Other Nations' Forests," *Dow Jones International News*, March 8, 2005.

20. Michael McCarthy, "Your Planet: The State We're In," *Independent*, September 25, 2005.

21. "Renewable Energy: China Pledges $180b for Initiatives," *Greenwire*, November 7, 2005.

22. Richard Lloyd Parry, "Himalayas' Melting Glaciers Will Open Floodgates to Catastrophe," *The Times*, July 12, 2005. See also Janet Larsen, "Ice Melt Alert," *USA Today*, May 1, 2005.

7: THE COLLAPSE OF SOCIAL TRUST

1. Arthur Waley, *Three Ways of Thought in Ancient China* (London: Routledge, 1939), 115.

2. Ibid., 116.

3. Sophia Yow, "Historic Ruling for Education Violation," *South China Morning Post*, September 1, 2001.

4. James Kynge, "Phoney Police Add to China's Fakes List," *Financial Times*, June 21, 2002.

5. This assertion is based on personal experience and on testimony from people working in public relations companies in Beijing.

6. Author interview, February 2005.

7. "Local Officials Given Imprisonment for Fake Milk Powder Cases," Xinhua News Agency, August 12, 2004.

8. Pierre Haski, *Le Sang de la Chine* (Paris: Grasset, 2005). See also Philip P. Pan, "China's AIDS Orphans Feel Brunt of Power," *Washington Post*, September 14, 2004.

9. James Kynge, "The Pearl River Delta Attracting $1bn of Investment a Month," *Financial Times*, February 4, 2003.

10. Author interview, October 2004.

11. Mure Dickie, "China's High-Tech Hero," *Financial Times*, December 11, 2004.

8: COMMUNISM VS. DEMOCRACY

1. Nicholas D. Kristof, "China Update: How the Hardliners Won," *New York Times*, November 12, 1989.

2. A transcript of this speech was given to the author by Cao.
3. Yasheng Huang, *Selling China* (Cambridge, U.K.: Cambridge University Press, 2003), 343–50. This book deals extensively with the ideological, structural, and political impediments to the development of the private sector.
4. "Dialectical Materialism," *Economist*, July 3, 1999.
5. A full account of the Zhengzhou Baiwen scandal is contained in Carl E. Walter and Fraser T. J. Howie, *Privatizing China* (New York: John Wiley, 2003), 190.
6. Hu Shuli, "Enrons of China," *Newsweek International*, December 1, 2004. See also "China's Bourses Are Looking Up," *Business Times Singapore*, February 3, 2004.
7. David Barboza, "Wave of Corruption Tarnishes China's Extraordinary Growth," *New York Times*, March 22, 2005.
8. Ibid.
9. "China Kicks Off Trial over $3.1bn Finance Fraud," Reuters, June 10, 2004.
10. "China's Bourses Are Looking Up."
11. Andrew Yeh, "Bank Refinance May Cost Beijing $190bn," *Financial Times*, April 29, 2005.
12. James Kynge, "Officials in China Face 'Mafia' Probe," *Financial Times*, June 22, 2001. See also Larry Teo, "Triads Could Overwhelm China's Local Govts," *Straits Times*, November 20, 2004.
13. Liu Li, "Audit Reveals Breadth of Fund Abuse," *China Daily*, June 29, 2005.
14. Pei Minxin, "China Is Paying the Price of Rising Social Unrest," *Financial Times*, November 7, 2005.

9: CAN WE BE FRIENDS?

1. Anne-Marie Brady, *Making the Foreign Serve China* (Lanham, Md.: Rowman & Littlefield, 2003). I am indebted to Brady's research for much of the material on *waishi*, or foreign affairs, mentioned in this chapter.
2. Ibid., 18.
3. Author interview, 2003.
4. Kathy Chen, "Seagram Wants Orange Juice to Be Chinese Staple," *Dow Jones International*, January 2, 1998.
5. Quoted from the unpublished diaries of Edgar Snow in Brady, *Making the Foreign Serve China*, 44–45.
6. Leslie Chang, "China Battles the Present with the Past—'Us Against the

World' Mentality Dominates the Nation's History Lesson," *Asian Wall Street Journal*, June 24, 1999.

7. Ibid.

8. Testimony of Ernest J. Wilson III, senior research fellow, Center for International Development and Conflict Management, University of Maryland, before the subcommittee on Africa, Human Rights, and International Operations, House Committee on International Relations, July 28, 2005.

9. "Asian-China Ties in 2020: Stronger and Deeper?" *The Nation* (Thailand), November 29, 2005.

10. I first heard this phrase spoken by Lester Brown, president of the Earth Policy Institute, a nongovernmental environmental organization based in Washington. Brown, who was speaking at a meeting in Beijing in early 2005, noted that China consumes more grain, meat, coal, steel, copper, cement, fertilizer, cell phones, and refrigerators than the United States.

11. David Zweig and Bi Jianhai, "China's Global Hunt for Energy," *Foreign Affairs*, September–October 2005, 25. I am indebted to this fine, comprehensive article for many of the points quoted in the next several paragraphs.

12. Ibid.

13. Glen Kessler, "Rice Puts Japan at Center of New U.S. Vision of Asia; China Challenged in Major Speech," *Washington Post*, March 19, 2005.

14. Peter S. Goodman, "Blood and Oil," *Washington Post*, April 24, 2005.

15. Ibid.

16. Ibid.

17. "U.N. Security Council Deadlocked over New Sudan Resolution," *Dow Jones International*, March 2005. See also Evelyn Leopold, "U.N. Council Votes for Sanctions on Darfur Offenders," Reuters, March 29, 2005.

18. "China Strengthens Alliance with Embattled Uzbekistan Leadership," *Voice of America*, March 26, 2005. See also "Guest of Dishonour," *Globe and Mail*, May 28, 2005, and Mark Magnier, "Slaking the Dragon's Thirst: China's Energy Quest," *Los Angeles Times*, August 7, 2005.

19. "Iran Leaves Europeans Out in the Cold," *Petroleum Intelligence Weekly*, March 7, 2005.

20. "U.S. Seeks China as Global Partner, Assistant Secretary of State for East Asian and Pacific Affairs Says," *U.S. Fed News*, June 7, 2005.

21. Transcript of daily press briefing, State Department Press Releases and Documents, March 8, 2005.

22. David Shambaugh, "Lifting the China Arms Ban Is Only Symbolic," *Financial Times*, March 5, 2004. The point about the shift in the military balance was made in conversations with the author in late 2005.

23. Robert S. Ross, "Assessing the China Threat," *National Interest*, October 1, 2005.

24. James Boxell, Demetri Sevastopulo, and Daniel Dombey, "China's Defence Spending More Than Double Disclosed," *Financial Times*, October 26, 2005. The London-based International Institute of Strategic Studies estimated that China spent $62.5 billion on defense last year, compared with the Beijing government's official figure of $25 billion. Indeed, most independent estimates are considerably higher than the official figures released by Beijing.

25. Jonathan Broder, "Balancing Fuel and Freedom," *CQ Weekly*, September 13, 2005.

Bibliography

★

Banister, Judith. *China's Changing Population*. Stanford: Stanford University Press, 1987.

Becker, Jasper. *The Chinese*. London: John Murray, 2000.

Bonavia, David. *The Chinese*. London: Allen Lane, 1981.

Brady, Anne-Marie. *Making the Foreign Serve China*. Lanham, Md.: Rowman & Littlefield, 2003.

Brown, Lester R. *Who Will Feed China? Wake-Up Call for a Small Planet*. Worldwatch Environmental Alert series. New York: W. W. Norton, 1995.

Burstein, Daniel, and Arne de Keijzer. *Big Dragon*. New York: Simon & Schuster, 1998.

Buzan, Barry, and Rosemary Foot, eds. *Does China Matter? A Reassessment*. New International Relations series. London: Routledge, 2004.

Cabestan, Jean-Pierre. *L'Administration Chinoise après Mao: Les Réformes de 1'ère Deng Xiaoping et Leurs Limites*. Paris: Éditions du Centre National de la Recherche Scientifique, 1992.

Chang, Gordon G. *The Coming Collapse of China*. New York: Random House, 2001.

Chase, Michael S., Kevin L. Pollpeter, and James C. Mulvenon. *Shanghaied?: The Economic and Political Implications of the Flow of Information and Investment Across the Taiwan Straits*. Santa Monica, Cal.: RAND Corp., 2004.

Chetham, Deirdre. *Before the Deluge: The Vanishing World of the Yangtze's Three Gorges*. New York: Palgrave Macmillan, 2002.

China: Air, Land, and Water. Environmental Priorities for a New Millennium. Washington, D.C.: World Bank, 2001.

Clissold, Tim. *Mr. China: A Memoir*. London: Constable & Robinson, 2004.

Cronin, William. *Nature's Metropolis*. New York: W. W. Norton, 1991.

★

Economy, Elizabeth C. *The River Runs Black.* Ithaca, N.Y.: Cornell University Press, 2004.

Faber, Marc. *Tomorrow's Gold: Asia's Age of Discovery.* Hong Kong: CLSA Books, 2002.

Farrell, Chris. *Deflation.* New York: Harper Business, 2004.

Gerth, Karl. *China Made: Consumer Culture and the Creation of the Nation.* Cambridge, Mass.: Harvard University Asia Center, 2003.

Giley, Bruce. *Tiger on the Brink: Jiang Zemin and China's New Elite.* Berkeley: University of California Press, 1998.

Gittings, John. *Real China.* New York: Pocket Books, 1997.

Hersey, John. *A Single Pebble.* New York: Bantam, 1956.

Hu, Angang. *Great Transformations in China.* Beijing: Center for China Studies, 2004.

Huang, Yasheng. *Selling China: Foreign Direct Investment During the Reform Era.* Cambridge, U.K.: Cambridge University Press, 2003.

Hutchings, Graham. *Modern China: A Guide to a Century of Change.* New York: Penguin Books, 2000.

Jenner, W.J.F. *The Tyranny of History: The Roots of China's Crisis.* London: Allen Lane, 1992.

Joint Economic Committee, Congress of the United States, ed. *China's Economic Future: Challenges to U.S. Policy.* Armonk, N.Y.: M. E. Sharpe, 1997.

Landes, David S. *The Unbound Prometheus.* Cambridge, U.K.: Cambridge University Press, 2003.

Lardy, Nicholas R. *Integrating China into the Global Economy.* Washington, D.C.: Brookings Institution Press, 2002.

Li, Zhisui. *The Private Life of Chairman Mao: The Inside Story of the Man Who Made Modern China.* London: Chatto & Windus, 1994.

Lieberthal, Kenneth. *Governing China.* New York: W. W. Norton, 2004.

Link, Perry. *Evening Chats in Beijing: Probing China's Predicament.* New York: W. W. Norton, 1992.

McGregor, James. *One Billion Customers: Lessons from the Front Lines of Doing Business in China.* New York: Wall Street Journal Books / Free Press, 2005.

Miles, James A. R. *The Legacy of Tiananmen: China in Disarray.* Ann Arbor: University of Michigan Press, 1996.

Miller, Donald L. *City of the Century.* New York: Simon & Schuster, 2003.

Moore, Oliver. *Reading the Past: Chinese.* London: British Museum Press, 2000.

Mosher, Steven W. *Hegemon: China's Plan to Dominate Asia and the World.* San Francisco: Encounter Books, 2002.

Nathan, Andrew J., and Robert S. Ross. *The Great Wall and the Empty Fortress.* New York: W. W. Norton, 1997.

Nolan, Peter. *China and the Global Economy.* New York: Palgrave Macmillan, 2001.

Nolan, Peter. *China at the Crossroads.* Cambridge, U.K.: Polity Press, 2003.

Overholt, William H. *China: The Next Economic Superpower.* London: Weidenfeld & Nicolson, 1993.

Pomeranz, Kenneth. *The Great Divergence: China, Europe, and the Making of the Modern World Economy.* Princeton, N.J.: Princeton University Press, 2000.

Pomeranz, Kenneth, and Steven Topik. *The World That Trade Created.* Armonk, N.Y.: M. E. Sharpe, 1999.

Pun, Ngai. *Made in China: Women Factory Workers in a Global Workplace.* Durham, N.C.: Duke University Press, 2005.

Richardson, Philip. *Economic Change in China, 1800–1950.* Cambridge, U.K.: Cambridge University Press, 1999.

Sachs, Jeffrey. *The End of Poverty.* New York: Penguin Books, 2005.

Saich, Tony. *Governance and Politics of China.* New York: Palgrave Macmillan, 2004.

Short, Philip. *Mao: A Life.* London: John Murray, 1999.

Spence, Jonathan. *The Search for Modern China.* New York: W. W. Norton, 1990.

Spence, Jonathan. *The Chan's Great Continent.* New York: Penguin Books, 1998.

Studwell, Joe. *The China Dream.* London: Profile Books, 2002.

Sull, Donald N. *Made in China.* Cambridge, Mass.: Harvard Business School Press, 2005.

U.S.-China Economic and Security Review Commission. Compilation of hearings, 2001–2002.

U.S.-China Economic and Security Review Commission. "U.S.-China Trade and Investment: Impact on Key Manufacturing and Industrial Sectors." Field hearing, Akron, Ohio, September 2004.

Waley, Arthur. *Three Ways of Thought in Ancient China.* London: Routledge, 1939.

Walter, Carl E., and Fraser J. T. Howie. *Privatizing China.* New York: John Wiley, 2003.

White, Theodore H., and Annalee Jacoby. *Thunder Out of China*. London: Victor Gollancz, 1947.

Wilson, Dick. *China: The Big Tiger*. London: Abacus, 1997.

Woetzel, Jonathan R. *Capitalist China*. New York: John Wiley, 2003.

Wolf, Martin. *Why Globalization Works*. New Haven: Yale University Press, 2004.

Wood, Frances. *No Dogs and Not Many Chinese*. London: John Murray, 2000.

Zhongguo Ke Chizu Fazhan Zhanlue Baogao. Beijing: Kexue Chuban She, 2004.

Zweig, David. *Freeing China's Farmers*. Armonk, N.Y.: M. E. Sharpe, 1997.

Index

★

★

257